Hiking
Oregon's History

Hiking
Oregon's
History

William L. Sullivan

Navillus Press
Eugene, Oregon

The Heceta Head lighthouse (Hike #35).

Published by the Navillus Press
1958 Onyx Street
Eugene, Oregon 97403
www.oregonhiking.com

Printed in USA

Frontispiece: Western governors touring the newly opened Columbia River Highway at Multnomah Falls in 1917.

SAFETY CONSIDERATIONS: Some of the trails in this book pass through wilderness and remote country where hikers are exposed to unavoidable risks. On any hike, the weather may change suddenly. The fact that a hike is included in this book, or that it may be rated as easy, does not necessarily mean it will be safe or easy for you. Prepare yourself with proper equipment and outdoor skills, and you will be able to enjoy these hikes with confidence.
Every effort has been made to assure the accuracy of the information in this book. The author has hiked all of the featured trails. Nonetheless, construction, logging, and storm damage may cause changes. Corrections and updates are welcome and are often rewarded. They may be sent in care of the publisher.

Contents

Portland

Salem

Baker City

Bend

Eugene

Coos Bay

Medford

Hiking
Oregon's
History

Location of featured hikes

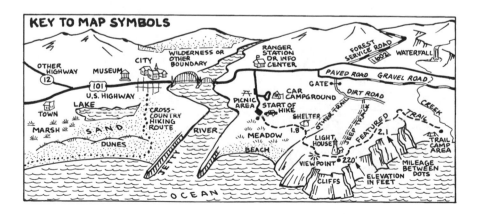

Mt. Hood from Timberline Lodge (Hike #53).

Introduction

Oregon was settled by walkers. Not only did North America's tribes arrive here on foot via an Alaskan land bridge, but most Oregon Trail pioneers also walked—hiking beside their covered wagons toward the dream they called Oregon.

Today the best way to explore the region's history is still by trail.

On Tillamook Head, for example, you can retrace the Lewis and Clark expedition's steps through the rainforest, breathing the tangy salt air they breathed upon discovery of a sudden Pacific Ocean viewpoint.

In Hells Canyon you can hike amid towering badlands on the actual route of Chief Joseph's tragic trail of tears. In Southern Oregon you can prowl through redwood groves to the bomb crater left by a daring Japanese attack in World War II. Gold mines, lookout towers, and wagon trails—the story of Oregon is printed on the land for hikers to read. Oregon's grandest museum is the great outdoors.

This remarkable outdoor museum tells us much about ourselves as Oregonians, too. The trailside exhibits reveal, for example, that we are a stubbornly independent folk, willing to homestead the intractable Eastern Oregon desert in a gamble for freedom. We are competitive, capable of building two rival railroads through a rimrock river gorge where even one would seem impossible. At times we have been foolish with our natural heritage, churning mountain valleys into wastelands in the search for gold.

At other times our conservation efforts have been improbably far-sighted, sparing beaches, headlands, and forests from the crush of development.

Through it all we have remained a peripatetic clan. Oregonians are not gladly caged inside California-style freeway jams. Similarly, we shy from the claustrophobic urban canyons of megacities "back East." When the rains lift, we find ourselves looking out the window with an inexplicable longing. Perhaps it is an echo of our wandering past, the call of the trail still beckoning us into the map's white open spaces.

Start your exploration of Oregon's past by reading through the main portion of this book as you would a historical novel. Curl up in an armchair by the fire. You'll find the history here strewn with more plot twists and outlandish characters than you'd ever find in fiction. The land itself is a central player in this drama, so tales of trailside geology, plants, and wildlife share the stage too.

When you're suitably inspired to lace up your hiking boots and hit the trail, pay special attention to the book's boxed inserts. These "how-to" sections describe exactly how to find each trailhead and featured site. The boxes also rate the difficulty of each hike, noting length and elevation gain. Tips on nearby museums and roadside attractions make it easy to round out the day. A "Hiker's Checklist" at the back of the book provides more general advice on hiking preparation and the trails' managing agencies.

The trails in this book have been chosen not only for their historic merit, but also because they are among the most beautiful and accessible in the state. Nowhere is Oregon's natural scenery better preserved than along these paths, where the footprints of pioneers and settlers still rest gently on the land. Come explore 14,000 years of legends, discoveries, scandals, and triumphs—come hike the history of Oregon.

William L. Sullivan
Eugene, Oregon

CHAPTER I

The First Tracks

There is no better place to begin a walking exploration of Oregon's past than beside a vanished Ice Age lake where a mysterious clan manufactured shoes. Here, in a cave overlooking what is now the sagebrush country of arid Fort Rock Valley, archeologists in 1938 were astonished to unearth a 9000-year-old cache of more than seventy sandals—an enormous heap of footgear, fastidiously woven from sagebrush bark.

The find shattered the prevailing assumption that humans had arrived in most of North America hardly 1000 years ago. Even today, the discovery raises questions. Who were these people, opening a Paleolithic version of a Nike superstore? Why did their culture—and their lake—evaporate? And what has become of their former domain?

Sandals from Fort Rock Cave.

Many of the answers to those questions are waiting in the pungent sagebrush landscape below Fort Rock's sudden circular cliff. Begin your investigation by hiking across that desert fortress to a viewpoint of the cave itself. Then track down the missing lake at a "lost" forest and follow what may be the clan's petroglyphs along an eerie dry riverbed cut dead by ancient lava flows.

Fort Rock

The Ice Age did not bring snow to Eastern Oregon, but rather rain. While glaciers crawled south across Canada and capped the Cascades 14,000 years ago, the Fort Rock Valley filled with rainwater. The lake

Fort Rock was once an island in an Ice Age lake.

swelled to become Oregon's largest ever, inundating 1500 square miles as much as 250 feet deep. Plovers, ducks, and geese flocked to its reedy shore. Buffalo, elk, and deer roamed the grass savannas on its bank. And people arrived, following the game that fled the glaciers. The people's ancestors had walked from Asia to Alaska on dry land exposed when the polar ice caps' growing ice reserves lowered the oceans of the world hundreds of feet.

Today, as you drive through a sea of sagebrush toward Fort Rock State Park, it's hard at first to visualize the immense lake that once lapped this desert rock's walls. It's easier to picture the lake after you've left the car and followed a park trail a few hundred yards up to the ancient beach. There, ringing the base of the rock's orange, pock-marked cliff, is a rounded, ten-foot notch carved by the vanished surf.

Originally, Fort Rock did not have cliff edges at all, but rather the gently sloping sides of a *maar*—a volcanic explosion crater. Dozens of similar maars erupted 50,000 to 100,000 years ago when bubbles of magma rose to the surface of this Eastern Oregon landscape and burst. Like boiling mudpots, the maars left craters ringed by slopes of gas-bubbled tuff and debris. Hole in the Ground, a relatively intact maar six miles to the west, is often mistaken for a mile-wide meteorite crater. Flat Top, a mesa ten miles to the north, is actually a maar that filled its crater brimful with basalt lava. Because Fort Rock erupted lower in the valley, it suffered a very different fate. For millennia Fort Rock was an island, battered by storm

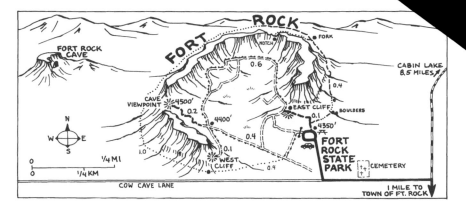

1. Fort Rock

HIKE LOCATION

Easy
1.7-mile loop
250 feet elevation gain

Explore a fortress-shaped outcropping in an Ice Age lakebed.

Getting There: From Bend, drive 25 miles south on Highway 97, turn left at a "Silver Lake" pointer on Highway 31 for 29.2 miles, and turn left at a "Fort Rock" sign for 6.5 miles. Turn left again just beyond the Fort Rock store, following signs 1.7 miles to Fort Rock State Park. The route is entirely paved. Park at the far end of the picnic area's lot.

Hiking Tips: From the picnic area, take a paved path 100 feet and continue on a rougher trail uphill 200 yards to a viewpoint beside Fort Rock's east cliff. Then keep right at all junctions, following an abandoned road around the inside of Fort Rock 0.6 mile to a 4-way junction. Here you have three options. To find the cave viewpoint, climb to the right on a faint path 0.2 mile. To see the west cliff viewpoint, go straight 0.1 mile. To return to your car, turn left 0.4 mile.

Season: May and June are lovely, and fall is pleasant. Avoid the heat of July and August. Winter months are windy and very cold.

While You're in the Area: The Fort Rock Homestead Village Museum, on the west edge of the town of Fort Rock, is open 10am-4pm Friday-Sunday (and holidays) in summer from Memorial Day to Labor Day. Hike #2 (Fort Rock Lake's Mysteries) is also nearby. If you need to overnight, head for the RV park and motels in Christmas Valley.

th winds. The surf eventually breached the crater's
the ring into the steep-walled crescent you see today.
und the inside of Fort Rock, contouring from one horn
the other, keep an eye out for the blooms of the high
he ancient beach's sagebrush you'll find brilliant red
ne, yellow clumps of sunflower-like Oregon sunshine in
summer, ellow-tipped rabbit brush in fall. Meanwhile, cliff swallows
swoop from mud nests high on the guano-stained rock walls. Hawks that
hunt the swallows cruise overhead. And the huge blue sweep of desert
sky is as intoxicating as the bittersweet smell of sagebrush.

But where is Fort Rock Cave, the sandal site? Actually the cave isn't
on Fort Rock itself, but you can see it from there. Turn right at a four-way
junction near the far side of Fort Rock's crescent and climb to a gap high
atop the rim wall. Look for the cave's dark spot at the base of a small knoll
more than a mile away, across a flat expanse of private ranchland. Waves
from the Ice Age lake once rolled across this gulf and smashed into the
knoll, carving the cave's fifty-foot-deep overhang by washing soft earth
from beneath a hard lava layer. The first people arrived when the lake was
slightly lower. By then the knoll had become an attractive peninsula, surrounded by lakeshore wildlife and easily defended against intruders.

The first scientist to investigate the cave was Luther Cressman, a University of Oregon archeologist who had won second-hand renown for his

The wave-cut notch on Fort Rock's cliffs resembles a gigantic bathtub ring.

brief marriage to the flamboyant South Sea island anthropologist Margaret Mead. Following their separation in 1928, Cressman began exploring Eastern Oregon with a Model A Ford, a notebook, and a revolver, intent on building a scientific reputation of his own. Hearing that pothunters had scavenged artifacts from this cave, he undertook a methodical excavation, marking the cave floor into square meters and sifting the sand with a quarter-inch screen. To his disappointment, the earlier souvenir diggers had left the top layer jumbled, destroying 3000 years of archeological record. But below that, and particularly beneath a multi-ton boulder that had fallen from the cave roof in an ancient earthquake, the intact strata began revealing astonishing finds: campfire wood from pinyon pine trees that no longer grow in Oregon, fishing net sinkers from a lake that no longer exists, and bones from an extinct species of buffalo.

Even more surprising, the richest finds lay below a thick layer of yellow volcanic ash. The eruption had apparently wiped out the area's forests and grasslands, leaving the cave virtually uninhabited for 2000 years. Could this be Mt. Mazama ash, blasted here when Crater Lake's volcano exploded 7700 years ago? In 1938, there was no dating system that could prove Cressman's guess, but his theory shook the archeological world.

In a move that Cressman would later regret, he carefully treated every scrap of the cave's sandals and mats with preservatives. A few years later, when researchers developed a radiocarbon system to determine the age of organic materials, Cressman realized with dismay that the preservatives had ruined all his samples for dating. Proof of his theory had to wait until 1948, when a man digging illegally in the old cave turned up a sandal fragment Cressman had overlooked. The scrap of woven sagebrush revealed a radiocarbon age of about 9053 years. Cressman was vindicated, and is known today as the "Father of Oregon archeology."

In 2008, U of O archeologist David Jenkins revealed that 14,300-year-old human DNA had been found in coprolites (dried feces) at the Paisley Caves, 50 miles southeast of Fort Rock. The discovery not only pushed back proof of human arrival in the Americas by additional thousands of years, but genetic analysis revealed that the people here were descendants of Siberians, lending credence to the Alaska land bridge theory.

Fort Rock Lake's Mysteries

The hotter, drier climate that followed the Ice Age did not drive human settlers out of the Fort Rock Valley permanently, nor did it completely eliminate Fort Rock Lake. From the viewpoint on Fort Rock's rim the

Hole in the Ground resembles a meteorite crater, but was created by a volcanic blast.

modern marks of settlement are obvious: mile-wide circles of irrigated alfalfa, moored to the former lakebed like great green flying saucers. But the valley is also hiding traces of the past—geologic oddities that may explain what happened to the Ice Age lake. To look for answers, try investigating four of these curiosities on foot. Start at a crater that shows what Fort Rock might have looked like if it had erupted on slightly higher ground.

Hole in the Ground. An explosion that leaves a mile-wide crater 400 feet deep would have the power of an atomic bomb. The fuel for Hole in the Ground's crater, however, was volcanic. Just before the bubble of molten magma that rose here reached the surface it hit a layer of ground water from the Fort Rock Valley. The water flashed to steam, blew out the crater, and cooled the magma enough that it stopped rising.

Since then a few ponderosa pines have managed to grow on the shady side of the rim, but this remains one of the most perfect volcanic bowls anywhere. You could simply admire Hole in the Ground from the parking turnaround on the rim, but if you're up for a 2.1-mile loop hike through the crater, you'll have a better feel for the scale of the explosion. The walk is also a nice introduction to the magical margin where pine woods give way to the pungent high desert.

Fort Rock's Valley. After visiting Hole in the Ground, drive on to the desert village of Fort Rock, a dusty Old West hamlet with a homestead museum on the west edge of town. As early as 1906 the federal government opened this region to homesteaders, offering free land to anyone willing to risk dry land farming. Promoters hyped the scheme heavily in the early 1910s, publicizing reports that the former lakebed's soil was indeed fertile.

The hucksters charged three hundred dollars to pick up settlers at the rail-head in Bend and drive them to "prime" farmsites. Other hopeful families came by covered wagon from as far away as Nebraska, and still others drove across the country in cars piled high with housewares. They built plank cabins, cleared sagebrush, planted rye, and prayed for rain.

But precipitation in the Fort Rock Valley currently averages just nine inches a year, and can be as low as four. The growing season has only twenty frost-free nights. After the summer of 1913, when dry winds blew out the rye seed as often as it was planted, nearly all of the farms stood abandoned. Since then, nostalgia buffs have moved dozens of weather-grayed buildings to the town's museum grounds.

Sixty years later, a second land rush swept Fort Rock. Farmers realized that the Ice Age lake's water had been here all along—underground! If huge powerlines could be strung south from the Columbia River dams, electric pumps might irrigate the former lakebed's fertile fields. To-day, as you drive east through the agricultural boomtown of Christ-mas Valley, you'll see power py-lons, sprinklers, vast hay sheds, and metal roofs glinting in the desert sun. What you won't see are lavish farmhouses. The money is here, but the new settlers know the boom can't last. Each year they drill their wells a little deeper to keep pace with the retreating subterranean lake. When the fos-sil water is gone and the desert winds again rake barren fields, this generation of homesteaders

Store at the Fort Rock Homestead Museum.

won't leave empty houses behind. They'll hitch up their mobile homes and move on.

The Sand Dunes. Fort Rock's desert winds have already raked togeth-er several miles of sixty-foot sand dunes on the remote far end of the an-cient lakebed. To visit them, drive half an hour beyond Christmas Valley, trading paved road for gravel and then rough dirt. Finally you'll have to park the car and set out on foot into a trailless Sahara.

Between the dunes' long ridges of dusty, wind-rippled sand you'll find

2. Fort Rock Lake's Mysteries

HIKE LOCATION

Easy (four short hikes)
0.4 to 2.3 miles each, round trip
50 to 390 feet elevation gain

Four short desert walks explore sand and lava oddities.

Getting to Hole in the Ground: From Bend, drive Highway 97 south 29 miles and turn left at a "Silver Lake" pointer onto Highway 31 for 22 miles. At milepost 22, follow a "Hole in the Ground" pointer left onto gravel Breakup Road 3125 for 3 miles. Then fork right onto washboard gravel Road 3130 for 1.2 miles to a powerline, and turn left on bumpy Road 200 for 0.2 mile to the crater rim. Park here and hike straight ahead on a steep, dusty trail 0.5 mile down to a small central playa. Continue straight on an (undrivable) old road for 1.2 miles, spiraling up to the right through ponderosa pine woods. Then continue 0.6 mile to the right around the rim on a dirt road back to your car.

Getting to the Sand Dunes: From Hole in the Ground, drive back to Highway 31, follow it south 7.2 miles, and turn left 6.8 miles to the town of Fort Rock. Continue straight, following signs for 27 zigzagging miles to Christmas Valley. Check your gas gauge here. Then continue straight 8 miles to a 4-way junction. Following "Sand Dunes" pointers, turn left on paved Road 5-14D for 8 miles to a T-shaped junction and turn right on gravel Road 5-14E for 3.3 miles. The main road turns left here, but go straight, passing a "Rough Road Ahead" sign. In fact, this narrow, sandy track can be impassable in wet weather. If it's dry, keep straight for 4.4 miles until you reach a wood-rail fence at a T-shaped junction. Turn right and drive the rough, sandy road 0.4 mile to a parking area. There is no trail, but you can see the dunes. Walk 0.3 mile southwest across the desert to them.

Getting to the Lost Forest: From the Sand Dunes' parking area, drive back to the north, keeping straight for 0.7 mile. A a T-shaped junction turn right for 2.2 miles on a very rough, bumpy, sandy road until you are near a large, orange rock bluff. A rough spur to the left, marked "Open Road," leads 200 yards to a turnaround at the rock's base. Park here and scramble up the trailless knoll 0.2 mile to a viewpoint overlooking the forest.

Getting to Crack in the Ground: Return to Christmas Valley. At the extreme eastern edge of this sprawling desert town, turn north off the main paved road at a "Crack in the Ground" pointer. Follow a good gravel road 7.2 miles to a signed parking area. A wide trail leads 0.2 mile to the lava crack. Then walk 0.2 mile along the bottom of this slot to a sandy gap. Beyond this point the crack is blocked by boulders, but you can follow the crack's upper rim as far as you like.

Season: Open all year, but avoid winter's cold and late summer's heat.

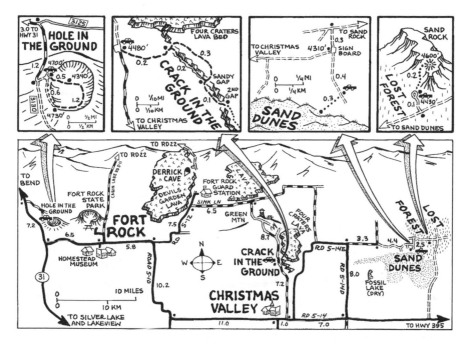

flat areas of hardpan where water briefly pools after rare rainstorms.

Look here for the tiny cratered entrances to the burrows of enterprising ants. In May, desert primroses dot the flats with clumps of showy petals. Tracks remain for months from passing deer and coyotes — and from the tires of all-terrain vehicles, a nuisance on summer holiday weekends.

The Sand Dunes consist of the same Mt. Mazama ash that blanketed ancient Fort Rock Lake and Fort Rock Cave 7700 years ago. As the lake dried, prevailing west winds herded the ashy deposits here. The last patch of open lake water stood five miles upwind, across the dunes at Fossil Lake — an alkali playa that is now dry for years at a stretch.

Fossil Lake, the withered heart of Fort Rock's ancient lakebed, was discovered by retired Oregon governor John Whiteaker during an 1876 desert camping trip. He promptly wrote University of Oregon paleontologist Thomas Condon that he'd found a playa littered with black, sand-blasted bones. Could they be fossils, he wondered? Intrigued, Condon mounted an expedition to the remote site. He later reported, "We staked our horses and went to work. We found the remains of elephants, camels and horses and other mammals; a good many bird bones, and some specimens of fossil fish. After a search of six or seven hours we packed our specimens and returned."

The Sand Dunes.

Condon's remarkably quick day's work opened a window onto Oregon's Ice Age life, revealing a relatively recent world of exotic mammoths and camels. Since then, other excavations have added to the picture and tried to answer several puzzling questions.

Puzzle #1: Why did so many animals die here? Answer: Evidently Fort Rock Lake has grown and shrunk many times during Ice Age fluctuations, repeatedly luring thirsty animals to their dooms in a remnant quagmire.

Puzzle #2: Could the mammoths and camels Condon identified have been hunted to extinction by humans? Answer: Perhaps. Condon discovered arrowheads among the mammal bones. He refused to jump to conclusions, however, arguing that winds might have blown away the sand of intervening strata, mixing old bones with recent artifacts. Later excavations showed Condon was right. The mammal bones at Fossil Lake belong to a layer that has been radiocarbon dated as more than 29,000 years old—quite a bit older than the first evidence of human occupation.

Puzzle #3: How could a landlocked desert lake have fossils of king salmon, a migratory fish from the ocean? Answer: Who knows? Could the lake have had an outlet somewhere after all? On a later hike you'll be able to investigate this puzzler in more detail.

The Lost Forest. Now it's time to get back in the car and bump up the sandy road another two and a half miles to the Lost Forest. Park the car and scramble up Sand Rock's craggy knoll to get a good overview of this "wandering" woodland, a five-square-mile stand of apparently misplaced ponderosa pines. Early Fort Rock homesteaders wryly suggested that these stately pines must have hiked here from somewhere else, because they obviously couldn't have sprouted out here in the desert.

Botanists who researched the Lost Forest agreed—not that the trees walked, but that the ponderosa pines should have died long ago. Since the Ice Age rainstorms tapered off several thousand years ago, pines have all but vanished from southeast Oregon. Ponderosas normally require seventeen inches of rainfall to survive. Here they seem to thrive on a meager nine. No other pine trees live within thirty miles.

The Lost Forest's secret ploy, it turns out, is to tap the ancient lakebed underground. The old lake was shallow here, barely deep enough to make

The Lost Forest from Sand Rock.

Sand Rock an island, but the lake's hardpan extends from the Sand Dunes up onto these rolling hills like a plastic swimming pool liner. Rainfall that might otherwise sink into the subsoil puddles up on this hidden hardpan below a thick covering of sand. Because ponderosa pines are one of the few conifers with a taproot, they are uniquely suited to pump up the water.

Crack in the Ground. After strolling through the Lost Forest, head back toward Christmas Valley to return to the unsolved puzzle of Fort Rock Lake's missing outlet. The problem deserves serious thought. Not only does this landlocked lakebed have fossils of ocean-run salmon, but it also harbors fossilized shells of *Limnaea* snails, a freshwater species now found only in the Columbia River drainage. And yet the pass blocking access to the Deschutes/Columbia watershed is 260 feet above the highest traceable shoreline of prehistoric Fort Rock Lake. No outlet river could have drained over that pass.

But could it have drained *under* the pass? The hills north of Fort Rock are draped with relatively recent lava flows. Perhaps one of them buried the old outlet river.

First take a look at the closest lava flow, where a two-mile-long crack in the lava extends from the base of four cinder cones. A gravel road from Christmas Valley leads seven miles north to a parking lot. From there a path ambles briefly amid sagebrush and juniper before ducking into the crack itself. For the next two tenths of a mile, the trail traces the bottom of this thirty-foot-deep lava slot, a rock chasm so narrow that boulders some-

Crack in the Ground.

times hang wedged overhead. Snow that drifts here in winter is so well protected from the desert sun that it often lingers until May. Wagonloads of early Fort Rock homesteaders used to picnic here on hot days, making ice cream from the snow. In summer the jagged slot's floor seems a secret garden, lush with gooseberries, dandelions—and some stinging nettles. Bright yellow and orange lichens decorate the lava walls. Gas bubbles in the lava flow have left honeycombed rock sculptures and small caves.

Crack in the Ground apparent-ly opened a few thousand years ago when the four cinder cones erupted nearby. Their activity emptied an underground magma chamber. The ground settled, and a tension crack formed along the edge of a broad depression.

It's unlikely that a river valley is underneath the Four Craters Lava Bed. But other lava flows nearby really could have dammed the lake. On the next hike, closer to Bend, you can walk through a dry canyon where an Ice Age river flowed. Perhaps it was a part of the missing link between ancient Fort Rock Lake and the sea.

Dry River

No water now flows in the lava badlands east of Bend, but during the Ice Age a tributary of the Deschutes River snaked across this barren land-scape, cutting through a narrow canyon and draining a vast lake on the present site of Millican, along Highway 20 toward Burns. If the larger lake at Fort Rock also overflowed, it too must have drained through this gorge.

Petroglyphs along the Dry River suggest the canyon was a popular fishing spot and travel route for early tribes. Luther Cressman, the archeologist who crisscrossed Oregon's high desert in the 1930s, recorded red-painted spirals, wavy lines, and indecipherable stick figures. None of Oregon's current tribes has a tradition of painting rocks in this fashion, so the meanings of the symbols are unclear. But the petroglyphs most likely were not written for people at all. They may well have been messages for the spirits, a touching point between the natural world and the unseen powers that lie beyond.

All Northwest tribes believed that salmon, for example, were actually a race of supernatural beings that lived under the sea. These spirits could take the shape of fish, if they so chose, and swim up the streams to aid people in times of hunger. If offended, the spirit-fish could easily change their minds and stay away. All the tribes living near salmon streams developed complicated rituals to assuage these powerful beings, honoring the first salmon of the season as a visiting chief and carefully returning fish skeletons to the stream, with the intact heads pointed upriver, to encourage the spirits to return next year. It seems likely that many Northwest rock paintings were once a part of these appeasement rituals, particularly because petroglyphs are so often found at river narrows where salmon fishing is easiest. Of course, this would mean that the petroglyphs along Dry River failed, driving away not only the fish but the river as well.

A cave overhang protects petroglyphs in the Dry River's channel.

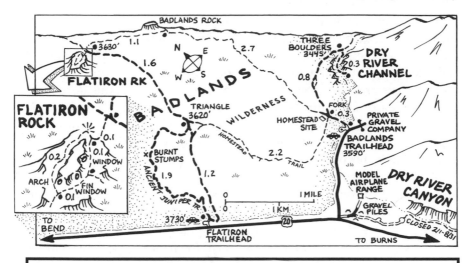

3. Dry River

HIKE LOCATION

Easy
3 miles round-trip
60 feet elevation gain

Explore a desert riverbed in a dramatic canyon near Bend.

Getting There: Drive east of Bend on Highway 20 toward Burns 18 miles. At an "Oregon Badlands Wilderness" sign at the bottom of a hill, turn left on a paved road for one mile. Then turn left into the fenced gravel Badlands Rock Trailead.

Hiking Tips: The trail starts as a gated dirt road that's closed to motor vehicles. Walk 0.3 mile to a 3-way fork. You'll want to go right here, but first explore the sagebrush area to the left, a homestead from the early 1900s. A wire fence protects an old cistern. All artifacts are federally protected. Then take the right-hand fork at the homestead and continue 0.8 mile. Leave the road when you reach *three* large boulders on the right. Take a downhill track sharply to the right and keep to the right for 200 yards to a pole fence at the mouth of the Dry River's channel. Beyond is a narrow canyon with 40-foot rock walls. An overhang to the right served as a cave campsite when the river ran with fish, perhaps 6000 years ago. The faint red ochre petroglyphs here can be camaged even by the oil of fingerprints, so don't touch! The canyon peters out after a few hundred more yards.

Season: Open all year, but avoid midwinter's icy winds and midsummer's blazing heat.

Today the hiking route to the Dry River crosses the Badlands Wilderness, set aside in 2009 as one of the strangest wilderness areas in Oregon. The region has no mountains, lakes, or streams. The entire valley here was buried by a basalt lava flow from the Newberry Volcano about 12,000 years ago. As the lava cooled, it wrinkled into pressure ridges—much the way a bad paint job on a refrigerator might wrinkle as it dries. Then in 5677 BC, the Mt. Mazama eruption that created Crater Lake dumped a foot of volcanic ash here, filling the gaps between the pressure ridges with what look like sandy paths. The result is a confusing labyrinth of random lava walls and winding sandy trails. Viewpoints are few. It is easy to get lost.

But there's a good chance you will make it to the Dry River's channel, where a cave overhang shelters faint red petroglyphs. The hike is nearly level, and it's not much more than a mile to your goal.

From the Badlands Trailhead you walk an old roadbed 0.3 mile to a trail junction beside an old homestead site. Pause at this junction to explore the sagebrush area to the left. You'll find a wire fence protecting an ancient water cistern. There are also rusty artifacts here from pioneer days, but resist the temptation to pick them up. Anything more than 25 years old is strictly protected by federal law. Leave artifacts as you found them, so that others can see them as well.

From the homestead junction, keep right on an old road for 0.8 mile. The track forks and rejoins, and passes some boulders that have been placed to block side tracks. Continue until you reach a track to the right blocked by three large boulders. Turn right right here on a side path that descends to the old riverbed.

Keep right 200 yards to a pole fence at the mouth of the Dry River's channel. Beyond is a narrow canyon with 40-foot rock walls. An overhang to the right served as a cave campsite when the river ran with fish, at least 6000 years ago. The faint red ochre petroglyphs here can be damaged even by the oil of fingerprints, so don't touch! The canyon peters out after a few hundred more yards, where circluar pits in the rocks remind of the vanished river's swirling waters.

This is a good place to rest and reflect before heading back. Imagine this canyon as it might have been at the end of the Ice Age. A family in deer skins and sagebrush sandals crouches beside the rushing river. They have trekked from the vast desert lakes to a sacred riverbend. Here they have built a fire beneath the rimrock.

They are watching, waiting for the salmon-spirits to return.

CHAPTER II

Angry Spirits

Oregon's first history was not written, but rather spoken. On long winter evenings, storytellers of the Northwest tribes used firesides as stages for the dramas of their gods and ancestors.

Some legends were strictly for entertainment—for example, the story of how the trickster god Coyote once ate his own broiled anus by mistake. Some tales held warning; a good example is the account of a little boy who ventured too near a river and was kidnapped by Seal people.

But the tales that early anthropologists sought most eagerly were legends of local history. After all, the Old Testament and Homer's *Odyssey* had begun as oral histories. The researchers hoped to find a basis of historical fact behind the Northwest tribes' legends too. They soon ran into a problem: The local tales seemed impossibly far-fetched. The Klamaths told of a missing mountain. The Kalapuyans described a flood that filled the entire Willamette Valley hundreds of feet deep. The Multnomahs told of a "Bridge of the Gods" spanning the Columbia River.

Years later, geologists discovered that each of these tales has a kernel of truth. Today, hiking trails descend into the Klamaths' missing mountain, climb the high ground above the Kalapuyans' flood, and cross the ruins of the Multnomahs' Bridge of the Gods. A walk on one of these paths is simultaneously an exploration of Oregon's geology and a journey among the spirits of the land.

Crater Lake's Wizard Island

Is it possible that the Klamath tribe could have preserved the memory of Crater Lake's formation for 7700 years? Consider the impact the original eruption must have had. Mt. Mazama, a 12,000-foot, glacier-clad volcano, had smoked sulkily for centuries. And then one day, in an explosion many times more massive than Mt. St. Helens' 1980 eruption, the mountain blasted 12.2 cubic miles of pumice and ash into the sky. The debris fell

Crater Lake's Wizard Island in winter.

two hundred feet deep on the Pumice Desert, and ten feet deep at Klamath Marsh, where the tribe has traditionally hunted waterfowl and gathered pond lily seeds. Thousands of people must have died. As the mountain collapsed, a glowing avalanche of pumice and superheated gas raced down the slopes at freight-train speeds as far as forty miles, killing still more.

Those who survived obviously left an enduring taboo on the mountain. Even into the nineteenth century, only shamans and power seekers dared to visit the spirit-infested lake in the sunken summit. No one spoke idly of such a place. Decades after United States explorers and settlers had crisscrossed Oregon, the secret lake remained uncharted. It was 1853 before John Hillman and a group of gold prospectors happened to reach the rim's startling cliffs. The report of their astonishment spread the lake's fame and eventually led to the establishment of Crater Lake National Park in 1902—and the trails you can hike today inside the ruined mountain's shell.

Although the Klamaths seldom spoke to outsiders about Crater Lake, their own legends reveal a surprising familiarity with the formation of the lake and its later mini-volcano, Wizard Island. The stories involve two of their most powerful spirit-gods: the wise and peaceful Skell, who usually took the form of a marten, and the jealous Llao, angry ringleader of evil spirits. The two rival gods ruled from opposite mountains. Skell lived with a host of friends on a high desert peak called Yamsay, "the home of the north wind." Llao lived on Mt. Mazama with his horde of minions.

In one of the early Klamath legends, Llao blew up Mt. Mazama in his rage for being denied the hand of a beautiful Klamath maiden. The only tribespeople to survive hid in the water of Klamath Lake. When the rain of fire subsided, the top of the Llao's mountain was gone. In another story — retold here — Llao set out to challenge his rival Skell, and ended up creating Wizard Island.

From his camp beside shattered Mt. Mazama, Llao devised a plan to overcome his rival, Skell. He disguised one of his ugly underlings as a beautiful maiden. "Go find Skell at Yamsay Mountain," Llao told her. "I can't seem to get him to fight, so seduce him and bring back his heart for me to eat."

When the strange temptress reached Yamsay Mountain, Skell suspected her at once. But his more gullible friend Weasel succumbed to her charms. Weasel soon lay with his head on the maiden's lap. When Weasel opened his mouth the girl tore out his heart with a digging stick. Then she ran back with Weasel's heart to Llao at the ruins of Mt. Mazama.

The treachery of the attack angered Skell more than anything Llao

Klamath tribespeople gathering reeds on Klamath Lake, circa 1890.

had done before. He called Antelope, Cougar, Jackrabbit, and his many other friends together. He assigned each of them a position on the route between the two mountains. Then Skell disguised himself as a withered old man and shakily approached the remains of Mt. Mazama.

The peak's shell had already filled with a deep lake. Skell found Llao and his underlings playing ball with Weasel's heart on the flats of the Pumice Desert nearby.

"Let an old man play too," Skell said.

Llao laughed. "This is no game for the feeble. Go away."

"I used to play pretty well," Skell replied, his voice weak.

"I said go away. When these players get hungry they sometimes eat old men."

"Just let me try catching the ball once," Skell persisted.

Llao scoffed and threw Weasel's heart at the old man as hard as he could.

Skell nimbly caught the heart one-handed. Then he tossed it to Antelope, waiting by the edge of the desert.

"After him!" Llao shouted, sending his fastest runners to chase Antelope. But when the runners were about to catch up, Antelope passed the heart to Cougar. Cougar sped onward until he too grew tired, then passed the heart to Jackrabbit. Each of Skell's friends took a turn in the relay until they had brought the heart back to Yamsay Mountain and restored Weasel to life.

Meanwhile at the Pumice Desert, Skell had changed himself back to his usual form, the shape of a marten. "Now, Llao, it is time I put an end to these attacks."

Llao's minions drew back with fear when they saw Skell. But Llao himself stepped forward, gloating. "At last I've lured you to fight. You'll soon learn who is stronger."

As the two gods circled each other warily for the battle, Llao's frightened followers hid in the nearby lake. From there they could hear the terrible roars of the gods' battle. The ground shook, breaking great rocks loose from the lake cliffs. Finally all was still. Then they saw their master Llao stride victoriously to the top of Llao Rock, the cliff overlooking the lake.

"I have killed the marten-spirit Skell," he roared, "And now I will tear up the remains of his body for you to eat, destroying him forever." The figure atop the cliff threw down the pieces of a body one by one. Llao's minions in the lake below eagerly gobbled them up—until they were thrown the last piece, the head. It was obviously not a marten's head. It was Llao's.

When they looked up, they realized the figure atop the cliff was actually the clever Skell, who had won the battle and disguised himself as his rival. He had tricked them into eating their own master's body. They wailed in mourning and left Llao's head untouched.

Skell returned triumphantly to Weasel and his friends at Yamsay Mountain, where he has lived in peace ever since. As for the evil Llao, all that remains of him is his head, poking above the water of Crater Lake, where it is now called Wizard Island.

Today Crater Lake National Park's most popular trail—and the only route to the lakeshore itself—switchbacks down to a boat dock at Cleetwood Cove. From there you can take a tour boat around the lake. And for an extra charge you can stop at Wizard Island to hike a little-known spiral trail up Llao's pointy head.

As you set off hiking down the wide Cleetwood Cove Trail you'll pass lodgepole pines, Shasta red firs, mountain hemlocks, manzanita bushes, and lots of glimpses down to the glowing blue lake. The amazing color results partly from the lake's purity (it has no inlet other than precipitation) and also from its depth, at 1943 feet the world's third deepest. In recorded history the lake's surface has only frozen twice and its level has only fluctuated sixteen feet. When you reach the rocky shore at Cleetwood Cove's dock you're not likely to find many people swimming. The water is barely fifty degrees even in summer.

You won't see many fishermen either, although the National Park Service has waived the need for fishing licenses in their push to get rid of the lake's fish. The problem is that fish aren't native here. In fact, they're

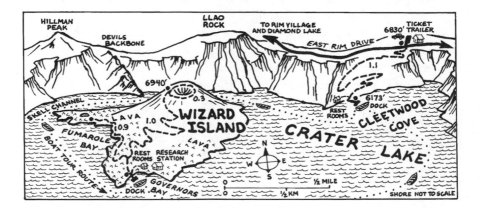

endangering the lake's renowned purity.

Rainbow trout were introduced in 1888 by William Gladstone Steel, a Portland outdoorsman who spent decades tirelessly promoting Crater Lake for national park status. On his 1888 trip Steel stopped at a farm

4. Crater Lake's Wizard Island

HIKE LOCATION

Moderate (to Cleetwood Cove)
2.2 miles round trip
700 feet elevation loss

Difficult (to Wizard Island summit)
4.2 miles round trip
1460 feet elevation gain

Ride a boat across Crater Lake to climb Wizard Island's cinder cone.

Getting There: From Crater Lake National Park's Rim Village, take the Rim Drive clockwise 10.6 miles to the Cleetwood Cove Trailhead. If you're coming from the park's north entrance off Highway 138, turn left along the Rim Drive for 4.6 miles. The national park itself has an entrance fee of about $10 per car for a week-long pass or $20 for an annual pass.

Hiking Tips: If you plan to take the boat tour, put a warm, waterproof coat in your pack and get your ticket in the large parking lot across the road from the trailhead. Plan to be there soon after the ticket kiosk opens at 8:30am. You can also reserve tickets in advance at 888-774-2728 or *www craterlakelodges.com* or from an automated kiosk in Crater Lake Lodge. Weather permitting, boat tours leave every 60 minutes between 9:30am and 3:30pm from early July to mid-September, but only the boat that leaves at 9:30am will stop at Wizard Island. Pickup times for the return trip are 2:30pm and 5pm.

A private concession company sets the prices. For the standard boat tour, expect to pay about $37 for adults and $25 for kids under 12. To disembark on Wizard Island you'll need to pay about $15 extra per person. To make sure hikers don't miss their boat, sales for each tour stop 40 minutes before it leaves. Overnight stays on Wizard Island are not permitted, and pets are not permitted on any trail in the national park.

Season: Snow closes the trail except in summer, from early July to early September.

While You're in the Area: Climb to The Watchman, a lookout atop Crater Lake's rim (Hike #49) and stop by Crater Lake Lodge (Hike #42) for a hike up Garfield Peak.

Llao Rock.

along the upper Rogue River and paid two boys to fill a bucket with six hundred fingerling trout. He put the bucket in his wagon, but it sloshed so much he wound up carrying it in his hands more than forty miles. With great care he freshened the water at each stream. When Steel finally scrambled down the lake's steep rim slopes with the bucket, only thirty-seven sluggish fingerlings remained alive. Nonetheless, his effort sufficed to change the lake's ecosystem, irrevocably damaging the park he had set out to save. Later visitors introduced Kokanee salmon as well.

Today park officials are still puzzling over how to remove the fish from four cubic miles of water. Fishing with bait isn't allowed because eggs and worms might introduce still more alien species. Anglers who try with artificial lures say the lake is simply too big for fish to find them.

The tour boats sailing from Cleetwood Cove look like roofless blue school buses, each packed with up to forty passengers and an interpretive ranger. On the cruise to Wizard Island you'll sail below Llao Rock's 1870-foot sheer cliff, where Skell threw the evil god into the lake. Llao Rock is composed of an enormous rhyodacite lava flow that helped trigger the mountain's final collapse. About two hundred years before the peak's final blast, a small gas explosion blew out a deep crater here on the mountain's flank. Pasty magma oozed out to fill the hole. Before long, similar lava flows had drained nearly three cubic miles of molten rock from the mountain's interior. These large flows caused Mt. Mazama's explosion by "uncorking" gas in the magma below, just as a popped champagne cork lets loose a sudden froth of gas bubbles.

Very few people get off the tour boat when it docks at Wizard Island, but then most people don't know about the spectacular trail that spirals up this island's cinder cone. The summit trail sets off amid blocky black lava colonized by golden-mantled ground squirrels. You'll also see the pink blooms of bleeding hearts and the gnarled trunks of Shasta red firs struggling from the rock. At the top, the panoramic path circles a ninety-foot-deep crater.

Notice that Wizard Island's summit pit really is a crater, while "Crater" Lake's basin is not. Geologists have two different words for mountains with holes in the top. If the hole formed as the mountain was being built up, it's a crater. If the mountain collapsed, it's actually a *caldera*. Wizard Island was one of two cinder cones that erupted in Mt. Mazama's caldera. The other, Merriam Cone, never saw the light of day. Rain and snow are heavy enough here that Crater Lake only took about 740 years to fill. Merriam Cone erupted entirely underwater, and remains 486 feet beneath the surface.

Wizard Island was named by Crater Lake's early promoter, William Gladstone Steel, because he thought it resembled a sorcerer's hat. Hat or spirit's head, the top offers unforgettable views of the blue lake in every direction.

After you hike back down from Wizard Island's crater and catch a tour boat toward home, you'll sail around Phantom Ship, a much smaller island. Named for its mast-shaped pinnacles and its relatively hidden moorage by the lake's south shore, the islet is the oldest rock visible on the lake, a 400,000-year-old remnant of a volcanic cone that preceded Mt. Mazama. Geologically, Crater Lake's two islands reflect the entire timeline of the mountain's eruptions—Phantom Ship was buried when Mt. Mazama was born, and Wizard Island is the cinder cone that decked its deathbed.

As you sail back toward Cleetwood Cove, you may not want to look at Crater Lake geologically. After all, this is the interior of a recently active volcano. Instead remember the Klamaths' legends, and the story of the peace-loving Skell, whose triumph laid the evil spirit Llao to rest for all time.

Marys Peak

Little is known about the Kalapuyans, the tribe that occupied the Willamette Valley, because so few natives were alive by the time pioneer settlers arrived. As much as a hundred years earlier, seafaring explorers had unknowingly brought measles, smallpox, diphtheria, influenza, and other diseases to the Northwest coast. The strange plagues had swept through native villages, killing as many as nine out of ten. The survivors, their culture in ruins, offered little resistance when farmers claimed their lands. The Luckiamute band of Kalapuyans, including the Marys River subgroup at Corvallis, might once have numbered a thousand. By 1905, only twenty-eight survived. By 1910, there were only eight.

As a result, most Kalapuyan legends have been lost. But fragments reveal that the trickster Coyote was a central character in their dramas. As with most Northwest tribes, the Kalapuyans set their tales in a protean age before humans. In those days, animal-spirits walked the earth as people do now. Coyote, a schemer whose plans often went awry, was the most powerful of these legendary demigods. And Marys Peak, the highest point in the Coast Range west of the Willamette Valley, was Coyote's favorite retreat.

The Kalapuyans knew Marys Peak as Chateemanwi, "the place where spirits dwell." Today, an easy hike to the summit's stunning viewpoint crosses meadows of strange wildflowers. Why are the odd flowers here? There's a surprising touch of truth to the explanation in the Kalapuyans' legends — recreated here from the remaining fragments.

> Long ago when spirits lived on the earth as animals, a terrible monster roamed the Willamette Valley by night. The monster seemed unstoppable, devouring any animal-spirits it met, and then retreating to the safety of a cave by day. Even Panther, who often hunted at night, was terrified. He went to ask Coyote for advice.
>
> "Of course I'm not afraid for myself," Panther explained, "but I worry about my beautiful young wife."
>
> "I see," Coyote replied, his thoughts straying already as he tried to picture Panther's beautiful wife.
>
> After a moment Panther prodded, "So what do you suggest doing?"
>
> "About what?"
>
> "About the monster."
>
> Coyote waved his paw. "Oh, that's easy enough. Obviously the monster can't stand sunlight. That's its weakness. Trick it out of the cave by day, and it'll be blind. Then you can finish it off in no time."

Hikers in the summit meadow of Marys Peak.

"That might work. But how can we trick it out of its cave?"

"Well, I'll just—" Coyote hesitated. No ideas sprang to mind. "Wait here a moment. I'd better make sure my son's watching the fire." Coyote slipped out, but didn't bother checking on his son. Instead he slapped his hip to call out his feces for advice. Surprising as it may seem, they usually knew what to do, and he'd learned to trust them. He whispered to them, "How can I trick a monster out of its cave?"

The feces sang quietly, "Hide the sun, hide the sun."

Coyote slapped the feces back in his anus. "Oh, I knew that all along." He went back to Panther and told him to be ready for battle outside the monster's cave. Then he took his bow and climbed to the top of Marys Peak. There he shot an arrow into the sun. He shot another and another, each squarely into the tail feathers of the last. When the arrows formed a long chain that reached down to earth, he pulled down the sun, walked back into the valley, and tied the sun to the bottom of the Willamette River.

Right away it was so dark you could see the stars dancing overhead. Before long Coyote could hear the growls and roars of a distant struggle. "That must be Panther and the monster fighting," Coyote thought. The plan seemed to be working. Fooled by the darkness, the monster had evidently decided it was time to come out for the night, and had run straight into Panther. "Now I just need to blind the monster."

Coyote dove back into the river and cut loose the sun. As soon as the sun popped back up into the air, the sky was blazingly bright. Coyote rested on the riverbank, listening again to the distant roars of the fight. The battle seemed to be lasting a very long time. He couldn't tell from the sound who was winning, Panther or the monster.

"If Panther wins," Coyote reasoned, "He'll be so grateful for my help that he'll want to give me an excellent gift—probably his beautiful wife. On the other hand, if the monster wins, I really should take it upon myself to care for Panther's widow. Either way I might as well go get her now."

Ancient forest along a Marys Peak trail.

Satisfied with this logic, Coyote went to Panther's home. Panther's wife was even more beautiful than he had imagined. Coyote explained the situation as best he could, but was disappointed when she didn't want to go with him. So Coyote simply took her away. He didn't let her out of his sight for weeks to make sure she wouldn't escape.

One day when they returned home from a hunt, Coyote asked, "Where's my son? He should be here watching the fire."

Panther's wife replied, "Can't you see the tracks? Panther's been here. He must have taken your son hostage because you took me."

"He can't do that!" Coyote roared. "I'll track him down and get my son back."

Panther's wife shook her head. "You'll never find them. Panther is much stealthier than you are. He's a better husband."

Coyote had never been so angry. "We'll see if I can't flush Panther out." He stormed down the valley and dug an enormous dam across the Willamette River. Then he took Panther's wife with him to the top of Marys Peak. There he waited while the valley slowly filled with water. Before long all the plants and animals were retreating before the flood, seeking high ground. After a few days they were clustered at the top of Marys Peak, begging Coyote to breach the dam.

"We'd rather face a monster than have floods like this," one of them said.

Coyote wouldn't listen. Finally he saw Panther swimming toward Marys Peak with Coyote's son on his back. "Aha!" Coyote shouted. "So now you're ready to give back my son."

Panther kept swimming. "No, I like swimming. I came to see if you were ready to trade your son for my wife. Or would you rather wait some more?"

Panther's wife whispered to Coyote, "He's a much better swimmer than you are. He's a better husband all around."

Coyote was beginning to think he could live without Panther's wife. He decided to make the trade and tear down the dam.

After the flood had finally ebbed, most of the plants and animals came down from Marys Peak. But quite a few liked it up there and stayed.

How much truth lies behind the Kalapuyan tales? Geologists report that the Willamette Valley was in fact filled from wall to wall three hundred feet deep by a series of Ice Age floods. The floods were triggered when a lobe of the continental glacier in Canada repeatedly advanced across a branch of the Columbia River in northern Idaho, temporarily damming a lake into the Rocky Mountains. Each time the glacier retreated and the ice dam burst, a gigantic flood poured across Eastern Washington.

The water churned through the Columbia Gorge and puddled up in the Willamette Valley before draining to the sea. Icebergs in the floods rafted boulders of Rocky Mountain granite as far as McMinnville.

But is the Kalapuyan tale a tribal memory of these glacial floods? Although the Ice Age brought at least eighty such floods, it is unlikely that anyone in the Willamette Valley would have survived to tell about them. Besides, the last glacial flood was 12,700 years ago—a very long time for a legend to persist.

The story of Coyote's flood might have been a way of explaining the strange plants the Kalapuyans found atop Marys Peak. The peak is a biological island, with alpine meadows of paintbrush wildflowers, stands of old-growth noble firs, and other species you'd expect in the High Cascades. Botanists believe these plants really did retreat here. In the colder climate of the Ice Age, similar alpine plants flourished throughout Western Oregon. As the weather warmed, increased competition drove these

5. Marys Peak

HIKE LOCATION

Easy (old road to summit)
1.2 miles round trip
340 feet elevation gain

Easy (Meadow Edge Trail)
2.2-mile loop
500 feet elevation gain

This Coast Range peak offers views from the Pacific to the Cascades.

Getting There: From Corvallis, take Highway 20 west through Philomath, fork left onto Highway 34 for 8.8 miles, and turn right on paved Marys Peak Road for 9.5 miles to its end at the observation point parking lot. A Northwest Forest Pass is required. The $5 per car fee can be paid at a box by the trailhead, or you can pick up a $30 per car annual permit in advance from a ranger station or outdoor store.

Hiking Tips: The easiest and only crowded hike at Marys Peak is the 0.6-mile stroll up a gated gravel service road from the observation point parking lot to the summit. The Meadow Edge Trail is only a mile longer and offers a quieter, more interesting loop to the summit. To find this path, drive Marys Peak Road only 8.8 miles up from Highway 34, turn right at the Marys Peak campground entrance, and 100 yards later fork left to a picnic area and trailhead. Keep left when the path splits after 150 yards. After 0.7 mile turn left at a junction, and 80 yards later turn right, climbing to the summit viewpoint. To finish the loop, head back down and keep left at all junctions.

Season: Wildflowers are at their best in June and July. Snow closes the summit trails sporadically between December and May.

While You're in the Area: The Benton County Historical Museum, in downtown Philomath's restored pioneer school building, is open 10am-4:30pm Tuesday-Saturday.

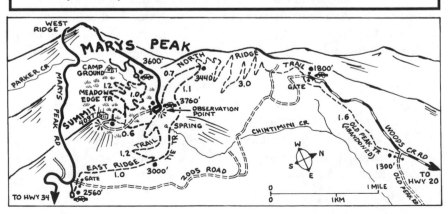

species to Marys Peak's summit, their last Coast Range stronghold.

Today the easiest hike atop this legendary peak of strange plants is the stroll to the summit from the observation point parking lot. It's a walk of about a half mile along a gated gravel service road. On a clear day, views extend from Mt. Rainier to Mt. Thielsen, with the ocean on the horizon to the west. July colors the summit meadows with red paintbrush, purple penstemon, white yarrow, and blue butterflies.

For a less crowded route to the summit, try the slightly longer Meadow Edge Trail. This loop begins at the Marys Peak campground, climbs to the summit through the unusual grove of huge noble firs, and returns alongside a quiet wildflower meadow. If you're interested in an even longer hike, two other paths explore the ancient forests on the steepish sides of Marys Peak: the East Ridge Trail and the North Ridge Trail.

The Kalapuya tribe once sent young men to the summit of Marys Peak on vision quests. The boys would wait alone for days, fasting until they received a vision from the animal-spirit that would serve as their lifelong spiritual guide. Chateemanwi, "the place where spirits dwell," still draws those who seek quiet contemplation and far-ranging views. It's as close to the sun as you can get in the Coast Range — and a good safe spot in a flood.

Bandon

For tales of perseverance, try the Southern Oregon coastal village of Bandon. This is a city that twice burned to the ground, yet refused to die. The area's Coquille tribe seems just as stubborn. Marched off to distant reservations and then officially disbanded, the tribe is now back in force. Even the heroes of the Coquilles' ancient legends never gave up, despite the angry spirits they faced.

The best way to tour the setting for these inspirational dramas is to walk through town to the pinnacled islands of Bandon's ocean beach. The hike begins in Old Town, where seagulls screech from the pilings of the Coquille River. Behind the docks of a marina rise Bandon's three downtown blocks of gift shops, boutiques, and galleries.

The picturesque coastal town you see here is actually the fourth on this site. The first was a Coquille tribal village of cedar-plank longhouses, built in the shadow of Tupper Rock, a sacred rock monolith on a hill where good spirits dwelled. In those days the tang of woodsmoke, kelp, and fish drifted from the houses past a row of dugout canoes on the river beach.

The Coquilles' thirty-foot cedar canoes were ideal for river travel, but too small to ply the choppy ocean. Elders told of a time long ago when

Bandon after the fire of 1936.

the tribe had been tempted to travel the seas like their powerful Yurok neighbors on California's redwood coast. The evil ocean spirit Seatka had left a huge redwood log on the village's beach after a storm. Many in the tribe had avoided the foreign log as an omen. But two young brothers had dared to carve it into a sixty-foot canoe that could challenge the Yuroks. As soon as the brothers paddled it onto the rough river bar, however, they capsized and drowned. Then the tribe knew Seatka had been using the redwood log as bait to capture foolish people.

The tribe was even more suspicious when strangers began arriving from the ocean in giant, white-winged canoes. After the California Gold Rush peaked, miners searched the Pacific Coast for gold. They found it five miles north of Bandon in 1853, in the black sands of Whiskey Run Beach. In 1854 a group of forty miners decided it would be safest to exterminate the natives before trouble arose. Without provocation, the miners suddenly attacked the village one morning at dawn, killing fifteen men and one woman. The Army took the survivors to a reservation at Fort Umpqua in 1857. When settlers wanted that land in 1861, the Coquilles were marched to a new reservation at Yachats. And when even that rocky shore was opened to settlers in 1876, the tribe was forced farther north to the Siletz Reservation.

Shipyards and sawmills dominated the pioneer city that sprang up on the ruins of the Coquille village. By 1900 Bandon boasted the largest fleet between San Francisco and Astoria. Riverboats docked here from the Coquille River hinterland. Ocean steamers crossed the treacherous river bar regularly. Then fire swept through Bandon on June 11, 1914, leaving little more than ashes. For the next two decades the town clawed its way back onto its feet. By 1936 it again boasted five hundred buildings and a population of nearly two thousand. Bandon had risen for the third time.

In the summer of 1936 the hills about Bandon glowed with the yellow blooms of Irish gorse. It was a wildflower that Lord Bennett of Bandon, Ireland had brought in the 1800s to remind him of his homeland. Since then the prickly, oily bushes had spread to the edge of town. On September 26, 1936, a wildfire raced through the dry gorse toward Bandon.

Bandon's Coquille River lighthouse.

All night, fishermen desperately ferried people across the river. From the safety of the far bank, the townspeople watched their homes burn again. By morning only sixteen buildings still stood.

The current "Old Town" is surprisingly quaint, considering that it is so new. After touring the shops, head west along the riverfront toward the sound of the ocean. Soon you'll pass a 1939 Coast Guard building that has been converted to offices.

As you continue toward the ocean, you'll see the forty-foot tower of the Coquille River lighthouse across the river. The beacon was built in 1896 to guide ships across the treacherous bar. But ships continued to founder. In fact, a three-masted lumber schooner nearly rammed the lighthouse in 1904, smashing into the rock just thirty feet away.

In the early 1900s the Army Corps of Engineers decided to protect ships by building jetties at the river mouth. To save money, they quarried the necessary rock nearby—from Tupper Rock, the town's landmark. Although this monolith had been the Coquille's sacred site, the Army blew it up and dumped the boulders into the sea. Then, in a final indignity, the

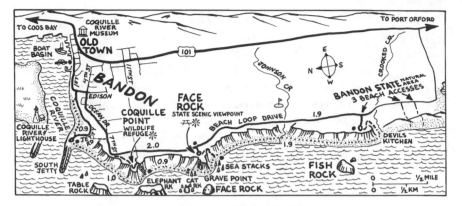

6. Bandon

HIKE LOCATION

Easy (to South Jetty)
1.8 miles round trip
No elevation gain

Moderate (to Face Rock Wayside)
4.8-mile loop
100 feet elevation gain

Stroll from a quaint coastal village to a beach with craggy islands.

Getting There: From Coos Bay, drive 24 miles south on Highway 101, turn left through an archway proclaiming "Welcome to Old Town Bandon," drive a block to the riverfront, and turn left to a parking area beside the boat basin.

Hiking Tips: Walk toward the ocean on First Street along the riverfront. Beyond the converted 1939 Coast Guard building, turn right on Jetty Road. Because this narrow street has no sidewalk, consider climbing over some boulders (after the Lighthouse Bed & Breakfast) to follow the river beach most of the way to Jetty Road's end at the South Jetty. If you're continuing, walk south along the beach 1.9 miles to the rock pinnacles at Grave Point, opposite Face Rock. Just beyond Grave Point climb a staircase to Face Rock Wayside and turn left on Beach Loop Drive for 2 miles through town to your car.

Season: Open all year.

While You're in the Area: Tour Bandon's Historical Museum, open 10am-4pm daily, on Highway 101 two blocks east of Old Town. Then drive Highway 101 north across the Coquille River and turn left past Bullards Beach State Park's 192-site campground to road's end at the Coquille River Lighthouse, with a small exhibit in the first floor room open 11am-5pm from mid-May to mid-October. Farther afield, check out Cape Blanco State Park (Hike #36) to the south and Shore Acres State Park (Hike #40) to the north.

government announced that the Coquilles no longer existed. They were declared "Americanized" and stripped of tribal status.

But the descendants of the Coquilles refused to give up their heritage. They started coming back to their homeland. They helped with excavations at the old village site, organized salmon bake festivals, and lobbied for reinstatement. In 1989, they won back tribal status. In 1990, they won back the quarry where Tupper Rock had stood. And in 1994 they built a retirement home there called Heritage Place, reclaiming for their elders the tribe's most sacred place.

Have the people here always been so patient and yet so enduring? If you doubt it, walk down the beach to Face Rock, the setting of another legend. Along the way you'll pass needle-shaped rock spires in the surf. Thousands of seabirds circle up from offshore islands. About two miles south of Bandon's jetty you'll see a giant island at sea with the striking profile of a girl's uplifted face in stone. According to a legend that has been reworded and revised many times over the years, this is Ewauna, the most obstinate of all the ancients.

Ewauna was the young daughter of a Takelma chief from far inland. When the Coquilles invited their neighbors to a great potlatch feast, Ewauna insisted on coming along.

"I've never seen the ocean," she explained to her father. "This is my chance."

Ewauna also had never heard of Seatka, the evil ocean spirit. When she reached the Coquille village, the locals warned her that Seatka could capture his victims with a single gaze of his eyes.

She shrugged as if she didn't care. Her father forbade her to visit the beach alone. But that made her even more determined to see the ocean for herself.

That night Ewauna slipped out of their longhouse and stole down to the shore. In the moonlight, the ocean seemed more wild and beautiful than anything she had seen before. Delighted, Ewauna splashed through the waves and went for a swim. But before long a dark cloud slid across the moon and Seatka's cold hands began closing about her from behind.

Frightened, she tried to shake free. "Let go!"

"Come now," Seatka murmured, turning her about, "Just look at me."

Suddenly she remembered the warning that Seatka controlled people with his eyes. "No, I won't look at you!" She turned her face away.

Bandon's beach.

"Oh yes." He pulled his head closer. "Yes you will."

Defiantly she looked up into the sky and fixed her eyes on the most constant thing she could imagine — the North Star. And there she stubbornly gazes to this day, though time has turned the headstrong girl to the stone of Face Rock.

Bridge of the Gods

Oregon's most enduring and endearing native legend describes a natural "Bridge of the Gods" across the Columbia River near Cascade Locks. The tale was long discounted by scientists as a fanciful fiction. But now investigations have proven the river really was spanned here by a natural walkway. In fact, hikers have been using the remains of the ancient crossing for years.

The setting for the legend — and the geologic explanation — is a vanished Columbia River rapids called the Cascades. Before the waters of Bonneville Dam covered it in 1937, this whitewater narrows had been a valuable fishing site for the Multnomah tribe. It had also been a hazardous bottleneck for Oregon Trail immigrants. John Fremont, a flamboyant U.S. Army explorer who accompanied the first of the large wagon trains to Oregon, wrote in 1843, "The river forms a great cascade, with a series of rapids, in breaking through the range of mountains." The cataract, he added, "gives the idea of Cascades to the whole range; and hence the name."

Fremont hired Multnomah villagers to portage his equipment around the narrows while his boats shot through the whitewater empty. Other immigrants tried running the rapids with their wagons perched on make-shift rafts. Some drowned, and many lost the supplies they had brought thousands of miles across the continent. The following year, in 1844, news of such tragedies led immigrants to try hacking out two rough wagon road detours—a short bypass on the Washington shore and the more desperate Barlow Road around Mt. Hood. Travel remained difficult along this stretch of the Columbia River until 1851, when steamboats arrived. In that year, a settler converted the portage route on the Washington shore to the Northwest's first railroad. Its primitive wood-railed track used carts pulled by mules. An odd little steam locomotive—again, the Northwest's first—was put to work on the portage track in 1862. Called the "Oregon Pony," it resembled a moonshiner's still on wheels. Today the little loco-motive is on display in a park at Cascade Locks.

Throughout these early years, travelers had plenty of time at the por-tage to repeat and embellish the Multnomah legends they heard. "The Indians have a tradition," one tourist commented in 1872, "That formerly there was a long, natural tunnel, through which the Columbia passed under a mountain. They assert that a great earthquake broke down this tunnel, the site of which they still point out, and that the debris formed the present obstructions at the Cascades."

A librarian named Katharine Judson, who worked in the periodicals

Table Mountain and the (now vanished) Cascades of the Columbia River in 1867.

section of the Seattle library, set out to piece together an "authentic" version of the Bridge of the Gods tale in 1910. She scavenged the library's holdings for anthropological articles and travelers' reports.

The central character, she decided, was Tyee Sahalie, the spirit chief of the Multnomahs' creation legends. The plot line that emerged from her research was colored in part by her era's romantic conception of the Indian world, but it has formed the basis for retellings ever since—including the version here.

> In the time before tribes lived along the Columbia River, Tyee Sahalie came downstream to choose places for his two sons to settle. He decided to shoot one arrow far to the west and another far to the east. He told his sons to found their tribes where the arrows landed. So one son went west and started the Multnomah tribe, while the other went east, founding the Klickitats. To keep the two tribes from arguing, Tyee Sahalie built the Cascade Range in between. But he also wanted a place where they could meet in peace. So he built a sacred walkway across the river in the middle of the mountain range.
>
> Time passed and the tribes would have been content, but they were constantly cold. The only fire in the world was hoarded by an old spirit-woman named Loowit. The people of the tribes complained about the problem to Tyee Sahalie. "Loowit has been taunting us," they said, shivering. "She's set up her fire right in the middle of the sacred bridge, where everyone can see how nice and warm it is."
>
> Tyee Sahalie felt sorry for them. "I'll see what I can do," he said. So he went to visit Loowit on the bridge.
>
> "I know what you want," the spirit-woman said right away when she saw Tyee Sahalie walking up, "and I'm not giving you any fire."
>
> "Not even if I offered a trade?" Tyee Sahalie asked.
>
> "A trade? What have you got?"
>
> "If you give the people fire, I'll give you eternal youth."
>
> "You can do that?"
>
> Tyee Sahalie nodded.
>
> Loowit eyed him cautiously. "And beauty too. I'd have to be the most beautiful girl anywhere."
>
> It was more than Tyee Sahalie had wanted to offer, but they struck the deal. Soon the people of the tribes had fires to cook their food and to warm themselves in winter. Meanwhile, Loowit became a beautiful young girl.
>
> The people's troubles, however, were just beginning. Loowit had

The Oregon Pony, *the Northwest's first locomotive, at Cascade Locks.*

enjoyed taunting them with her fire. Now she found she could tease them even more with her beauty. She lounged seductively in the middle of the bridge, flirting with the passing men until they were crazy with jealousy. Smitten worst of all were the two tribal chiefs, Wy'east of the Multnomahs and Klickitat from the eastern tribe.

The two lovestruck chiefs waged such a bloody war over Loowit that Tyee Sahalie finally became angry. He shook the ground, destroying the sacred walkway he had built across the river. Then he turned the rival chiefs into mountains, frozen under eternal snow. Chief Wy'east became Mt. Hood, overlooking the land of the Multnomahs. And Chief Klickitat became Mt. Adams, by the land of his own people.

Loowit, who had escaped the bridge's collapse, didn't seem sorry to lose her two suitors. When Tyee Sahalie saw she was already winking at other men, he turned her into a mountain too—the beautiful Mt. St. Helens.

The legend provides a nice explanation for the numerous minor eruptions of Mt. Hood and Mt. Adams in recent centuries: Wy'east and Klickitat are still fighting over Loowit, hurling lava bombs at each other across the Columbia River. Of course, the legend could not predict the fate of the heartless Loowit. Her contract for eternal youth and beauty obviously expired with the self-destruction of Mt. St. Helens' elegant cone in 1980.

But is there a factual basis for a natural bridge across the Columbia?

First, it's important to avoid visualizing a bridge in the conventional sense. No Northwest tribe is known to have built bridges, so the term "bridge" is almost certainly an inaccurate translation. Imagine instead a "walkway that allowed people to cross the river dry-footed." Certainly that more accurately describes what geologists have found.

The Columbia River was not bridged, but rather dammed. About 560 years ago a massive landslide sheared away half of Table Mountain and sent it thundering across the river to the Oregon side. The landslide covered fourteen square miles with debris and left a natural dam 270 feet tall.

---

7. Bridge of the Gods

HIKE LOCATION

Moderate (to Gillette Lake)
5 miles round trip
300 feet elevation gain

Difficult (to Greenleaf Overlook)
7.6 miles round trip
600 feet elevation gain

Follow the Pacific Crest Trail to a lake and a Columbia Gorge viewpoint.

Getting There: Drive Interstate 84 to Cascade Locks exit 44, pay $1 to cross the modern-day Bridge of the Gods, and turn left on Highway 14 for 2 miles to the Bonneville Trailhead on the right. A Northwest Forest Pass is required here. It costs $5 per car per day or $30 per year and can be purchased at ranger stations or outdoor stores.

Hiking Tips: From the Bonneville Trailhead, walk briefly up a gated gravel road to a sign announcing the Tamanous Trail to the PCT. Equestrians share this route, so be sure to step off the trail on the downhill side if you meet horses. After 0.6 mile, turn left on the PCT for 1.7 miles to a regrowing 1990 clearcut. Then the path meets a gravel road, continues on the far side 50 feet to the right, and descends under a powerline. Soon a side trail to the left leads to green Gillette Lake—a pleasant picnic spot, but beware of patches of poison oak brush nearby. For a better view, hike another 1.3 miles along the PCT to Greenleaf Overlook.

Season: Open all year.

While You're in the Area: Inspect river locks and sternwheelers at the Historical Museum in the riverfront park of Cascade Locks, open noon to 5pm from May through September (closed Mondays). Then tour the site of an 1856 Army stockade (and see a nice petroglyph) on the Fort Cascades Trail, a packed gravel 1.2-mile loop; the trailhead is on Washington Highway 14, west of the Bridge of the Gods 3.2 miles.

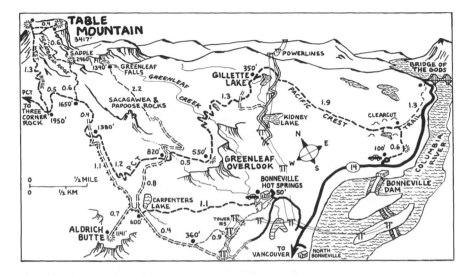

The dam lasted several months. During that time, people could easily have walked across it with dry feet. A reservoir gradually backed up as far as The Dalles. The lake killed riverside forests, leaving snags that could still be seen in the 1800s. When the dam finally washed out, it exposed the Cascades rapids. It also left a new riverbend where the Columbia squeezes hard against the Oregon shore. Bonneville Dam took advantage of that natural narrows. So did the modern Bridge of the Gods, a steel span built beside the town of Cascade Locks.

Today the famous Pacific Crest Trail crosses this modern steel version of the Bridge of the Gods, ambles across the old slide, and climbs past the fresh-looking cliff where Table Mountain was torn in half. For an easy, nearly level hike through this legendary landscape, start on the Washington side beside Bonneville Dam. The forest has regrown atop the slide, but souvenirs of the colossal collapse are everywhere: house-sized boulders, lakes, and hummocky terrain. After two and half miles you'll reach the grassy bank of Gillette Lake, a perfectly good turnaround point.

If you're still going strong, however, continue a little more than a mile on the Pacific Crest Trail. You'll pass two pretty creeks and end up at Greenleaf Overlook, a clifftop viewpoint where you can see the entire sweep of the ancient landslide. Here it's not all that hard to imagine the sacred walkway Tyee Sahalie built across the river, hoping in vain to bring peace to his sons' people.

CHAPTER III

The Explorers

Just over two centuries ago the Oregon Country was one of the last great blanks on North American maps. Long after the Yukon River and the waterways of the Canadian Arctic had been charted, white men still did not know that the legendary River of the West — the Columbia — actually existed. Oregon was a fortress of the wild, palisaded by mountain ranges, entrenched by Hells Canyon to the east, and moated by a harborless Pacific shore in the west.

Even the word "Oregon" rang of mystery. The name's origin has long been disputed. Most likely it derives from *wauregan*, the word for "good, beautiful" in the language of the Connecticut Mohegan tribe. The Mohegans apparently also used the word to refer to a great, westward-flowing river — probably the Ohio. But after British army Major Robert Rogers took Mohegan guides on his exploration of the Ohio River in 1758-60, he wrote an unsuccessful petition to the British crown in 1765, seeking finances for a longer expedition to find the "Ouragon" River, which he brazenly claimed would lead across the uncharted side of the continent to the Pacific.

The explorers who first ventured into Oregon's mysterious natural stronghold left a legacy of adventure. Today you can share in that legacy by hiking in their footsteps, following clues to a Spanish treasure, tracking Captain Cook on his quest for the legendary Northwest Passage, and tracing Lewis and Clark's path to a Pacific Ocean viewpoint.

Neahkahnie Mountain

The beach below this mountain might be where Europeans first set foot in Oregon. Jutting 1600 feet above a treacherous sand spit, Neahkahnie Mountain seems an unlikely place for a first landfall. And yet tantalizing clues keep reviving the legend of a chest buried on this peak by survivors of a wrecked Spanish galleon.

Today a portion of the Oregon Coast Trail crosses the mountain's summit

Neahkahnie Mountain.

to a breathtaking, aerial view of the beach south to Tillamook Bay. The peak is an inspiring place, where the Tillamook tribe believed their most powerful god resided. In fact, the name Neahkahnie comes from their words *Ne* ("place of") and *Ekahnie* ("supreme deity"). For some hikers, there's additional inspiration in the thought they might stumble over hidden gold.

Gold was in fact what brought the first European sailors to this Pacific shore. In 1577, the swashbuckling Englishman Sir Francis Drake became the first to venture north of California by sea. In those days, Spanish conquistadors were shipping boatloads of Aztec and Incan gold to Spain. England, virtually at war with Spain, allowed its merchant ships to loot any Spanish treasure ships they could find. The daring Drake took up the offer. He filled his hold with pirated gold off the Pacific coast of South America. Then he realized that bringing his booty back around Cape Horn would mean facing the entire Spanish fleet on the trip home.

In desperation Drake struck north, hoping to discover a "Northwest Passage" — a sea route to England around the unmapped shore of North America. It's unclear how far north he sailed, or whether he actually landed in Oregon, but he certainly didn't like the weather. His log complains of "most vile, thicke, and stinking fogges." When storms forced him to abandon hopes of a shortcut, he tried the unthinkable: He sailed west, circling the globe via Africa. Drake made it back to London the long way, and was hailed a hero.

In the years that followed, Spanish galleons routinely crossed the Pacific between colonies in the Philippines and Mexico. Several treasure

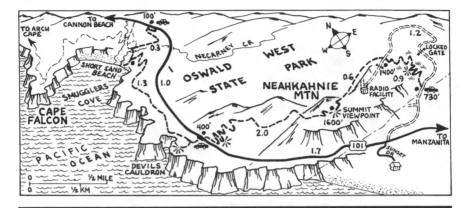

8. Neahkahnie Mountain

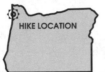

HIKE LOCATION

Moderate
3 miles round trip
900 feet elevation gain

Climb a legendary treasure mountain to a sweeping beach view.

Getting There: Drive Highway 101 south of Seaside 20 miles (or north of Tillamook 28 miles) to a brown hiker-symbl sign opposite Sunset Drive, between mileposts 41 and 42. Turn east on a gravel road for 0.4 mile and park at a wide spot. At the far end of this small pullout, look for a tiny trail sign on the left where the trail begins.

Hiking Tips: Steep switchbacks lead up through meadows 0.9 mile to a ridgetop junction. Continue straight on a path that contours 0.6 mile around the wooded back of the mountain before emerging at the summit meadow viewpoint. This is the recommended turnaround point, although the trail does continue, dropping for 2 miles to a Highway 101 crossing.

Season: Open all year, but skip stormy days when there's no view.

While You're in the Area: Two state parks have picnic areas on the beach near Neahkahnie. To see the shipwreck beach, drive 2 miles south on Highway 101 to milepost 44 and follow signs to Nehalem Bay State Park, where there's a nice campground. To stroll through an ancient rainforest to a hidden "Smugglers Cove," drive 2 miles north on Highway 101 to Os West State Park. If you'd prefer a train ride pulled by a steam locomotive, take the scenic 5-mile ride between Garibaldi and Rockaway Beach. Trains leave Garibaldi at 10am, noon, and 2pm, and leave Rockaway Beach at 11am and 1pm daily in summer, and on weekends from mid-May to mid-June and in September. The round-trip fare is about $18 for adults.

ships were lost at sea—and several tribes along the Oregon Coast have legends of ancient shipwrecks. But people didn't connect the two until the 1850s, when Gold Rush miners began spreading out from California, snooping after rumors of gold.

The most widely circulated treasure story describes an early Spanish wreck on the Nehalem spit at the base of Neahkahnie Mountain. Thirty survivors made it to the beach, ferrying the ship's treasure ashore in a longboat. The men dragged the treasure chest up onto the mountain's slopes and dug a hole. Knowing that Indians feared disturbing the graves of the dead, the captain shot his black Caribbean slave and buried him on top of the treasure. Then the captain shot or drove away the crew members who wouldn't fit in the ship's longboat, and he ordered the remainder to row him back across the ocean toward Mexico.

View south from Neahkahnie Mountain.

By 1870 a gold digger named Pat Smith had become so infatuated with the legend that he married a Clatsop woman to get inside information from the tribe. In 1890 Smith's excavations revealed several strange boulders, now on display in the Tillamook County Museum. The rocks are inscribed with arrows, crosses, and the letters "DEW." Smith believed they were coded directions to the treasure site. Speculation mounted when beachcombers found chunks of beeswax washing up on the sandy spit nearby, some stamped with old insignia, and one with the number "67." Beeswax was a common cargo on Spanish trading ships. It could have washed free from the old wreck.

In 2007, a team of twenty researchers announced that they had narrowed the identity of the missing ship to one of two galleons, the *Santo Christo de Burgos,* lost in 1693, and the *San Francisco Xavier,* lost in 1705. The researchers sent divers to inspect magnetic irregularities in Nehalem Bay, but instead of a treasure chest, they found discarded railroad rails.

To date, the most spectacular treasure anyone has found in the area is the inspiring view from the summit trail of Neahkahnie Mountain.

Cape Perpetua

An easier hike climbs to a stone shelter and ocean view atop Cape Perpetua, near Yachats on the central Oregon Coast. Cape Perpetua was named in 1778 by Captain James Cook, the renowned British explorer who set out to find Drake's missing Northwest Passage. To be sure, Drake's 1577 description of Oregon's "stinking fogges" had dampened British enthusiasm for the Pacific Northwest for nearly two centuries, but the notion of a sea shortcut around North America lingered like the tale of Atlantis.

The Spanish, meanwhile, had already responded to Drake by sending several expeditions of their own. Their results were decidedly mixed. The first Spanish reconnaissance party, under the Greek captain Juan de Fuca

The view from Cape Perpetua's shelter.

in 1592, claimed to have discovered what looked like a Northwest Passage near present-day Victoria. Juan de Fuca dubbed this deepwater inlet the "Straits of Annian." He gushed that he'd sailed eastward through it for twenty days in a land rich with gold, silver, and pearls. But because he returned empty handed, the cagey Spanish governors doubted his story. They sent a more sober captain, Sebastian Viscaino, who reported in 1603 from Southern Oregon (where he turned back, plagued by scurvy) that the shore had no such inlet—in fact it had no navigable harbors at all. The unfriendly Indians, Viscaino groused, didn't even know what gold was. Spain, and most of the world, promptly turned its attention elsewhere. No explorers visited Oregon for over 170 years.

As the British Empire grew, however, so did the hunger for a Northwest Passage. Such a shortcut would allow the Union Jack to rule the North Pacific as far as China. Already James Cook had dazzled the world with two voyages around Africa to the South Pacific. He had sailed in search of a fabled "Southern Continent" and had actually found Australia. And so in 1776, three days after America signed her Declaration of Independence in far-off Philadelphia, the British admiralty launched Cook from London with a new, secret assignment in a sealed envelope. At sea Cook opened his orders to find he had been sent in quest of the Northwest Passage. A reward of 20,000 pounds sterling encouraged success.

Cook sailed around Africa and across the Pacific for nearly two years before he sighted Oregon near Coos Bay on March 7, 1778. Eager to start looking for Juan de Fuca's alleged strait, he turned north and fixed his sights on a prominent cape about sixty miles distant. But the renowned "stinking fogges" of Drake's visit struck again, whipping choppy seas against the ship. Four days later Cook still hadn't reached the frustrating cape. Because the headland seemed perpetually ahead, and because March 11 was the holy day of the faith-tested martyr St. Perpetua, he irritably labeled it Cape Perpetua.

Cook continued onward, charting the coast north to Canada. Incredibly, he managed to overlook both the Columbia River and the twenty-mile-wide Juan de Fuca Strait, precisely the kind of inlet he was seeking. During a chilly winter on Vancouver Island, which Cook mistook as mainland, his men bundled up in sea otter furs casually acquired from local Indians for a few metal trinkets. The next spring Cook continued his futile search north to Alaska's Bering Sea. When pack ice turned him back, he retreated to warmer climes and discovered the Hawaiian Islands. The crew liked the place, but Cook thought the natives pilfered too much from the ship's stores. To teach them a lesson, Cook ordered his men to fire into a crowd. While his men were reloading, the outraged natives charged. Five sailors died in the melee, including Cook himself.

Cook's ship continued without him, sailing next to China. And it was there, in Canton, that Cook's crew made the most surprising discovery of the entire trip. The sea otter pelts they had been using to pad their bunks were worth the staggering sum of $120 apiece. The men nearly mutinied in their eagerness to return to America for more. Ship officers forced them to sail to England, but the secret was out: The Northwest Coast's treasure was not gold, but rather the silky fur of its lovable, nearly tame sea otters. Within a few decades, enterprising sea captains had shipped 200,000 pelts to China and Europe. By 1812, sea otters were extinct in Oregon.

Although Cape Perpetua's sea otters are gone—an unfortunate side effect of Cook's 1778 visit—the wild landscape at this rainforest headland has otherwise weathered the centuries well. Start your exploration at the Cape Perpetua Interpretive Center on Highway 101. From there, trails fan out in five directions. If you hike a mile inland along Cape Creek, you'll penetrate the ancient, moss-draped woods to a giant Sitka spruce tree fifteen feet in diameter. It sprouted four hundred years ago on a log that

9. Cape Perpetua

HIKE LOCATION

Easy (to tidepools)
0.8-mile loop
50 feet elevation gain

Easy (to Giant Spruce)
2 miles round trip
100 feet elevation gain

Easy (to Devils Churn and shelter)
0.2-mile loops
100 feet elevation gain

Short paths visit tidepools, a giant spruce, and a viewpoint shelter.

Getting There: Drive Highway 101 south of Yachats three miles (or north of Florence 23 miles) to the Cape Perpetua Visitor Center turnoff between mileposts 168 and 169. If you don't have a Northwest Forest Pass, expect to pay a $5 per car day-use fee.

Hiking Tips: From the Visitor Center's front door, follow a "Tidepools" pointer to the left 0.2 mile, duck under the highway, and keep left on an 0.2-mile loop to Cooks Chasm and the tidepools. If you'd like to see a giant spruce's walk-through root tunnel, return to the Visitor Center, follow a "Giant Spruce" pointer, and keep right at all junctions for a mile. To see the stone shelter's viewpoint, drive a quarter mile north on Highway 101, turn right at a campground sign, and then keep left for 1.5 miles to a parking lot and 0.2-mile loop trail. To visit the Devils Churn, drive north on Highway 101 another one-tenth mile to a parking area and a 0.2-mile loop trail on the left.

Season: Open all year.

While You're in the Area: Don't miss the Heceta Head lighthouse (Hike #35), located 11 miles south on Highway 101.

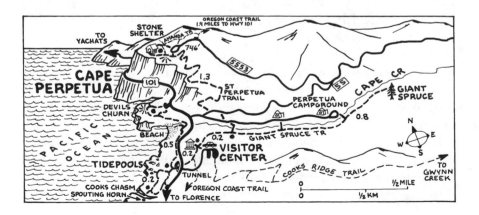

has since rotted away, leaving the tree's arching roots as a walk-through tunnel.

The most popular trail from Cape Perpetua's Interpretive Center visits the tidepools and spouting horns of the rocky shore. Just a few feet down this path you'll pass the overgrown foundations of Cape Creek Camp, a 1933 Civilian Conservation Corps work center that employed hundreds of young men from families on the relief rolls during the Depression. The men built the area's original trails and the sturdy stonework shelter on top of Cape Perpetua. Their barracks, however, were so flimsy that the men were sometimes ordered to huddle together against the walls during winter storms to keep the buildings from blowing over. The Forest Service burned the barracks when the camp closed after World War II.

A trail junction by the old CCC camp marks the crossing of a 1914 Florence-Yachats wagon road, now converted to the Oregon Coast Trail. This coastal route began as an Indian path that skirted Cape Perpetua's cliffs. Even after the perilous original trail around the cape was widened to three feet in 1897, a slip by a mounted mail carrier sent his horse and mailbag plummeting into the sea. Following World War I, the government set out to complete a "Roosevelt Coast Military Highway" along Oregon's shore as a defense against foreign attack. One of the route's final stretches was completed here in 1930. It remains largely unchanged today as the serpentine and vertiginous Highway 101.

The trail to the tidepools ducks under Highway 101 through a tunnel. The best pools are to the left. At low tide look for spiny purple sea urchins, bulbous green anemones and gooseneck barnacles. Early tribes collected mussels here as much as 6000 years ago. Their middens of cast-off shells remain as white mounds twenty feet tall. Collecting marine life is banned here now. Beyond the middens you'll find Cooks Chasm, a spouting horn where waves blast water out of a sea cave at high tide.

Trails also lead from Cape Perpetua's Interpretive Center to two other top attractions, the Devils Churn and the cape's stone lookout, but most people take shortcuts in their cars. From a parking area along Highway 101 it's only a few hundred yards down to the Devils Churn, a seething fifty-foot-wide slot in the lava shore. The churn began as a crack in the rock. Over thousands of years, waves hollowed out a long cave and then collapsed the roof.

The shortcut trail to Cape Perpetua's stone shelter begins on a spur road past the area's campground. The path ambles out through headland meadows where blue camas, red paintbrush, and a few lupine bloom in May and June. The rustic shelter itself frames views that extend 37 miles to sea and south 104 miles to Cape Blanco. To the north, look for Cape Foulweather. Not surprisingly, that headland's dreary-sounding name was also picked by Captain Cook, the day after he passed Cape Perpetua in his stormy search for a Northwest Passage.

Cape Disappointment

Far from being disappointed, Lewis and Clark celebrated when they first sighted the Pacific Ocean from Cape Disappointment, a dramatic headland on the Washington side of the Columbia River. Those stalwart explorers had trekked 2000 miles across the continent. Today the trail up Cape Disappointment is still inspiring, but the hike is much shorter. It also features a number of additional historic attractions, including a lighthouse, an artillery bunker, and a museum.

Considering that the Columbia River is seven miles wide at its mouth, explorers to the Oregon Coast had failed to discover this "Great River of the West" for a surprisingly long time. Neither Drake nor Juan de Fuca noticed it on their voyages in the late 1500s. The second flurry of sea explorations in the late 1700s also had bad luck. Juan Perez piloted Spanish ships along the coast here in both 1774 and 1775. The second time, steering Bruno de Heceta's vessel, he reported a bay here that he thought might be a river. But the crew was sick with scurvy and there was no time to investigate. Three years later Cook sailed by without even reporting a bay.

By 1788, freelance fur trading ships were routinely plying the coast. British captain John Meares, sailing under a Portuguese flag of convenience, stumbled into a storm here and desperately sought a harbor. He fled toward the Columbia River opening "with every encouraging expectation" that it would be the great river of legend. But breakers on the river's shallow bar convinced him he must be mistaken. Angrily, he named the river mouth Deception Bay, and the nearby headland Cape Disappointment.

In 1792 the British admiralty sent Captain George Vancouver with two ships to chart every nook and cranny of the Pacific Northwest coast, hoping that Cook had missed an inlet or navigable river that might yet allow some kind of Northwest Passage. When Vancouver reached Meare's Deception Bay, he noted that the blue ocean suddenly turned the color of a muddy river, but decided this was "the probable consequence of some streams falling into the bay." He sailed past, "not considering this opening worthy of more attention."

Two days later Vancouver paused alongside a small American trading ship, the *Columbia*, captained by one Robert Gray of Boston. Gray told

Cape Disappointment.

the Britishers that he'd just sailed past Deception Bay too, and believed it really was a river. The current, Gray said, had been so strong he couldn't sail his ship against it. Vancouver scoffed and sailed north to map Puget Sound. Meanwhile, Gray went back to take another look at the deceptive bay. On May 11, 1792, he plowed across the bar's breakers and suddenly found himself sailing on the long-sought River of the West. He christened it the Columbia for his ship, traded with the local Clatsop tribe for sea otter furs, and sailed a few days later toward an outpost at Nootka, where he left a sketch of his findings as a courtesy to fellow travelers.

Two months later Vancouver stopped at Nootka too. As soon as he saw Gray's sketch, he realized he had been beaten to the discovery of the great river by a Yankee trader, and that the United States now had a viable claim to the whole of the Oregon Country the river drained.

Trying to recover from his error, Vancouver immediately sent the smaller of his two ships across the river bar. Under the command of Lieutenant Broughton, a crew spent three weeks carefully charting the waterway as far east as the Sandy River, near present-day Troutdale. They named Mt. Hood after the British admiral who had outgunned the Americans in the Revolutionary War. They named Mt. St. Helens for a town near Liverpool. They named Broughton's Bluff and Point Vancouver. They performed an official claiming ceremony for Britain. But it was no use — the damned Yankee had found the river first.

When Thomas Jefferson became President ten years later, he was painfully aware how tenuous the United States' claims to the Oregon Country were. Gray had not actually planted an American flag. His captain's log noted that he landed merely "to view the Country." The words "and take possession" had been added to Gray's log later, but they were obviously in a different hand.

Jefferson envisioned an American empire, convinced that the United States must one day expand to the Pacific. In one of his first official acts as President, he quietly negotiated purchase of the vast Louisiana country from the French, annexing land from New Orleans to the Rocky Mountains. Then he sent Congress a secret request for $2500 to finance an

overland exploration of the new tract. Jefferson chose his personal secretary, Captain Meriwether Lewis, to lead the expedition, and explained to him that the goal was grander. The Corps of Discovery would not go merely to the Rockies. They would continue an extra thousand miles beyond United States territory to the Pacific Ocean. There they would plant a flag at the Columbia River's mouth to back up Gray's claim.

William Clark and Meriwether Lewis.

Lewis chose a co-leader with frontier experience, William Clark, and together they left St. Louis with forty-three men on May 14, 1804. Their Corps of Discovery had barely reached present-day North Dakota before weather forced them to set up a winter camp. There they met Sacajawea, a sixteen-year-old Shoshone girl. She agreed to come along as an interpreter with her French-Canadian husband and baby. The following spring the troop set off slowly, believing they could simply portage their canoes across the Continental Divide to a navigable branch of the Columbia. But the Rocky Mountains were higher and more rugged than anything Lewis and Clark had anticipated. Late in summer they abandoned their canoes. They trekked hundreds of miles through the snowy Bitterroot Range, starving and cold, before staggering down to the lands of the Nez Perce tribe. There they were welcomed and fed. Then they built dugout canoes and paddled down the Snake and Columbia rivers toward the ocean.

On November 7, 1805, Clark exulted in his journal (with the freestyle spelling of his era), "Great joy in camp we are in View of the Ocian, this great Pacific Octean which we been So long anxious to See. And the roreing or noise made by the waves brakeing on the rockey Shores (as I suppose) may be heard distinctly." Unfortunately, it wasn't really the ocean. Clark had been fooled by the breadth of the lower Columbia's estuary. The expedition still had eight days of paddling ahead before they finally landed on the north shore and climbed Cape Disappointment to see the ocean itself. Carrying out Jefferson's orders, Lewis planted the expedition's largest American flag on the spot.

Today the view from this cape is still stirring, but there have been some changes. As you walk up the short path from the Lewis and Clark Interpretive Center parking lot, the first thing you'll notice is the concrete ruin of Battery Harvey Allen. From 1906 until after World War II, this artillery battery guarded the Columbia River entrance against foreign invasion. The bunker's three six-inch guns are gone, but concrete passageways remain for the curious to investigate.

Just beyond is the grassy bluff where Lewis and Clark most likely planted their flag. The Lewis and Clark Interpretive Center is planted here now, with walk-through exhibits describing their expedition. To the west, the ocean view includes a three-mile-long jetty. The jetty has changed the shape of the coastline since the Corps of Discovery's visit. Over the years, sand dunes have drifted against the breakwater from the north, leaving Cape Disappointment stranded a mile from the current river mouth.

After touring the museum area, hike about a quarter mile along the bluff to the Cape Disappointment lighthouse, the oldest lighthouse still in use on the West Coast. The trail route skirts Dead Man's Cove, a picturesque chasm in the cape's cliffs with a hidden beach where a shipwreck casualty once washed ashore.

In fact, the Columbia River bar is known as the "Graveyard of the Pacific" because of the appalling frequency of shipwrecks here. Over the years, the treacherous mouth of this well-traveled river has swallowed over a hundred ships and nearly a thousand lives. The very first company of Oregon settlers, hired by John Jacob Astor to found Fort Astoria in 1811, lost two yawls and eight men trying to find a channel across the bar for their main ship. Later, when the U.S. Navy sent the *Shark* in 1846 to display American military might in the still-disputed Oregon Country, the schooner broke up so thoroughly on the Columbia bar that the largest remaining piece was a chunk of deck with a cannon attached. It washed ashore at what later became known as Cannon Beach, twenty-five miles to the south.

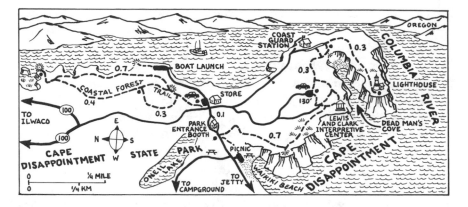

10. Cape Disappointment

Easy
1.2 miles round trip
200 feet elevation gain

A Lewis and Clark museum and a lighthouse top this Washington cape.

Getting There: From Astoria, take Highway 101 across the Columbia River bridge and continue north 11 miles to Ilwaco. In the center of town go straight on Loop 100, following signs for Cape Disappointment State Park for 3.3 miles. At the crossroads for the park's boat launch go straight another half mile to the Lewis and Clark Interpretive Center's parking turnaround.

Hiking Tips: At the far right end of the parking lot, climb the paved trail 300 yards to the Interpretive Center, open 10am-5pm daily all year. It's $5 for adults, but kids age 7-17 are $2.50. When you leave the museum, turn right and keep to the right to find the trail to the Cape Disappointment lighthouse. After 0.3 mile there's a confusion of trails above Dead Man's Cove. Keep right and go down the stairs to visit the cove's hidden beach. Then reclimb the stairs and turn right on a concrete pathway that skirts the cove's clifftops for 0.3 mile to the lighthouse.

Season: Open all year.

While You're in the Area: Cape Disappointment State Park, half a mile before the trailhead, has 220 campsites and a picnic area at a cove called Waikiki Beach. Also stop by the Heritage Museum in the town of Ilwaco, 3 miles away. A block off Highway 101 at 115 SE Lake Street, the museum has Native American artifacts, a pioneer village, and a restored railway depot.

Heedful of such disasters, Congress dispatched a freighter in 1853 with a lighthouse kit—bricks, windows, lantern, lens, and other lighthouse materials—to be assembled at the mouth of the Columbia. Unfortunately, that ship capsized in the Columbia's breakers too, taking its cargo with it to the river bottom a mile short of Cape Disappointment. Three years later, a second ship with a lighthouse kit made it through, allowing the current 53-foot brick tower to be built. The five wicks that lit the original beacon burned 170 gallons of kerosene a month—all carried up the circular stairway in cans—until installation of an electric beacon in 1938. The original one-ton French lens, after serving in several other lighthouses, has ended up close to home as a display in the Lewis and Clark Interpretive Center.

Even with the lighthouse, the Columbia bar kept wrecking ships. So in 1892 the Coast Guard took the unusual step of stationing a floating lighthouse in the middle of the river entrance. Three massive anchors held the 123-foot lightship in place. But in a ferocious November 1899 storm, all three cables snapped. The lightship beached a mile north of Cape Disappointment. Despite the pounding surf, the solidly built ship refused to break up, and the entire crew was rescued. Sand soon drifted around the derelict lightship, repeatedly frustrating attempts to tow it back to sea. After fourteen months of futile efforts, the Coast Guard finally put the salvage operation up for bid. Surprisingly, the low bidder was a house mover from Astoria. Even more surprising, he jacked up the massive ship, put it on wheels, and rolled it inland two miles through the forest. There he launched it into the much calmer waters of Baker Bay. Before long the diehard lightship was back in service, blinking from the bar, warning other ships from first-hand experience of the dangers at Cape Disappointment.

After hiking at Cape Disappointment, consider swinging through Astoria to see the last of the Columbia River's floating lighthouses. In 1979, after a lighted buoy made the lightship obsolete, the Coast Guard docked it permanently at the Columbia River Maritime Museum on Astoria's waterfront. An admission ticket to this world-class interpretive center includes a boarding pass to the peculiar ship.

Tillamook Head

The farthest point reached by the Lewis and Clark expedition was not at the mouth of the Columbia River, but rather twenty miles south at Tillamook Head, where they went hiking in search of whale blubber.

The thousand-foot cliff of Tillamook Head rises like a wall from Seaside's beach. Today an eight-mile section of the Oregon Coast Trail follows the explorers' route across this formidable cape to Cannon Beach. Along the way, the path passes viewpoints that made even Captain Clark exclaim in wonder.

After Lewis and Clark's first sighting of the Pacific Ocean from Cape Disappointment, they soon realized they needed a more protected place to spend the winter. On December 5, 1805, Lewis and three men crossed the Columbia to find a less stormy site. They chose a clearing on what became known as the Lewis and Clark River, a lazy backwater six miles south of present-day Astoria. Soon the whole group was there, busily building a fifty-foot-square log stockade. Today excavations have still not pinpointed the fort's site. A replica built at a probable location by the National Park Service in 1955 burned in 2005. It was replaced by a more accurate replica the following year. Today park rangers in frontier garb lead tours of the cramped, smoky rooms.

The 1955-2005 replica of Fort Clatsop.

Rain fell on all but twelve of the 106 dreary days the expedition spent at Fort Clatsop. They celebrated Christmas listlessly with what Clark described as "pore Elk, so much Spoiled that we eate it thro' mear necessity. Some Spoiled pounded fish and a fiew roots." By January Clark was arguing with Lewis over the need for salt to preserve and spice their meager fare. Perhaps sensing his cabin fever, Lewis let Clark lead an excursion to Killamuck, a beachside village of friendly Clatsops. There, a hundred feet from what is now the Promenade in the city of Seaside, he boiled seawater in five large kettles, obtaining nearly a gallon of salt a day.

While unwinding at this beach retreat, Clark heard from locals that a whale was stranded at the next village south, on the other side of Tillamook Head. He passed word back to Lewis at Fort Clatsop that tribespeople from up and down the coast were going to help butcher the whale—should he go too? Oil was also lacking in the expedition's diet, and the beached whale might provide a source. As soon as Sacajawea heard the news, she begged to go along. "She observed that she had traveled a long way with us to see the great waters," Lewis wrote, "and now that monstrous fish was also to be seen, she thought it very hard she could not be permitted to see either."

Tillamook Rock lighthouse, circa 1890.

So Sacajawea joined Clark and a small group of men on a mossy rain-forest trail tracing the edge of Tillamook Head's colossal cliff—essentially the same path that crosses Ecola State Park from Seaside today. Clark gazed back across a twenty-mile sweep of wilderness beach to the distant blue of Cape Disappointment, and later wrote, "I beheld the grandest and most pleasing prospects which my eyes ever surveyed." A modern trail-side sign commemorates a likely location for "Clark's Point of View."

On the far side of Tillamook Head, Clark's group followed the beach two miles to a cluster of five huts, the forerunner of Cannon Beach's crowded mishmash of artsy boutiques and motels. There, beside a creek, lay the skeleton of a 105-foot gray whale. Unfortunately for Clark, the entire animal had already been dissected for meat or blubber, and the locals weren't keen on sharing. Clark had to bargain hard to get a mere three hundred pounds of blubber and a few gallons of whale oil, which the group then lugged back to Fort Clatsop.

By mid-March, the Corps of Discovery were heartily sick of their rainy fort. They traded Lewis' frilly dress coat to the local Clatsop chief for an extra canoe and headed east . By September they were back in St. Louis, already spreading word of the wonders awaiting adventurers in Oregon.

As you hike across Tillamook Head today, it's easy to wonder why such an enormous basalt cliff is sticking out into the ocean at all. The answer is far from obvious, and took geologists years to accept. The headland is the tip of a massive, 400-mile-long lava flow from Idaho. About 15 million

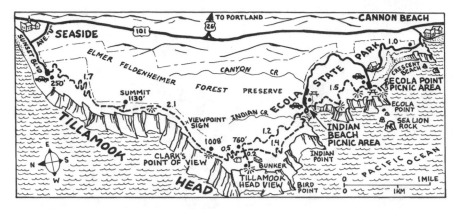

years ago, when the Coast Range was just emerging from the ocean, vast lava floods welled up from cracks in the earth's crust near Hells Canyon. Known as the Columbia River basalts, this rock buried much of Eastern Oregon and Eastern Washington, sometimes a mile deep. Lava repeatedly poured down the Columbia River Gorge and fanned out to the sea. Virtually every headland and island from Newport to Astoria is a remnant of these colossal inundations.

On the remote tip of Tillamook Head you can now see two features Clark could not. One is an abandoned six-room concrete bunker that housed a radar installation in World War II. The other is Oregon's strangest lighthouse, a desolate tower a mile offshore on a small, barren island named Tillamook Rock.

When Congress approved $50,000 for a lighthouse south of the Columbia River in 1878, most people assumed it would be built atop Tillamook Head's thousand-foot cliff. But engineers decided the headland is shrouded in fog so often that ships wouldn't see a beacon up there. Instead they suggested building closer to sea level, on the 120-foot-tall island offshore. They admitted this might increase the difficulty of construction. That proved to be a serious understatement.

Even in the calmest weather, the Pacific rolls past cliff-edged Tillamook Rock with ten-foot swells. The first builder sent to survey the rock in 1879 attempted to leap ashore from a lifeboat. Before he could get his footing, a wave swept him away and he drowned. His replacement found that the accident had made locals so leery of the project that he had to hire workers from distant towns and transport them to the site without letting them stop in Astoria along the way.

The new builder decided he would transport men and materials to Tillamook Rock with a "breeches buoy," a 300-foot cable rigged up between

11. Tillamook Head

HIKE LOCATION

Moderate (to WW II bunker)
3-mile loop
900 feet elevation gain

Difficult (shuttle across headland)
6.1 miles one way
1350 feet elevation gain

Follow Sacajawea's footsteps across a panoramic cape.

Getting There: Take Highway 101 south of Seaside 7 miles to the north exit for Cannon Beach and follow signs to Ecola State Park, keeping right for 2 miles to the park's entrance booth. A $5 day-use parking fee is collected here. Then turn right for 1.5 miles to the Indian Beach picnic area. Dogs must be on leash.

Hiking Tips: The trail starts behind the restroom on the right. After 200 feet ignore a footbridge to the left and keep straight on the main trail, an old roadbed that climbs 1.2 miles to a trail crossing near a primitive campsite with three open-sided shelters (available on a first-come, first-served basis). In another 0.2 mile you'll find the concrete bunker and a cliff-edge viewpoint of Tillamook Rock.

To return on a loop, walk back to the trail crossing and turn right on a path 1.4 miles downhill to the Indian Beach parking lot. If you'd prefer to continue across Tillamook Head, turn left at the trail crossing. This longer route passes Clark's viewpoint before switchbacking down to Sunset Boulevard. To leave a shuttle car there, drive Highway 101 to Seaside's southernmost traffic signal, turn west on Avenue U for two blocks and turn left on Edgewood (which becomes Sunset) for 1.2 miles to road's end.

Season: Open all year.

While You're in the Area: Don't miss Lewis and Clark's stockade at the Fort Clatsop National Memorial. To find it, drive Highway 101 north of Seaside 11 miles (or south of Astoria 4 miles) and follow signs. The interpretive center and fort are open daily 9am-5pm (6pm in summer).

For a stroll through the old resort town of Seaside, start at the Lewis and Clark statue at The Turnaround (in the middle of Seaside's beachfront) and take the broad, paved Promenade half a mile south along the beach, where a sign points left half a block to a park with a replica of Clark's salt works.

the island and a supply ship. Wearing a body harness attached to a pulley, each worker would slide through the air to the island. Although no one died with this system, the bobbing of the ship routinely dragged men through the waves or snapped them into the air as if from a rubber band.

Using the breeches buoy, the builder finally succeeded in landing four men and a large supply of dynamite onto the island on October 21, 1879. He set them to work blasting a level foundation for the future tower. The job took the men a full seven months. During that time, a midwinter storm swept their storehouse off the island. But the stalwart crew kept working. By the following May they had blasted 4,630 cubic yards of basalt into the ocean, lowering the island's summit from 120 feet to 91. That summer the builder raised a derrick and a long beam beside the leveled site. Then he

Clark's view from Tillamook Head.

had a daring ship captain maneuver close enough to the island that granite blocks and other building materials could be hoisted ashore.

Construction of the actual lighthouse took yet another seven months, pushing costs to 250% of the original budget. When the work was nearly done, on the stormy night of January 3, 1881, workers thought they heard a ship captain shouting orders in the dark. The lighthouse builders rushed outside with lanterns, but saw nothing. When morning dawned, however, they noticed the topmost mast of a ship protruding from the surf at the rocky base of Tillamook Head. Bound for the Columbia River from Japan, the British bark *Lupata* had gone down on the unlit shore with all hands. Only an Australian shepherd dog made it to the beach alive.

Tillamook Rock's beacon first shone four weeks later. Mounted on a 62-foot tower 133 feet above the sea—high enough that the engineers felt sure it could weather any storm—the light probably saved many a ship from the *Lupata's* fate. However, it soon became clear that the engineers had underestimated the North Pacific's fury.

In January of 1883 a storm tossed rocks through the foghorn roof. In December 1886, waves ripped loose a half-ton block of concrete from beside the tower's base. The following December, seas broke continuously over the tower itself, smashing the lantern and flooding the stairwell. Again in December 1894, gigantic waves broke thirteen lantern panes, chipped the lens, flooded the tower, and perforated the roof with rock debris.

Hoping to improve emergency communication with the isolated lighthouse, the Coast Guard laid a $6000 telephone cable to the island in 1897. Within months the cable was useless, snapped by storm waves. Crews began calling the rock "Terrible Tilly," complaining that it was the most isolated and dangerous post in the service. Repair bills mounted. In an October, 1912 storm, the entire tower shook when waves ripped a 100-ton block of basalt from the island's face. Yet again the sea smashed the lantern windows and filled the foghorn with rocks. The drenched lighthouse crew, heroically working all night amid broken glass and debris, managed to keep the light burning through the gale for all but fifteen minutes.

The final blow came in October, 1934, when a typhoon with 109-mile-per-hour winds drove sixty-pound rocks, seaweed, and even fish through sixteen smashed lantern-room windows. The beacon's delicate glass lens was so badly damaged it never shone again. The next year the light was replaced by a whistling buoy anchored nearby.

The Coast Guard declared Terrible Tilly surplus property in 1957 and put the whole complex up for auction—island and all. A Las Vegas businessman was the high bidder, but even he couldn't find a practical use for the inaccessible crag. After shifting ownership two more times, the lighthouse ended up with Eternity At Sea, a funeral business that catered to people who want to be stored in a lighthouse when they die. Inspectors eventually closed the operation because the guano-covered building didn't meet state mortuary standards. But for a time helicopters ferried urns with cremated remains to a stormy final resting place on Tillamook Rock—in the midst of the grandest and most pleasing prospect Captain William Clark had ever beheld.

Sauvie Island

At the tip of Oregon's largest island, a woodsy trail along the Columbia River leads to the tiny Warrior Rock lighthouse and a secluded, sandy beach. The path ambles through what is now the Sauvie Island Wildlife Area, where you can expect to spot great blue herons, geese, or even a bald eagle. It's a surprisingly quiet place, considering it's hardly ten miles from Portland.

But Sauvie Island has not always been a pastoral backwater. Early traders and trappers followed rivers into the Oregon Country's interior. This island, at the confluence of the Columbia and the Willamette, was a key stopover point and a contested crossroads for rival fur companies.

British Lieutenant Broughton, who scouted the Columbia River for

Lake on Sauvie Island.

Vancouver in 1792, visited several villages here belonging to the Multnomah tribe. He reported that their hundred-foot-long lodges, built of giant cedar planks, featured a separate doorway for each of the many families that lived inside. Broughton named the place Wappato Island after a plant that provided the local Multnomah tribe with their main food source. Wappato plants are rare on Sauvie Island today, but they once grew like pond lillies in the island's marshy lakes. The plant's large, arrowhead-shaped leaves stretch to the water's surface, while fleshy, bulbous roots grow in the mud underneath. Multnomah women would wade out in the lakes, digging up wappato roots with their toes. The roots were stacked in dugout canoes and later baked like potatoes.

When Lewis and Clark stopped by Sauvie Island in 1805, geese and ducks were even more plentiful than now. Clark complained that the incessant honking of waterfowl kept him awake at night. Lewis spotted an enormous bird overhead and shot it down for closer examination. It turned out to be a previously unknown species, a condor with a wingspan of nearly nine feet.

Fort Astoria and Fort Vancouver may have been the most famous pioneer fur trading posts along the lower Columbia River, but for a time they were rivaled by Fort William, a Sauvie Island settlement built by Nathaniel Wyeth, a Massachusetts ice merchant. Wyeth had made a modest fortune by figuring out how to ship ice from Cambridge to the Caribbean, where it sold high in summer. By 1832, bored with ice, he found himself daydreaming about riskier business thrills in the legendary land of Oregon. Why not start his own trading empire?

Surely, Wyeth reasoned, he could avoid the misfortunes that had ruined John Jacob Astor's trading post at Astoria twenty years before:

•Astor's men had built their fort at the mouth of the Columbia, hoping to buy sea otter pelts—but by then sea otters were almost impossible to find. Wyeth would settle inland, concentrating on beaver pelts and farming instead.

•Astor had hired a tyrannical captain whose foolish orders killed most of the men and blew up the expedition's ship. Wyeth would train and lead his expedition in person.

•Astor had launched his luckless venture just before the War of 1812 broke out against Britain, and had soon been forced to sell his feebly defended fort to the British at a loss. Since 1818, however, the entire Oregon Country was at peace, with a joint occupancy agreement allowing both British and American citizens to do business wherever they pleased. What could go wrong?

Fired with enthusiasm, Wyeth began posting advertisements in the spring of 1832 to enlist fifty craftsmen and farmers for an Oregon expedition. The men were to be given three months of wilderness training before setting out. The first sign of trouble came when only twenty-three men signed up. Time was running short, so Wyeth trimmed their "frontier" training to a ten-day campout on an island in Boston's harbor. Then he dressed them up in smart uniforms and took them to St. Louis for the overland trip west. All the trading supplies and farming equipment they would need had already been sent off toward Oregon by chartered ship around Cape Horn. The few things they would need on the overland trip would be packed in ingenious wheeled keelboats Wyeth himself had invented. Wyeth planned to pole the boats up to the Rocky Mountains and then simply roll them across the Continental Divide like wagons.

Genuine frontiersmen in St. Louis took one look at Wyeth's wheeled contraptions and guffawed. They convinced him to trade the boats for horses and join a caravan as far as the Rocky Mountain fur traders' annual rendezvous in western Wyoming.

The farther west they traveled, however, the more squeamish Wyeth's Boston recruits became. Three called it quits at the rough-looking frontier town of Independence, Missouri. Another three turned back when a Pawnee war party rode by, waving scalps from an enemy tribe. Seven more of Wyeth's brigade quit when they saw the coarse debauchery of the mountain men's Wyoming rendezvous.

Only ten men followed Wyeth when he finally struck off across the Snake River country toward Oregon. The little troop lost the Indian trail repeatedly, and would have starved but for the generosity of Shoshone villagers along the way. Exhausted, they stumbled into the Hudson's Bay Company trading post at Walla Walla, where they traded their ribby horses for a barge and drifted downriver to meet their supply ship.

It was late October by the time they reached Fort Vancouver, another Hudson's Bay post run by the far-reaching British company that had expanded to fill the void left by Fort Astoria's failure. The administrator there, John McLoughlin, informed Wyeth that his chartered ship had been lost at sea. All of the trading supplies and farming tools Wyeth needed for his settlement had been lost. At that point, the last of Wyeth's crew deserted him, borrowing equipment from McLoughlin to trap or farm on their own. Wyeth's expedition had been an even greater disaster than Astor's.

Incredibly, Wyeth refused to give up. Vowing to break the British company's trade monopoly in Oregon, he returned alone across the Snake River Country, crossed the Rockies, and went back to Boston to raise money for an even larger expedition. By the spring of 1834 he was marching back to Oregon with fifty new men, and a new shipload of supplies was on its way around Cape Horn. This time Wyeth had not only rounded up a tougher bunch of craftsmen, but he was also taking along a Methodist missionary named Jason Lee and a renowned Philadelphia naturalist named John Townsend.

On Wyeth's second trip west he stopped in Idaho to build Fort Hall, a fur trading post named for his Boston financier. Within weeks, however, the Hudson's Bay Company built a rival fur trading post at Fort Boise nearby, cutting Wyeth off from most potential Shoshone customers. Undaunted, Wyeth marched on to Oregon to meet the British challenge head on. Just eight miles from the Hudson's Bay Company headquarters at Vancouver, Wyeth set up his own central trading post, Fort William, on the southwest edge of Sauvie Island. This time Wyeth's chartered ship arrived in good condition. He promptly filled the ship with logs and sent it to Hawaii to trade for cattle, sheep, goats, and hogs. Soon Fort William was a bustling settlement, surrounded by grazing livestock.

But things did not go well on Sauvie Island. Wyeth had arrived too late for the runs of salmon he had hoped to ship back to Boston. Most of the local tribes, under pressure from the Hudson's Bay Company, refused to trade with him at all. Hunger and sickness plagued Fort William through the winter. He wrote that his workers were "sick and dying off like rotten sheep of bilious disorders," perhaps from a diet of "trash and dogs." Wyeth himself ate a lamprey eel, which resulted in "vomiting and purging."

Wyeth's rough and tumble craftsmen caused other troubles. One day the fort's tailor discovered a two-gallon whiskey jug that the naturalist Townsend had carefully filled with preserved specimens of Oregon's lizards and snakes. The tailor strained off the reptiles and drank the whiskey, much to Townsend's outrage. To this day, Townsend's chipmunk and Townsend's warbler are well-known Oregon species, but there is no Townsend's newt.

The same scurrilous tailor later got into an argument over a native woman with the fort's blacksmith. In a jealous rage, the tailor armed himself with a gun and knife. But that night when he crept into his rival's cabin, the able blacksmith simply pulled a gun from under his pillow and shot the tailor dead. This murder was the first among white men in the Oregon Country. Because the region had neither a British nor an American government, no one was sure how to conduct a proper trial. Finally Wyeth asked the learned Townsend to preside as judge. Perhaps Townsend was still smarting from the loss of his reptiles when he pronounced the tailor's death "justifiable homicide."

Warrior Rock lighthouse on Sauvie Island.

After two difficult years on Sauvie Island, Wyeth finally pulled in his horns. He sold Fort William to the Hudson's Bay Company and went back to his Cambridge ice business, never to return. In 1846, when Fort Vancouver needed more farmland, John McLoughlin sent one of his French-Canadian trappers, Laurent Sauve, to start a dairy on the site of Fort William. In the years that followed, "Sauve's Island" gradually filled with homestead farms. The southern end of the island, diked against floods in 1941, now is a patchwork of vegetable and berry crops.

The island's undiked northern tip, including the trail to the Warrior Rock lighthouse, still floods occasionally in winter and again in late May, when Rocky Mountain snowmelt swells the Columbia. Even in dry weather, the trail can be muddy enough you'll want to wear boots. Tall

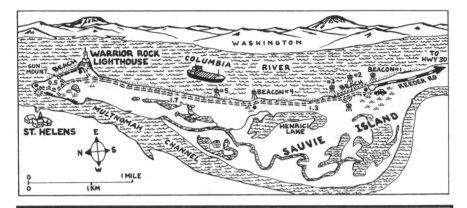

12. Sauvie Island's Warrior Rock

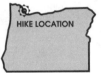

HIKE LOCATION

Moderate
7 miles round trip
No elevation gain

Hike along the Columbia River to a lighthouse at Sauvie Island's tip.

Getting There: From downtown Portland, drive north on Highway 30 toward St. Helens. After ten miles, turn right across the Sauvie Island Bridge and head north along Sauvie Island Road to the Cracker Barrel Grocery. You can stop here to get the required Sauvie Island Wildlife Area parking permit ($7 a day or $22 a year). Then drive 1.8 miles past the store on Sauvie Island Road, turn right onto Reeder Road, and follow this road for 12.8 miles to its end at a gravel turnaround with a parking area and an outhouse.

Hiking Tips: Unleashed dogs and overnight camping are prohibited in this wildlife area. Wear boots because the trail can be muddy. From the parking lot at the end of Reeder Road, the main hiking route to Warrior Rock is an old dirt service road. However, it's pleasant to start out walking along the beach itself for half a mile or so. When the sand narrows at the third beacon, climb up to the road and continue. After 2.8 miles the road fades in a meadow and forks. Keep right to find the road leading 0.2 mile through the woods to the lighthouse beach. To find a hidden viewpoint of the town of St. Helens, hike 200 yards along the beach from the lighthouse to a small concrete artillery platform. Turn inland to the left on a small road for 100 yards to a T-shaped junction. The route back to your car is to the left, but first go right 0.3 mile to the viewpoint on the tip of Sauvie Island.

Season: Although the trail is technically open all year, floodwaters can close the access road and cover the trail itself after heavy winter rains or during the high water of late May and early June.

cottonwood trees and August-ripening wild blackberries line the route. Further on, the forest shifts to ash trees with licorice ferns sprouting from the mossy branches. Given the jungly setting, it's a little surprising when ocean-going freighters steam past in the adjacent Columbia River channel.

After about three miles, a right-hand fork leads through the woods to a small rocky headland. A white-sand beach beside the little lighthouse here makes an ideal lunch spot—and a good place to imagine buckskin-clad voyageurs paddling dugout canoes along the shore of this pivotal Oregon island.

Humbug Mountain

Like a misplaced mountain, this forested peak juts straight out of the Southern Oregon Coast's beach, forcing Highway 101 to detour inland. The protected vale behind the strange mountain shelters a handy, all-year campground, a picnic area, and the trailhead for a loop path that scales the peak itself, with glimpses up and down the coast for miles. It's a beautiful, unspoiled corner of Oregon.

So why was the mountain given the unfortunate name, "Humbug"?

The story begins in 1851, when Captain William Tichenor decided to found a seaport at the nearby cove of Cape Orford. Originally from New Jersey, Tichenor had panned out seventy-five pounds of gold dust in California's 1849 Gold Rush. In 1850 he had used the money to buy a steamship named the *Sea Gull,* sail to Mexico, and collect turtles. Upon his return to San Francisco, he had sold his catch to restaurants at a substantial profit. Now, looking for an even bigger business venture, he had steamed north along the wilderness coast toward Oregon.

Tichenor knew gold had just been discovered along the Klamath River, deep in Northern California's mountains. The overland route from the Sacramento Valley to the new diggings crossed a hundred miles of rugged ranges. But he reasoned that there must be a shortcut to the mines from the ocean—and the man who platted a city where that shortcut reached the sea might be building a new San Francisco. Such a man would be wealthy beyond imagining.

The biggest obstacle to this scheme was that Tichenor really didn't have any training as an explorer. All the rivers on the coast looked a lot the same to him. As he steamed north with nine hired men, he mistook the Rogue River for the Klamath, and began looking for a place to stake out his seaport there.

Battle Rock on the beach at Port Orford.

Now a second problem emerged. The Spanish had noted 250 years earlier that this stretch of coast has no natural harbors. Tichenor couldn't find any either. The only feasible landing site was twenty miles north of the Rogue River, where a small cape at what is now Port Orford shelters a sandy cove from the worst of the Pacific's surf. So he anchored the *Sea Gull* there and began shuttling his nine pioneers to the beach in dinghies. He told them he would be back in two weeks with a shipload of supplies from San Francisco. Then they would blaze a trail inland to the Klamath River gold mines and be ready for business.

Tichenor's hired men were more than a little nervous about being left behind on this remote shore. What if the natives weren't friendly? To put their minds at ease, Tichenor left them the ship's four-inch cannon before sailing away. But trouble wasn't far away.

Today the ocean scenery at Port Orford's beach is so peaceful that it's easy to forget the troubles of Tichenor's men, at least for a while. When you're driving Highway 101 south toward Humbug Mountain, park at the south edge of town and stand on the bluff edge above the beach. To the right you'll see the cape that serves as a breakwater for the town's only dock. Because Port Orford's harbor really is on the ocean, a crane has to lift fishing boats out of the water each night for safer storage on top of a wharf. To the left you'll see the beach arcing out six miles to the dark hump of Humbug Mountain. And directly in front of you, resembling a derelict steamship with its prow beached just beyond the surf, is an almost-island called Battle Rock.

Tichenor's men had been left on the beach right beside this 400-foot-long rock on June 9, 1851. As soon as Tichenor sailed away, his hired men noticed

Indians among the trees of the shore. Alarmed, they dragged their gear up the steep, narrow neck of Battle Rock, where they would be protected on three sides by water. More and more Indians arrived, armed with bows and striped with what looked like war paint. The next day a canoe arrived from the south with still more natives, led by a chief in a red shirt.

Preparing for the worst, the nine men on Battle Rock set up their cannon on the rock's natural causeway. They loaded it with a double handful of nails and inch-long chunks of bar lead. Then two men stood ready to light the charge, crouched behind a fifteen-inch-wide plank.

All at once, nearly a hundred Indian men charged up onto the rock. Within seconds, thirty-seven arrows had thunked into the cannoneers' protective plank. When the red-shirted chief leading the charge was just eight feet from the cannon's muzzle, Tichenor's men fired.

The cannon's blast killed seventeen Indian men. The rest fled back to the woods, terrified. Later that day, an unarmed Indian chief appeared on the beach. Using hand signals, he indicated that the tribe wanted to retrieve their dead. They carried away all but the red-shirted chief. When Tichenor's men signaled that they should remove this warrior as well, the Indians shook their heads. They ripped his red shirt down the middle, kicked him in the ribs, and left him where he had fallen. That night, as Tichenor's men dragged the body down to bury it in the beach sand, they saw that his face was freckled and his hair was blond. One of Tichenor's men later claimed he learned from the Indians that the dead man was actually a Russian sailor, shipwrecked here years before.

Tichenor's men were more than ready to leave Port Orford, and they knew they were low on gunpowder. But as they explained to the Indians in a parley, their ship had promised to come to get them in fourteen days. Both sides agreed to a truce for that long. What they didn't know is that Tichenor had stopped for engine repairs in San Francisco and would be three days late.

And so on the fifteenth day the Indians massed again on the shore with their bows and war paint. When they began advancing under a new chief, Tichenor's men picked him off with a rifle shot. The Indians regrouped and approached with yet another leader. A rifle shot felled him too. This time the Indians retreated to a campsite where they chanted and performed war dances long into the night.

Tichenor's men decided they couldn't wait for the *Sea Gull* any longer. Under cover of darkness they slipped down from Battle Rock and fled through the woods toward the nearest white settlement — Fort Umpqua, eighty miles to the north.

When Tichenor sailed in to Port Orford two days later and saw the blood stains on Battle Rock, he assumed his men had been killed. Immediately he returned to San Francisco with news of the massacre. Citizens called for retaliation against the killers, unaware that Tichenor's men were safe at Fort Umpqua, and the ones who had actually been killed were nine-teen Tututni tribesmen. Within days Tichenor enlisted sixty-seven unemployed gold miners for a second expedition. When they reached Port Orford they quickly chased off the Tututnis and built two log blockhouses on the shore overlooking Battle Rock.

Now Tichenor could get back to the business of opening a trail inland to the Klamath River gold mines. Of course, Tichenor still wasn't aware that he had set up near the Rogue River by mistake.

Humbug Mountain from Port Orford.

The Rogue's daunting canyon twists inland through virtually impenetrable, jagged mountains. Not surprisingly, the first trailblazing party Tichenor sent to find the Klamath River mines got lost. After a week, thirteen of them made it back to Port Orford. The others wandered north to the Coquille River, lost five men in an Indian ambush, and ended up at Fort Umpqua, eighty miles in the wrong direction.

Stirred to action, Tichenor announced that he would lead a second trailblazing party himself. All they needed to do, he explained, was climb the mountain at the south end of Port Orford's beach. On the far side they would see the route to the gold mines. So they set off, arduously slashing their way up the mountain's steep slope through a jungly forest. When they reached the summit, all they could see on the other side was more ocean. The men angrily named the mountain "Tichenor's Humbug" and went home.

After that, the town of Port Orford probably would have vanished altogether if miners had not discovered gold dust two years later in the sand at Battle Rock, and at most Southern Oregon beaches. The mines Tichenor sought had been under his feet from the first.

Today, of course, the ocean view and the ancient forest that so infuriated Tichenor's men have become Humbug Mountain's enduring attractions. The modern-day path from Highway 101 sets off through a glen of huge maple and myrtlewood trees, with sword ferns and maidenhair ferns. The trail soon climbs into an old-growth forest of Douglas firs, some six feet thick. After a mile the trail forks at the start of a large loop. The shorter, slightly steeper North Trail to the right passes the hike's best viewpoint (looking north to Redfish Rocks, Port Orford, and Cape Blanco). Where the routes finally rejoin, you can take a short uphill spur to the small, steep summit meadow of grass and bracken fern. At the top, Tichenor's humbug view has become so overgrown that the name still fits.

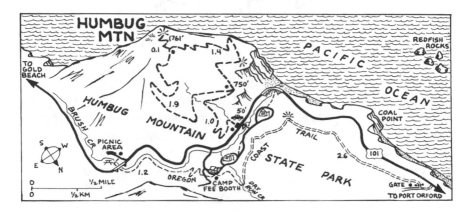

13. Humbug Mountain

HIKE LOCATION

Difficult
5.5-mile loop
1710 feet elevation gain

Climb through an ancient forest to a coastal peak's ocean views.

Getting There: From Coos Bay, drive 51 miles south on Highway 101. Beyond Port Orford six miles (and 21 miles before Gold Beach) park at a large brown "Humbug Mountain Trail Parking" sign a quarter mile north of the state park's campground entrance.

Hiking Tips: Walk a mile up the trail to the start of the loop. Turn right on the shorter, more scenic North Trail for 1.4 miles and take a 0.1-mile spur up to the mountain's overgrown summit. Then return to continue the loop.

Season: Open all year.

While You're in the Area: Humbug Mountain State Park's campground offers 55 tent campsites and 40 trailer spaces. A short path from the campground ducks under Highway 101 to a secluded sandy beach.

CHAPTER IV

The Settlers

The rivers that roll through Oregon brought settlers long before wagons creaked overland from the Oregon Trail. The Willamette Valley's early settlers were a motley mix of French-Canadian voyageurs, failed fur traders, shipwrecked explorers, bawdy mountain men, and stern missionaries. One and all, they knew the temperate valley's gentle prairies as an easy Eden, with the Willamette River as everyman's main street.

Ten thousand times more people live in the Willamette Valley now than in 1843. But because development has largely turned its back on the rolling river, the sites of the oldest settlements remain lost amid the cottonwoods, slumbering in the mist. Just minutes from the gray whine of Interstate 5, trails descend past stubble farmfields and brambles to the nearly forgotten landings of history—to Champoeg, where Oregon's government began; to the Willamette Mission, where missionaries gained a shaky foothold; and to Minto-Brown Island, where two of the fledgling capital's pioneers squared off. Today these paths are an opportunity to come home to Oregon's original main street, the river.

Champoeg

Halfway between the sleepy Willamette Valley hamlets of Butteville and St. Paul, the pastureland of Champoeg State Heritage Area hardly looks like Oregon's most important polling place. Vanished with hardly a trace are Champoeg's once busy streets, church, mills, and houses. But this is where the first American government west of the Rockies formed in 1843, after a deadlocked vote in the old town's riverbank meadow. Today a loop trail tours the town's tale.

The vote in Champoeg's meadow was a turning point in the long battle between Britain and the United States over control of the Oregon Country. That rivalry had begun in 1792 when American Captain Gray found the Columbia River just ahead of British Captain Vancouver. Britain won

The Willamette River at Champoeg State Park.

the upper hand in 1834 when Hudson's Bay Company chief McLoughlin crushed the upstart Yankee trader Nathaniel Wyeth. At Champoeg the two nations' fortunes also seesawed. But the story begins long before 1843, and the town's riverside meadow is at center stage.

For centuries, the Kalapuyan tribe had set fires in the Willamette Valley each autumn to burn brush so deer would be easier to hunt. The fires also encouraged the spread of *champooick,* a local variety of edible camas that gave the townsite its name. Over the years, the fires had cleared a patchwork of prairies spreading twenty miles north from present-day Salem. Only here at Champoeg, however, did that savanna reach the river itself. The grassy bank became a natural stopping point for travelers by either land or water.

The United States beat the British to the Willamette Valley in 1811, when coonskin-capped Americans, exploring south from Fort Astoria for furs, noticed the riverbank meadow and set up a Willamette Outpost two miles west of here. But their little fur trading post folded two years later when Fort Astoria fell into British hands.

The Hudson's Bay Company took over and ran the fur business with a very different style. English gentlemen of the company dined at Fort Vancouver with silver, crystal, and bone china. Each year one of these chief traders would lead a fur trapping expedition south through the Willamette Valley. In 1825, for example, the expedition camped at Champoeg along the way, allowing their guest scientist, the Scot David Douglas, to investigate and name new species, such as the Douglas fir and the Douglas squirrel. On such expeditions the troop's English leader would ride up front, mounted on a strong Nez Perce horse and armed with the best rifle available. Behind him rode his proud Indian wife, decorated with beads, bells, and a broad hat. Then came the chief trader's children on ponies. Following these were the actual trappers, French-Canadians with bright red knitted caps, beaded tobacco pouches, and long rifles.

But not all of the American Astorians had left Oregon, and few had forgotten the pleasant prairies of the Willamette Valley. By 1826, a French-Canadian former Astorian named Etienne Lucier had retired to a farm just west of Champoeg. In 1834 an American trapper, Ewing Young, settled across the river. Theirs was an easy life. The prairies were ready-made farmfields. Even casually sown crops never failed in the mild climate.

The idyll particularly impressed John McLoughlin at Fort Vancouver. Cagily, he decided to retire his aging French-Canadian employees to the Willamette Valley prairies. Most of his hired men were originally from distant Montreal and Quebec, and they didn't want to go back, even though Hudson's Bay Company rules dictated that retirees be returned to the place where they had signed up. So he offered to keep them on the books as part-time farmers if they retired on the plains like Etienne Lucier. Soon more than sixty French-Canadians took up the easy farming lifestyle on what became known as French Prairie.

McLoughlin had an ulterior motive for the retirement scheme. His French-Canadians were technically British subjects, and he knew that by settling them in Oregon he was shifting the balance of power in the Northwest even farther toward Britain. Since 1818 the U.S. and Britain had agreed to "joint occupancy" of the Oregon Country because no one could decide how to divide the territory. In practical terms, that meant there would be no government at all until one side or the other had enough settlers on the ground to force the issue.

As you drive from the Champoeg Park entrance toward the Riverside Day Use Area, you'll be traveling through the middle of an early, ragtag French-Canadian settlement that strengthened Britain's claim. A dozen crude log cabins were scattered along a half-mile track haughtily dubbed "Napoleon Boulevard" by Hudson's Bay gentlemen in the late 1830s.

But American settlers kept arriving. When Nathaniel Wyeth's Sauvie Island fort failed, many of his men ended up as farmers near Champoeg. In 1840, the flamboyant Joe Meek and four other American mountain men quit the rigors of Rocky Mountain fur trapping and retired to Oregon with

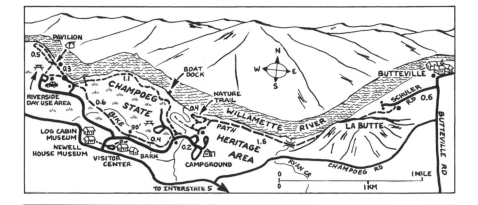

14. Champoeg Park

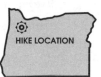

HIKE LOCATION

Easy
3.2-mile loop
No elevation gain

Stroll along the Willamette River to the site of Oregon's first government.

Getting There: From Portland, take Interstate 5 south 20 miles to the Donald exit #278 and turn right, following signs 5.7 miles to Champoeg Heritage Area's entrance. Stop at the visitor's center here to see its displays. Then drive on into the park, keeping left at junctions, to the Riverside Day Use Area.

Hiking Tips: Follow a "Pavilion" trail sign to the site of the famous 1843 meeting. Walk through the pavilion to the Willamette River. To the left, a 0.4-mile, paved path loops through the riverside woods. To the right, the main riverbank trail leads to a road. Continue 200 yards up the road to a curve where a paved bike path begins. Veer left on the Champoeg Townsite Trail. After 0.6 mile this bark dust river path circles a group camping area where pioneer plays were once held. Next the path skirts the Oak Grove Day Use Area lawns and ends at a wide, paved bike path beside a road. To complete the 3.2-mile hiking loop, turn right on the bike path.

Season: Open all year.

While You're in the Area: Near the park entrance, the Robert Newell House Museum preserves the only farmhouse to survive the 1861 flood. The restored house, furnished with antiques, is open 11am-3pm on weekends from March through October for $4. Next door is a 1931 log cabin museum with more pioneer exhibits.

their Indian wives and children, settling north of the Willamette on the Tualatin Plains. Also in 1840, a contingent of fifty Methodist missionaries arrived by ship around Cape Horn.

Meanwhile, "Oregon fever" had begun to spread through the Eastern states, fanned by anti-British sentiment and by tales of the Willamette Valley's farming paradise. The first large wagon train to take the Oregon Trail arrived in the fall of 1842, bringing 197 Americans to the valley. The balance of power was tilting back in America's favor, and Champoeg would be the site of a showdown.

Joe Meek.

Park your car at the end of the Riverside loop and follow the "Pavilion" trail sign a few hundred yards to a shelter and a granite monument with a bronze plaque. The riverside meadow that once sprawled here is now mostly overgrown with trees, but just ahead you can see a remnant lawn. Beyond it, the broad, lazy river reflects clouds, a few geese, and perhaps a great blue heron. To your right was the site of a warehouse the Hudson's Bay Company built about 1841 for buying and storing wheat.

The British company had been surprised by the amount of wheat their French-Canadian retirees produced, seemingly without effort. In 1836, the farmers harvested a thousand bushels. The next year the crop was five times larger. Each year the harvest increased. McLoughlin bought the wheat for fifty cents a bushel and sold it to the Russians in Alaska for three times that price. To keep settlers dependent on the British, he never paid them in cash, but rather in chit that could be traded only for Hudson's Bay Company goods. The company tacked a small store onto one wall of Champoeg's wheat warehouse so that, in the words of one disdainful American, "Mr. and Mrs. No-Shirt could return home arrayed in all the hues of the rainbow." McLoughlin offered free loans and assistance to the American settlers, but many felt oppressed by the monopolistic Britisher. In a land with no formal government, the Hudson's Bay Company ruled unopposed.

The Americans called for a general meeting at Champoeg on May 2, 1843, to challenge the British company's power once and for all. Every white adult male in Oregon was invited to vote on forming an American-style government "for civil and military protection of this colony," as proposed by a local committee of twelve Americans. McLoughlin called on his French-Canadian employees to vote down the committee's proposal as a block. The Americans tried to muster every independent settler, trapper, and mountain man they could find—but in 1843 there were scarcely two hundred adult white men in the entire Willamette Valley, and many of them could not come.

The day before the vote, men began arriving at Champoeg from all over Oregon. On the second of May a hundred French-Canadian, British, and American men packed into the Hudson's Bay store for the fateful meeting. In the wrangling clamor, the only point the men could agree on was to move the meeting to the meadow outside.

There the fiery American mountain man Joe Meek, fed up with indecision, called for the group to divide itself into two sides so they could take an accurate vote. He drew a line in the sand and shouted, "Who's for a divide? All for the report of the committee and an organization, follow me!"

When the crowd drew up sides, a count showed exactly the same number of men on either side of the line. The vote was tied fifty to fifty. But two French-Canadians had remained standing in the middle, uncertain whether to join the Americans or their fellow French-Canadians. One of the two was Etienne Lucier, the voyageur who had come west with the American Astor company in 1811. Lucier had lost his job when the British took over Fort Astoria. The other was F. X. Matthieu, who had been forced to leave Montreal for plotting an anti-British revolt. Matthieu had come west with the Oregon Trail wagon train in 1842. Both had no love for Britain, but voting against the other French-Canadians would not be an easy decision for them. Lucier also feared that forming a government would mean he'd have to start paying taxes. Matthieu finally convinced him to join the Americans, and the day was won, by a mere two votes.

"Three cheers for our side!" Joe Meek shouted, throwing his slouch hat in the air. The fifty defeated French-Canadians glumly went home. The victors later elected officers and declared Champoeg the seat of a legislative district stretching from the Rocky Mountains to the Pacific Ocean. Both Britain and the United States still claimed the Oregon Country, but the settlers knew the power of the Hudson's Bay Company had been broken.

The British claim on Oregon took another blow five months later when a massive influx of 875 Americans arrived in the Willamette Valley from the Oregon Trail. The next year, after President Polk won election on an anti-British campaign threatening war over the Oregon Country, wagon trains brought 1750 more Americans. In 1845, the wave of immigration swelled to 3000. The British finally admitted defeat in 1846, dropping their claims south of the forty-ninth parallel. The U.S. Congress officially established the Oregon Territory in 1848, completing the work that fifty-two men at Champoeg had begun.

Champoeg's importance did not last, however, and if you hike to the right along the riverbank trail you'll see why. The townsite here was simply too near the river, on dangerously low land. To be sure, the town prospered at first. Steamboats began landing here in 1851, and the townsite was officially platted in 1852. By 1860 Champoeg boasted two hundred buildings, including a hotel, Masonic hall, two blacksmith shops, an Episcopal church, and several saloons. Then, in a December, 1861 rainstorm, the river rose fifty-five feet, covering the townsite seven feet deep. No one drowned, thanks largely to the quick work of four young men in rowboats. But one by one the log cabins and frame houses floated off their foundations and vanished downriver. When the waters retreated, the townsite

Log cabin museum at Champoeg before it was moved away from the river in 2014.

was a bare, sandy plain. Only the massive Hudson's Bay Company warehouse remained near the river, and it had floated 150 feet to an unusable site. The church's bell was found in Champoeg Creek— a sluggish stream you'll pass after hiking a mile along the riverbank. The bell was salvaged for use in the Butteville church, two miles away, where it remains to this day.

After the flood of 1861, a few people rebuilt on higher ground. A barn from 1862 stands by the park's visitor center. As you're hiking on a loop back to your car, walk up to visit this museum and get an overview of the old townsite below. Only a few warehouses and mills were built on the lowlands after the flood of 1861, and all of those buildings washed away in a second great flood in 1890. Then the townsite was abandoned for good.

Finish the hiking loop by following a paved bike path across a sheep pasture where Champoeg's streets once ran. But before getting back in your car, stop one more time at the riverside meadow's Pavilion. The monument here has a final story to tell.

Celebration at Champoeg, 1905.

In 1900, when the newly founded Oregon Historical Society decided to place this marker at the site of Champoeg's historic meeting, they weren't sure precisely where to put it. The entire town had washed away twice, leaving few landmarks. The only person who might know the correct location was the eighty-two year-old French-Canadian pioneer F. X. Matthieu, the last survivor of the historic vote. To locate the exact spot where Joe Meek had drawn his line in the sand, the governor of Oregon himself, Theodore Geer, arranged to meet Matthieu at his Butteville home.

And so Governor Geer got on a large-wheeled bicycle at the Salem Capitol and rode twenty-four miles over the dirt roads to Butteville. Matthieu, meanwhile, had forgotten about the appointment and taken his buggy into Portland for the day. The governor decided to wait. He practiced pitching horseshoes for a while. Then he mowed Matthieu's lawn. When the old pioneer returned that evening, it was too dark to go to Champoeg, so the governor had to spend the night. Out in the riverside meadow the next morning, Matthieu tapped an oak stake into the ground where he said Joe Meek had stood.

Truth be told, the granite monument the governor later unveiled here is not actually where Matthieu drove his stake, but rather a few hundred feet closer to the river, where it could be admired more easily by passing steamboat passengers. Still the marker is close enough, and the festive unveiling ceremony in 1901 launched a tradition of summer celebrations. Until 1994, an annual Historical Pageant presented a reenactment of the Champoeg story. Now the open-air amphitheater near the river has become a group campsite with a boat dock. But those who know Champoeg's history may hear an old echo ringing across these fields — Joe Meek's stirring challenge, "Who's for a divide?"

Willamette Mission

A hike through Willamette Mission State Park not only visits the site of Oregon's first missionary outpost, but it also offers a look at the nation's largest cottonwood tree and a free ride across the Willamette River on a historic ferry. Along the way you'll find a reminder of a tragic romance that shook the Methodist mission here in 1838.

Start at the park's Filbert Grove Day Use Area, a picnic area set in an old hazelnut orchard. Some years the trees still produce a bumper crop of free, gatherable nuts in autumn. Walk from the picnic area about a quarter mile to the riverbank and turn right on a paved bike path. Follow this promenade about a mile to the Wheatland Ferry landing.

This is the oldest ferry landing in Oregon, dating to 1844 when pioneer settler Daniel Matheny's mules pulled a log barge across the river with ropes. The present steel ferry platform uses an electric winch and an overhead cable. Because it's the fifth boat to see service here, it's christened the Daniel Matheny V. Pedestrians ride free, but car drivers pay about $2. The trip takes about ten minutes each way.

After riding this quaint shuttle across the river and back, explore the gravel shore nearby. The bank is a pleasant place to watch the big, glassy river slide by, or to skip rocks out into the current. Children delight in finding tadpoles, frogs, and crawdads in the shallows. Look in the wet sand for the palm-sized tracks of great blue herons and the little hand-shaped tracks of raccoons. Cottonwood trees along the bank spread their honeyed smell in spring and the snowflake fluff of their drifting seeds in summer.

Before the ferry started service, dugout canoes probably crossed the river here, especially when the Methodists' Willamette Mission was in operation between 1834 and 1840. After the first Oregon Trail wagon train rolled into the Willamette Valley late in 1842, settlers needed something bigger than canoes to cross the valley's great river. Three of those new arrivals were brothers from the Applegate family. They spent the rainy winter of 1843 bivouacked in the old mission's abandoned log buildings. While they were there, Lindsay Applegate built a boat out of crude

The Wheatland ferry.

planks. He filled the cracks with religious tracts left by the missionaries, forcing the papers in with a chisel and sealing them with hot pitch.

The large Oregon Trail wagon trains of 1843 brought Daniel Matheny with his wife and seven children to the Willamette Valley. In the spring of 1844 Matheny bought Lindsay Applegate's boat and settled on the far side of the river. Within months Matheny had built a bigger barge that could carry an ox team. Because it was the only ferry on the Willamette, settlers from the fertile Yamhill country were soon bringing wagonloads of wheat here. Many camped or bartered while waiting for the slow, cumbersome ferry. Sensing an opportunity, Matheny platted the townsite of Atchison beside the west ferry landing in 1847 and began selling lots in exchange for wheat. In the early 1850s the young town changed its name to Wheatland.

To imagine the riverbank burg of Wheatland in its 1860 heyday, picture two hotels and a full wheat warehouse, with a sternwheel riverboat steamer from Oregon City snorting black smoke beside the ferry landing. The picture for that particular year might also include a strange little sidewheel paddleboat powered by oxen on a treadmill. Dubbed the "Hayburner" by its critics, this alternative-energy craft was the creation of a Corvallis inventor. On the boat's maiden voyage down the river past Wheatland, the oxen ate most of the fuel supply while the boat was hung up on a gravel bar. After the boat arrived in Oregon City the pilot stocked up more hay, but he sold the oxen when it became obvious they couldn't

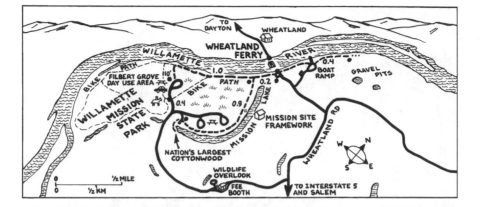

15. Willamette Mission

HIKE LOCATION

Easy
2.7-mile loop
No elevation gain

Ride the Wheatland Ferry and hike to Oregon's first mission site.

Getting There: Drive Interstate 5 north from Salem 9 miles (or south from Portland 36 miles) to the Brooks exit #263. Then drive 1.8 miles west on Brooklake Road, turn right onto Wheatland Road for 2.4 miles, and turn left at the Willamette Mission State Park sign. Follow the entrance road 1.8 miles (keeping left at junctions), pay a $5-per-car fee at an entry booth, and park at the Filbert Grove Day Use Area.

Hiking Tips: Take the path past the restrooms 0.2 mile to the riverbank and turn right for a mile to the Wheatland Ferry landing. The ferry runs 5:30am-9:45pm every day except Christmas, Thanksgiving, and several weeks in winter when it closes for high water. Call 503-588-7979 for information. To return to the loop, hike 300 yards back from the landing and turn left onto a road-like trail. This path passes the mission monument and eventually enters a developed picnic area in an old walnut orchard. Keep left at junctions for half a mile to trail's end at a road (where a sign points out the nation's largest black cottonwood). Walk along the road to return to your car, turning left at the first stop sign and right at the next.

Season: Open all year.

While You're in the Area: Visit Jason Lee's 1841 Salem house at the Mission Mill Museum, 1313 Mill Street SE, across the street from Willamette University. With a functioning pioneer woolen mill, it's open 10am-5pm Monday-Saturday. Call (503) 585-7012 for information.

power the boat upstream against the Willamette's current, no matter how much they ate.

The town of Wheatland had setbacks too. The 1861 flood that washed away Champoeg took the lower half of Wheatland, including the town's warehouse with seven thousand bushels of wheat. When trains later by-passed the town, Wheatland faded. Today only a road sign and a few farmhouses remain.

When you're ready to continue to the mission site, walk a few hundred yards back from the Wheatland Ferry landing on the bike path and turn left onto a grassy, road-like trail. This path follows the shore of marshy Mission Lake. Before the 1861 flood, this oxbow lake was the Willamette River's main channel. At a viewpoint with a plaque you can look across the water to a metal framework that represents the mission buildings built on the opposite shore of this old riverbank by Jason Lee in 1834.

The Methodist Board of Missions had actually sent Lee and two male assistants west in 1834 to preach among the "Flathead" tribe of what is to-day eastern Washington state. But after accompanying Nathaniel Wyeth's second Oregon expedition through the Rocky Mountains, Lee found the no-madic natives there so violent, and the sagebrush landscape so uninviting, that he decided to continue on to Fort Vancouver instead. When he reached the settlement he preached an awkward service to a polyglot jumble of Mult-nomah tribespeople, French-Canadians, imported Hawaiian laborers, and three shipwrecked Japanese fishermen. John McLoughlin counseled Lee to set up his ministry among the Willamette Valley's Kalapuyans instead.

Before Lee set out toward the south he prayed, "O, My God, direct us as to the right spot where we can best glorify thee and be most useful to these degraded red men," a remark reflecting the racial insensitivity of his day. With guides and provisions supplied by McLoughlin, Lee's party canoed past Sauvie Island, rode across the Tualatin Plains, and swam their horses across the Willamette River to Champoeg. Then they rode south through French Prairie a dozen miles to the riverbend here, near what Lee described as a "filthy, miserable company" of thirty Kalapuyans subsist-ing on camas roots. Lee set up a tent and asked for the rest of his supplies to be brought upriver by canoe. For the next month the missionary men hewed oak logs to build an 18-by-32-foot, two-room house.

The Methodist missionaries preached to the Kalapuyans and to the French-Canadian Catholics nearby, but a great deal of their time was oc-cupied clearing farmland and establishing a settlement.

The men also found themselves caring for three Kalapuyan children who had been orphaned when their parents died of disease. That first winter

Lee wrote to his Methodist supporters back East, "I have requested the Board not to send any more *single men*." To make sure he was understood, he added, "A greater favour could not be bestowed upon this country, than to send to it pious, industrious, intelligent females. I am not singular in this."

A year later, in 1836, the Methodist men were still single. Meanwhile they had fenced thirty acres, doubled the house's size, and added a large

log barn. Their mission school, however, only had an enrollment of eighteen Kalapuyans on weekdays and fifty-three on Sundays. Eight of their students died, probably from disease spread in the school itself, and many others eventually left or were removed by their parents. Nonetheless, Lee wrote back glowing reports of Oregon as an earthly paradise in need of guidance. In particular, he noted, "white females would be of the greatest importance to the mission."

Frameworks now show the size and location of the Willamette Mission's buildings.

In July, 1836 the Methodist mission board finally sent a reinforcement of thirteen missionaries—including several women. One of them, a thirty-three-year-old New York schoolteacher named Anna Pittman, had been picked as a possible match for Jason Lee. For ten months the group sailed via Cape Horn and Hawaii to Oregon. Anna had hardly finished unpacking at the dirt-floored mission when Lee proposed marriage. She asked for time to think it over.

A month later Anna Pittman handed Lee a poem she had written. It began, "Yes, where thou goest I will go." They agreed to keep their engagement secret a few days longer. Lee had been asked to officiate at a wedding for one of the other newly arrived women. On July 16, 1837, the missionary community gathered in a grove of trees two hundred yards east of the mission buildings. Lee married the other couple and performed the first communion ever given in the Willamette Valley, but first he surprised the crowd by exchanging vows with Anna himself. The romantic twist so charmed onlookers that they gave Anna an unexpected wedding present: a cutting from a rose bush that had been brought halfway around the world to brighten the missionary outpost with flowers.

When the rose bush budded that spring, Anna was pregnant. Jason reluctantly left her to travel back East, hoping to convince the Methodist mission board to expand the Oregon mission. Three months after he had left, Anna gave birth to a baby boy. But the baby was not healthy. Two days later it died. At once Anna's condition worsened. After a night of suffering she announced, "I am going to my rest." Anna passed away calmly just before dawn. She was buried with her baby in her arms, in the same grove where she had been married.

Messengers on horseback reached Jason Lee with the news sixty days later in the Shawnee country of the Great Plains. Shaken, he continued east. For nearly two years he lectured from St. Louis to Boston about his mission in Oregon. His talks fired thousands of everyday people with "Oregon fever." He convinced the Methodist mission board to authorize $100,000 for a "Great Reinforcement" of fifty people to Oregon. Meanwhile, he ordered an elaborate tombstone carved that he could take back to Anna's grave in Oregon.

Jason Lee sailed back around Cape Horn with the new recruits in the spring of 1840. The marker he raised on Anna's grave might as well have been a tombstone for the old Willamette Mission itself. Within weeks Lee had set up three new satellite missions, abandoned the buildings by the riverbank here, and moved his headquarters ten miles south to Chemeketa—a site now known as the city of Salem.

Lee had several reasons for abandoning the old mission site. Salem was better protected from floods, and had a creek that could power his planned sawmill. But Lee also thought the higher, drier site at Salem might prove healthier. Too many people had died in the old riverside log cabins—including his wife Anna and his infant son.

In the new settlement at Salem, controversy soon began to spread about Jason Lee's leadership. One of the new arrivals wrote that Lee had deceived them about the number of Kalapuyans in Oregon. "Instead of thousands I have found but a few hundreds, and these are fast sinking into the grave. Extinction seems to be their inevitable doom, and their habits are such that I am fearful that they will never be reached by the gospel."

The newly arrived missionaries were shocked that the Kalapuyans expected to be paid for attending church. Even when Lee organized a full-scale camp meeting at Chemeketa, holding communion with five hundred Kalapuyans and baptizing more than a hundred, the natives' heathen lifestyle seemed unaffected. Lee built a mill and a frame house for himself (now both preserved at Salem's Mission Mill Village), and in 1842 he founded the Oregon Institute for native students (now Willamette University), but so few native children attended that the school soon had to switch to teaching white settlers' children instead.

Jason Lee's disgruntled colleagues wrote to the Methodist mission board, complaining that he seemed more interested in commercial enterprises among the white settlers than in spiritual work among the natives. The mission board responded by removing Lee from office. They sent a new leader who shut down Lee's Salem mission in 1844 and sold the property. Outraged, Lee rushed back to New York to plead his case. After lengthy testimony, the mission board relented. They offered to give him back his job. But by then his health had begun to fail. Jason Lee died in the East at the age of forty-one.

When you leave the mission's monument to complete the loop hike through the park, you'll find a sign at the far end of Mission Lake pointing to the nation's largest black cottonwood. The stately tree is 155 feet tall and over twenty-six feet in circumference. It is one of the few survivors of that pioneer era more than a century and a half ago, when Jason Lee raised a tombstone to his wife.

On your hike through the modern state park you won't see much evidence of the original mission settlement. The apocalyptic flood of 1861 not only turned the old river channel here into a slough, but it also swept away the log cabin buildings. If you hike here in the spring, however, you may still catch an ethereal reminder of that earlier world: a hauntingly sweet fragrance wafting from a rose bush at the viewpoint of the mission site. The bush's blooms are of a rare, old-fashioned variety called the "Mission Rose." These are the delicate flowers of Anna Pittman, the young woman who was given a treasured rose cutting on her wedding day to help grace a lonely Methodist mission with her fragile dreams.

Minto-Brown Island

Two of Salem's least compatible citizens once settled on adjacent Willamette River islands. Today their islands have merged to become Salem's largest and wildest park, hardly a mile from downtown. A hike on the mostly paved paths of Minto-Brown Island Park almost guarantees you'll see great blue herons stalking the riverbank and Canada geese gleaning the fields. But you'll also be walking the awkward property line between two unlikely pioneer neighbors: a drunken sailor and an upstanding legislator.

Although the sailor's name was officially Isaac Brown, everyone called him by the more descriptive handle, Whiskey. He was originally stranded in Oregon when his ship wrecked on the Columbia River bar in 1853.

It may well have been the same freighter that sank that year with the materials for a Cape Disappointment lighthouse. After four years at loose

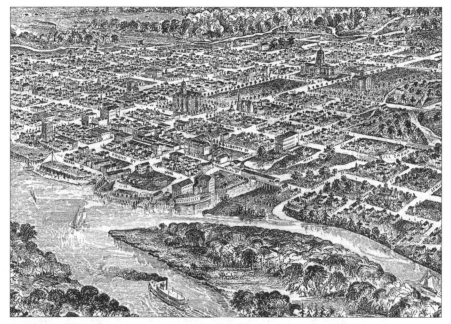

Salem in 1877, with Minto Island at lower right.

ends in the Astoria area, Whiskey Brown built himself a raft and poled upriver. He settled on what became known as Browns Island, an isolated patch of floodplain separated from the up-and-coming city of Salem by the main channel of the Willamette River and by a second, larger island. In those days the river cut between the two islands like the slash through a percentage symbol. On Browns Island, Whiskey built a shack on stilts, planted tobacco and melons, and began distilling his favorite beverage. Soon every boatman and rafter on the river—and many a canoeload of local Kalapuyans—had discovered Whiskey's ramshackle outpost. The old salt liked nothing better than to drink, smoke, and swap yarns with rivergoers.

Whiskey's laid-back lifestyle outraged the churchmen who had founded Salem. They denounced his devilish liquor and derided his stilted home. But the missionaries had recently lost some of their clout. Rumors still swirled about the disagreement that had shut down the Methodist mission and led to Jason Lee's suspension.

Another rivalry simmering in Salem at the time centered on the city's selection as Oregon's capital. Champoeg had been the seat of Oregon's provisional government, but when territorial status arrived, the legislature met in Oregon City. There, in 1851, they wrangled over where

16. Minto-Brown Island

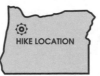

HIKE LOCATION

Easy
3.7-mile loop
No elevation gain

Watch ducks, geese, and herons from this riverfront park's paved trails.

Getting There: From Interstate 5, take the third Salem exit (#253) and head west on Mission Street 3 miles. Beyond Bush Park 2 blocks, turn left on Commercial Street for 0.2 mile. Then turn right on Owens Street, which becomes River Road. At the first light (after 1.4 miles), turn right into Minto-Brown Island Park and drive a mile to a parking area at road's end.

Hiking Tips: From the parking lot's map signboard, turn right at the restroom enclosure and then fork left to find the riverside trail. Follow this path 0.8 mile to a T-shaped junction in a field. If you like, you can turn right here to complete a short 1.4-mile loop back to the car. For a longer, 3.7-mile loop, turn left, skirting old farm fields. After 1.4 miles, ignore a footbridge to the left, cross the entrance road, and continue to the edge of a duck pond. Then keep right for another 1.3 miles to complete the loop back to your car.

Season: Open all year.

While You're in the Area: Drive to Salem's Bush Park (see map) to visit Bush House, the Victorian mansion of another prominent Salem pioneer, *Oregon Statesman* editor Asahel Bush. It's open for guided tours at 1pm, 2pm, 3pm, and 4pm Wednesday through Sunday (closed January and February). Also stop by the Deepwood Estate, at the far northeast corner of Bush Park, an 1894 Queen Anne house with stained glass windows and formal gardens. The delightful gardens are always open; the house itself opens only for special events.

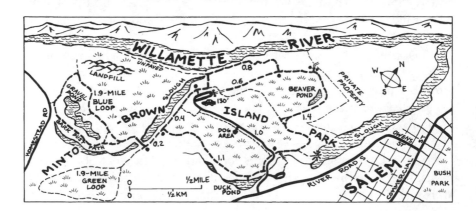

to place the capital permanently. Portland, Corvallis, Salem, and half a dozen other towns jostled for favor. In a fiercely contested vote, the legislators decided to give the penitentiary to Portland, the university to Corvallis, and the capital to Salem. The next legislature met in Salem in 1853 and voted to switch the capital to Corvallis after all. The 1855 legislature would have none of it, and promptly moved back to Salem. At this point the office buildings that had been used for the capitol in Salem mysteriously burned to the ground. The *Oregon Statesman* newspaper, trying to publish from the capital, had to move its press three times before landing in Salem for keeps.

Then came the flood of 1861 — the same deluge that erased Champoeg and the Willamette Mission's old buildings. Whiskey Brown simply loaded his jugs, a few pigs, and some chickens in a boat, tethered it to a tree, and rode out the flood in high spirits. His platform house survived fine, too. But when the waters receded, Whiskey realized that his island had changed dramatically. Suddenly the Willamette River no longer flowed between him and Salem. Both Browns Island and the larger island to the east had been joined to the city's riverbank. Whiskey's splendid independence from Salem was over.

Another blow to Whiskey's isolation came six years later when the adjacent "island," now only partially separated by a sinuous slough, was bought by John Minto. A staid Oregon legislator with muttonchop sideburns, Minto was everything that Whiskey Brown was not. Most of all, Minto was an achiever. Born in Newcastle, England, in 1822, Minto had started working in coal mines at the age of ten. At twenty-two, he had crossed the Oregon Trail and staked his claim to a farm in the South Salem hills. At the age of twenty-six, he had gone to the California Gold Rush and brought back enough cash to make his farm the pride of the region, planting a new orchard and importing prize-winning Merino sheep. He scouted a wagon road across the Cascades at what became known as Minto Pass. He wrote poetry extolling the beauty of Oregon. He was elected four times to the legislature. In 1867, this pillar of the community bought land next door to Whiskey Brown's.

Given their differences, it's surprising the two neighbors didn't declare outright war. While Minto trimmed his prize sheep or hunted pheasants, the drunken Brown would be staggering about a camp strewn with dirty dishes and garbage, cursing. Salem boys respected Minto, but they delighted in raiding Brown's melon patch. On one occasion Brown blasted at his tormentors with a muzzleloader, grazing the rear of a fleeing horse. And yet between Minto and Brown themselves, a wary truce remained in

Willamette riverbank path at Minto-Brown Island Park.

force all their lives, as if the river still ran between their lands in spirit.

Today, two of the best loop hikes at Minto-Brown Island Park follow paved paths on Minto's half of the merged islands. For a thirty-minute walk, take a short loop along the riverbank. If you have more time, continue around Minto's old farmfields past two ponds—one pool where beavers have been industriously gnawing at cottonwood trees, and another where a gaggle of resident ducks and geese wait for handouts. A different, partly unpaved loop trail crosses over the original Willamette riverbed to explore Whiskey Brown's island. Here you'll see that more recent controversies have left their mark on these islands.

By the 1960s, both Minto and Browns islands had fallen on hard times. Browns Island housed a landfill and a gravel pit. The north end of Minto Island was home to a paper mill's sludge ponds. A turning point came in 1970, when the City of Salem acquired a large part of the area and began planning a park. After much debate, proposals for a huge baseball stadium and a $12 million arboretum complex were finally defeated. The city decided to leave the area as undeveloped as possible. Today the sludge ponds and the landfill are being phased out, and the gravel pit on Browns Island has become a pleasant, forest-rimmed lake. A proposed pedestrian bridge would link the northern tip of the two former islands directly to downtown Salem's Riverfront Park.

The original settlers may have disagreed on how to use their islands, but the hikers and joggers who come here today seem to have found a consensus that this patch of wildness is a treasure to protect.

CHAPTER V

Wagon Wheels

After Lewis and Clark's harrowing description of the Rocky Mountains in 1806, sane men understood that wagons could not be driven to Oregon. The idea of an "Oregon Trail" for wagons was ridiculed as soundly as Nathaniel Wyeth's plan to wheel keelboats across the Continental Divide in 1832. But there have always been people who have a hard time with the word "impossible."

Among these dreamers were an upstate New York missionary couple named Marcus and Narcissa Whitman. Alarmed that the rival Methodists had sent Jason Lee to convert the West's heathens in 1834, the combined forces of the Presbyterian and Congregational churches had sent the Whitmans in 1836 to spread the correct gospel in Oregon.

The Whitmans and their four companions showed up at the Missouri frontier with two wagons piled high with furniture, religious books, and trunks of clothing. The mountain men who had agreed to guide the party west told them to leave the wagons behind. The Whitmans refused. After the Whitmans' fourteen horses had arduously dragged the caravan across the rivers of the Great Plains to Fort Laramie, the guides again insisted the wagons be left. The Whitmans eyed the Rockies' front range and sold one of the wagons. But they took the other.

Through the Rocky Mountain crossing, Marcus Whitman laboriously pried rocks from the route, chopped trees, and gradually discarded most of the wagon's contents. The wagon itself tipped over several times a day. When the missionaries finally got through to the fur trappers' annual rendezvous in western Wyoming, the rugged frontiersmen there shook their heads at the ungainly vehicle. If the Whitmans wanted to go any farther west, they warned, the wagon would definitely have to be left behind. The Whitmans still refused.

The Indian path into Idaho was a wagoneer's nightmare. Marcus Whitman chopped the wagon in half and continued with the front wheels as

Covered wagon at the Oregon Trail Interpretive Center near Baker City.

a makeshift cart. Finally at Fort Boise, with summer gone, the Whitmans abandoned their beloved wheels and continued on horseback to Walla Walla.

The Whitmans had failed to open a wagon road to Oregon. But the determination of the seemingly frail missionaries had dumbfounded the mountain men. And so when Joe Meek—the later hero of Champoeg's government-forming vote—decided to leave the Rocky Mountain fur trapping business in 1840, he bought himself a wagon, hitched up a team of sturdy oxen, and with a Herculean pathbreaking effort succeeded in dragging the wagon clear through to the Columbia River, hauling both his gear and his extended Indian family to Oregon. Word spread like wildfire among the restless souls of America: The impossible Oregon Trail was open after all.

Those who braved the Oregon Trail in the 1840s discovered that the most difficult part of the trek was not the Rockies, but rather the obstacles in Oregon itself, near journey's end: the Blue Mountains and the Cascade Range. Exhausted pioneers faced these fearsome barriers as winter snowstorms approached.

Today, hikers can follow the wagon route through the desert near Baker City to an ominous viewpoint of the Blue Mountains' sudden wall. And in Western Oregon, hikers can sample six different wagon routes across the Cascade Range. Although modern highways now crisscross the state, large sections of these historic routes have been preserved intact as hiking trails.

The Oregon Trail at Flagstaff Hill

A century and a half have erased most of the original ruts from the route of the old Oregon Trail. Even at the elaborate Oregon Trail Interpretive Center on Flagstaff Hill near Baker City, you'll need a bit of imagination to spot the dusty track amid the sagebrush. The view you're likely to remember from a hike here is the same one that startled early pioneers: a panorama of the jagged Blue Mountains, looming dead ahead to the west.

Oregon Trail pioneers usually reached Flagstaff Hill in September, after three months on the trail. They had crossed the Rocky Mountains via South Pass, where neither snow nor forests blocked their path. Here, however, they saw they still faced both of those dangers. The Blue Mountains had been named for the range's silhouette, which appears blue in the distance because of the range's pine and fir forests. When wagonmasters neared Oregon they would point ahead to the long silhouette and urge their caravans to hurry, warning of the Blue Mountains' early autumn blizzards, and snowdrifts that lock up the passes ahead for eight months of the year.

Today the Oregon Trail Interpretive Center perches on top of Flagstaff Hill like a giant white spaceship hangar. Inside, picture windows frame the colossal view of the Blue Mountains. Dramatically narrated dioramas tell of the Oregon Trail's trials. But to feel the pull of the trail, you'll need to experience this landscape as the pioneers did, with the sun at your back and the smell of sage in the air.

Surprisingly few tourists take the paved, one-and-a-half-mile path down to see the actual Oregon Trail. Most visitors turn back at a replica of a hard-rock gold mine mounted on the hillside below the interpretive center. Many others turn back at Panorama Point, a cliff-edged viewpoint with a deck and a shaded bench. As a result, the broad swale that served as the route for the Oregon Trail can seem nearly as lonely and silent as the day the Conestoga wagons arrived. To find the actual track, look for a small granite marker near a weathered replica of a covered wagon.

In 1841, the year after Joe Meek drove the first wagon through these dry hills, thirty-two people followed his tracks. The next year, 197 came. The "Great Migration" of 1843 brought 875, but even greater migrations followed: 1750 people in 1844 and 3000 in 1845. After a dip in popularity during the California Gold Rush, when most travelers veered south, traffic on the Oregon Trail shot back up to 8000 in 1853.

One of the pioneers of 1853 was 23-year-old Ezra Meeker (no relation to Joe Meek). Like many of the pioneers, Ezra long remembered the trip as

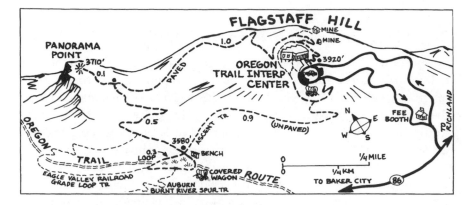

17. Oregon Trail

HIKE LOCATION

Easy
2.9-mile loop
340 feet elevation gain

Walk through the sagebrush to the Oregon Trail's route.

Getting There: From Interstate 84 exit 302, just north of Baker City, drive east 5 miles on Highway 86 to the National Historic Oregon Trail Interpretive Center entrance road on the left. Hiking trails are free, but museum admission runs $8 for adults and $4.50 for seniors, with kids under 15 free.

Hiking Tips: Start by touring the walk-through exhibits in the interpretive center building. After you come back out of the front door, take stairs down to the left to the paved trail network. First switchback downhill a few hundred yards to the replica hard-rock gold mine. Next follow "Panorama Point" signs a mile down to this viewpoint. Then continue downhill 0.5 mile to an X-shaped trail junction near a shade shelter with a bench. To the left is your return trail—a rough dirt path that climbs 0.9 mile to your car. But first go straight on a 0.3-mile loop path that passes a covered wagon on the actual route of the Oregon Trail.

Season: Open all year 9am to 4pm (6pm in summer), but the high desert here has icy winds in winter and 100-degree heat in late summer.

While You're in the Area: Drive into Baker City, where the entire downtown district is registered as a historic landmark. Stop for brunch beneath the stained-glass ceiling of the palm room in the Geiser Grand Hotel (1996 Main Street), built in 1889 and restored in 1998. For a tour of the nearby Blue Mountains gold rush country, see Hike #27.

Ezra Meeker promoting preservation of the Oregon Trail in Baker City, 1906.

a turning point in his life, and he regretted that the trail itself was gradually forgotten, replaced by more modern roads. His nostalgia probably deepened in 1905, when the nation riveted its attention on a New York-to-Portland race in which drivers vied to be the first to cross the continent by automobile. The following year, at seventy-six, Ezra set out to restore the dignity of the old Oregon Trail by retracing the entire route from west to east. Along the way he memorialized the route by placing scores of granite markers — including the one you see by the covered wagon here. For more than twenty years, until his death at ninety-eight, Ezra Meeker championed preservation of the old trail, an effort that others have continued ever since.

Hiking the short loop path near the covered wagon, however, reveals that time has taken its toll on the integrity of the old Oregon Trail, even here in the desert. A signed side path leads to the ruts of a later wagon road that led to Blue Mountain gold mines discovered at Auburn in 1861. Another marked detour visits a railroad grade built in 1905 for a never-completed railroad that would have connected Baker City with the Eagle Creek Valley. The grassy area in the middle of the little loop trail is actually the bulldozed remains of a cattle watering pond that a rancher built directly over the Oregon Trail. And of course a century of grazing has left the landscape riddled with confusing cow paths. But despite all of this, when you stand on the original wagon track beneath the giant blue sky of the desert, the thrill of the trail still pulls. And if you turn toward the ominous palisade of the Blue Mountains, it's hard not to shiver at the wild challenge and impossible adventure that drew so many to the old Oregon Trail.

The Barlow Trail

Deep in the Cascade Range, tractor-trailer rigs downshift and whine on the Laurel Hill grade from Mt. Hood to Zigzag. Carloads of skiers pull into overdrive to whoosh past. But on either side of the arcing asphalt ribbon, time has stopped in a different century. Ruts remain from the wheels of careening Conestogas. Ancient trees are still rope-burned where pioneers lowered wagons down harrowing inclines.

Sam Barlow.

Laurel Hill was a final challenge for Oregon Trail shortcutters—a near disaster on a route dreamed up by Sam Barlow. Now Barlow's terrible trail has softened into a moderate hiking path where travelers can stop to stretch their legs in the forests of old Oregon.

Samuel Barlow did not start out looking for trouble. Each year since Joe Meek's trip in 1840, "Oregon fever" had sent increasing numbers of travelers across the plains in wagons. So by 1845, Sam and his wife Susannah thought it would be safe for their family to join the rush. On March 30 they struck off from Illinois in four wagons pulled by fourteen oxen.

The Barlow entourage included three sons, two daughters, a son-in-law, and two small grandchildren. At Independence, Missouri, they joined an unprecedented three thousand emigrants. The wagons were soon grouped into companies of forty or fifty. Sam was chosen captain of one group. Partly due to his guidance, they crossed the prairies and the Rocky Mountains without the Indian attacks and disease that troubled many other companies.

But when they reached the Columbia River, they found an unexpected bottleneck. Hundreds of wagons were crowded on the riverbank six miles west of The Dalles, where the trail ended at the Columbia River's gorge. The river cut through the Cascade Range, but horrific rapids along the way had already wrecked countless jerrybuilt rafts, drowning many travelers. Everyone wanted an alternative. The safest option was to hire a sturdily built ferryboat for the trip downriver to a portage at the Cascades' rapids, site of the legendary Bridge of the Gods. Maddeningly, only two such boats were available. The ferrymen charged more than a wagon was worth, and their waiting list stretched into winter.

Could there be another way through the Cascade Range? Sam noticed a low point on the horizon south of Mt. Hood and announced, "God never made a mountain without a way over it or under it, and I'm going to try." He scouted thirty-five miles toward Mt. Hood through open grassland. The route seemed easy enough that far. So he rode back to The Dalles and convinced several families to join him on his shortcut.

On September 26, 1845, Sam led eleven wagons up toward Mt. Hood, away from the known Oregon Trail. Five days later a wagonmaster named Joel Palmer convinced another seventeen families to follow Barlow's tracks. Palmer's group caught up with the Barlows where the grasslands ended and the Cascades' forests began. Together the combined group arduously chopped, sawed, and burned trees, trying to clear a path up the White River. The going was slow.

Barlow, Palmer, and another man scouted ahead on October 11 to find an easier route. Palmer believed that by going high enough on Mt. Hood they could avoid the wearisome forests on its flanks. So the pathfinders climbed to the site of present-day Timberline Lodge. Of course, trees were not a problem at this dizzying elevation. But two miles west they came face to face with Zigzag Canyon's mile-wide glacial chasm. Barlow could see at once that no wagon would ever cross here. He sat down to wait while Palmer searched in vain for a still higher wagon route on Mt. Hood, clambering over the glacier that now bears his name.

When Barlow and Palmer returned to the wagon train, they brought bad news. A wagon road might be possible through the forests and swamps at the base of Mt. Hood, they said, but there wasn't time to build it before winter. The travelers would have to abandon their wagons, cache their belongings, and run for their lives over the high trail at timberline on Mt. Hood, hoping to reach help in Oregon City.

So as the cold rains of winter began, the travelers built a log cabin on the White River near what is now Barlow Crossing Campground. They named the cabin Fort Deposit and left a caretaker to watch over their goods until next spring. Then the families began hiking the trail across Mt. Hood.

18. Barlow Trail

HIKE LOCATION

Easy (to old wagon chute)
1 mile round trip
200 feet elevation gain

Moderate (entire hill, with shuttle)
4.1 miles one way
1100 feet elevation gain

Follow the Barlow Trail to a chute used by covered wagons.

Getting There: For a quick look at Laurel Hill's infamous wagon chute, drive Highway 26 east from Portland 51 miles toward Mt. Hood. Just before milepost 51, park at an "Oregon History" signboard on the right.

For the longer hike across Laurel Hill, plan on leaving a shuttle car (or bicycle) at the upper trailhead, so you can hike the Pioneer Bridle Trail one way. To find the upper trailhead, drive Highway 26 to between mileposts 52 and 53, a mile west of Government Camp. Opposite the western entrance to Mt. Hood Ski Bowl, turn north off the highway onto Road 522 past a "Dead End" sign. Park in 0.2 mile at a gate. To start your hike at the lower trailhead, drive Highway 26 to between mileposts 48 and 49. Just 200 yards before the intersection with Road 39, park on the north side of the highway by a "Pioneer Bridle Trail" sign.

Hiking Tips: To see the wagon chute, walk 0.1 mile from the "Oregon History" signboard to the abandoned Mt. Hood loop highway. Turn right a few yards to the bottom of the rocky chute. Then continue, following signs, to switchback 0.4 mile up through the woods to the top of the chute, where Barlow Trail wagon ruts are still visible.

If you're hiking the 4.1-mile Pioneer Bridle Trail across Laurel Hill, note that the route is shared with horses and mountain bikes. Also expect some highway noise. Starting from the lower trailhead near Road 39, hike 2.3 miles to a junction beside Highway 26. You could detour across the highway here to see the old wagon chute. Then continue 0.4 mile to a tunnel under the abandoned Mt. Hood Loop highway. Beyond the tunnel 0.3 mile you'll briefly follow the Highway 26 guardrail. Keep left at a fork, follow a creek, and cross the only boggy part of the trail, a 100-foot stretch that's tough in tennis shoes.

Season: The trail is usually snow-free from mid-March to mid-December.

While You're in the Area: Drive a couple miles east on Highway 26 and turn left to Timberline Lodge (Hike #53) to see the Timberline Trail scouted by Palmer. Then follow Highway 26 east another 0.2 mile and turn right at a "Still Creek" sign to drive a graveled portion of the Barlow Trail to three pioneer gravesites beside Summit Meadows. Keep left to return to Highway 26. Then take the highway 3 miles toward Hood River to Barlow Pass. Here a side road to the south traces the original Barlow Road over the pass.

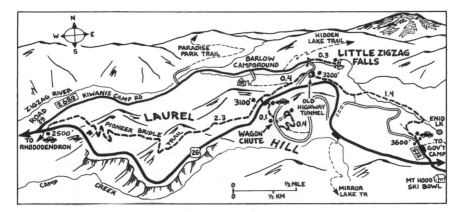

The last to leave Fort Deposit were the Barlows. When they finally set out on December 1, the timberline path was buried by snowdrifts.

Food supplies were low, their shoes were worn through, and the winter winds cut cold. Sam took his family on the lower, future wagon route instead. They became the first to cross Barlow Pass. They trudged past Trillium Lake through the snowfields of Summit Meadows and traversed swampy forests toward Laurel Hill's ominous dropoff. It was a miserable December trek, slowed by a jungle of rhododendrons. The Barlows mistook the tough-limbed bushes for laurel, and the confusion gave Laurel Hill its name. One glum night their starving horse, Old Gray, died from eating rhododendron leaves. When Sam returned to camp with the empty harness, the family broke into tears, despairing that they would all starve in the snow.

At that point Sam's stalwart daughter Sarah roused the family to courage. "We are in the midst of plenty," she admonished them. "Plenty of wood to make fires, plenty of snow to make water, and when it comes to starving, here is your old dog as fat as butter, and he will last us a week."

The next day Sam Barlow's son went ahead for help, sliding down Laurel Hill "like a shot on a shovel." He returned with more horses and led them down to Oregon City, where they finally arrived on Christmas Day. Incredibly, no one had died on Barlow's disastrous shortcut trail. Even their dog had survived.

For a quick look at the most harrowing part of the Barlow Trail, park at a Highway 26 historical marker in the middle of the Laurel Hill grade. From there a short path leads to a rockslide that was the steepest pitch on the old wagon trail. The route here is simply a thirty-foot-wide chute in a forty-five-degree slope. Old notched stumps remain to show where ropes were used to lower wagons down the hill.

Barlow Road tollhouse and gate in 1880.

In 1846 Sam Barlow won a charter from Oregon's provisional government to open a toll road on the route he had blazed. That spring he hired a forty-man crew to rough out a crude track, including the horrendous chute on Laurel Hill. After the wagons at Fort Deposit had been brought down to Oregon City, Barlow started charging immigrants the moderately high fee of five dollars to cross his road. He built a toll gate on the eastern side of the mountains, catching travelers before they had actually seen the road's condition. A later gate was added on the west side, near present-day Tollgate Campground. A sign marks the spot beside Highway 26, just east of Rhododendron.

One of the Barlow Road's biggest tests came in 1849, when the Army sent 250 tons of supplies from Fort Leavenworth, Kansas, to outfit Oregon forts. Most of the shipment's 429 wagons and 1716 mules were routed over Barlow's cutoff. The caravan stopped to regroup near the summit — lending the name "Government Camp" to the site. By then so many mules had died of starvation that forty-five wagons had to be abandoned. Then they faced the chute at Laurel Hill.

"The road on this hill is something terrible," an 1852 traveler wrote of Laurel Hill. "It is worn down into the soil from five to seven feet, leaving steep banks on both sides. Our wagon is in all shapes coming down the hill;

sometimes one forewheel would drop nearly three feet from a boulder in the road, while at the same time the opposite rear wheel dropped two feet or more into another hole." Wagon brakes were useless, and even "rough-locking" the wheels by wrapping them together with a log chain had little effect. Some travelers cut forty-foot trees to drag behind their wagons with the branches pointing downhill. Others simply dismantled their wagons and lowered down the parts. "Picture a train of wagons and cattle passing through a crooked chimney," an 1853 traveler's diary suggests.

If you have time for a four-mile hike, take the Pioneer Bridle Trail along the entire length of Laurel Hill. This path follows a slightly improved version of the Barlow Trail that avoided the grueling chute. The Civilian Conservation Corps converted the road to a hiking path in 1935. The path ducks underneath an abandoned portion of the first paved highway around Mt. Hood, from the early 1920s. So this hike actually tours portions of three different historic roads—all trying to scramble down Laurel Hill.

Take time on your hike to notice the lichen-draped, second-growth forest here, an odd mixture of trees from the east and west sides of the Cascades, including lodgepole pine, western hemlock, and red cedar. The quietest and prettiest portion of the trail is near the top, where you'll glimpse the whitewater of the Little Zigzag River and follow a lovely creek up toward Government Camp. In April, the "laurel bushes" of the Barlows brighten the route with magnificent pink rhododendron blooms. In December, snow usually decks Government Camp's marshy upland forests, as the Barlows learned

Laurel Hill wagon chute.

in 1845. Today the trail above Laurel Hill is marked for cross-country skiers in winter, so most December travelers now glide through the ancient woods where the Barlows once trudged, cold and hungry "in the midst of plenty."

Middle Fork Willamette River

A major problem with Barlow's road around Mt. Hood was that it did not actually reduce the Oregon Trail's mileage. A glance at the map told pioneers that they could shave one hundred and fifty miles off the route from Idaho by cutting directly across Central Oregon to the Willamette Valley. But their maps also showed ominous blank spots along the way. In 1845 and again in 1853, wagon trains ventured into that uncharted region trying to find a southern shortcut across the Cascade Range. The two groups became known as the "Lost Wagon Trains" of the Oregon Trail.

Today a thirty-mile trail follows the route of the 1853 Lost Wagon Train to the headwaters of the Willamette River. It's still a rarely visited corner of the Cascade Range, in the shadow of the Diamond Peak Wilderness. A short walk along the wagon ruts leads to several of the enormous springs where the Middle Fork Willamette River begins.

The story behind the lost wagon trains begins with Stephen Meek, the lanky older brother of the famous mountain man Joe Meek. In 1845, Stephen Meek announced to Oregon Trail travelers in Idaho that he could find a southern shortcut across the Cascade Range. A thousand people, including three families from Samuel Barlow's company, took the bait. They followed Meek up the Malheur River into Southeast Oregon's pitilessly hot, high desert wastes. When it became obvious they were lost, the men pulled three wagons into a triangle, tied the tongues together in the air as a makeshift gallows, and prepared to hang Stephen Meek. Cooler heads prevailed, and Meek escaped that night. In the desperate weeks that followed, thirst and sickness killed twenty-three people and most of the livestock. The survivors eventually wandered north to The Dalles.

The horrors of Meek's Cutoff wilted interest in Cascade Range shortcuts for some time. Word also spread of the 1846 Donner wagon train in California's Sierras, where a party trapped by mountain snows had resorted to cannibalism.

But seven years later, a group of Eugene-area settlers decided to try scouting the Cascade Range shortcut again—in the opposite direction. They figured the mountain crossing would be easier to find if they started from the Willamette Valley and worked east. And so John Diamond set out with six other men from the Eugene area in March of 1852 to explore a route up the Middle Fork Willamette River.

The Eugeneans made their way through the woods to a crossing they called Emigrant Pass. It's a heavily forested saddle between Summit Lake

Diamond Peak.

and Diamond Peak, a mountain Diamond climbed on the trip and named for himself. Then they crossed the Deschutes River near present-day Bend and continued east across the high desert to the Snake River in Idaho. There, Diamond and two others were so badly wounded in an Indian attack that they had to be hauled home in a wagon via the usual Oregon Trail route.

Back in Eugene, the explorers reported overoptimistically that a wagon road could be built on their shortcut route for a mere $3000. Early in 1853 they signed a contract to begin construction at twelve cents a mile, a trifling sum that later proved to be ridiculously inadequate.

Perhaps the most enthusiastic supporter of the new route was Elijah Elliott, a Eugene-area settler who had not been on the scouting expedition, but who was expecting his family to arrive on the Oregon Trail that summer. Eager to help his family, Elliott rode all the way back to Idaho to let them know about the new shortcut. Surprisingly, Elliott did not use the shortcut himself on his trip to Idaho. Because construction was only just starting on the new route, he rode east on the usual Oregon Trail via Oregon City and The Dalles. When he reached Fort Boise, Elliott explained to the crowds of travelers there that work was underway on a new shortcut. He announced that he would lead all comers across the route, saving them hundreds of miles. Won over by Elliott's enthusiasm, 1027 people with 215 wagons agreed to follow him west.

Elliott failed to tell the travelers that he had never actually been over the route himself. The only guide he had brought was John Diamond's sketchy notes. He also didn't know that the roadbuilders had decided not to start work that summer after all. There was no road.

Elliott followed Stephen Meek's eight-year-old wagon tracks as far as Malheur Lake, where the group became suspicious of his scouting ability and split up. Some wagons went north around the alkaline lake and some went south, bogging down in perilous marshes. Weeks were lost before the groups rejoined and continued west across the trackless desert. There, most of the livestock died of thirst. Elliott kept looking for Diamond Peak, the landmark John Diamond's notes said would stand beside the finished road. On October 2 the Cascade Range finally came in sight, a string of faint white mountains. The travelers argued about which of the snow-peaks on the horizon was actually Diamond's landmark.

To settle the question, two search parties were sent out—one to the Three Sisters and one to Diamond Peak. The first group scouted the windswept alpine notch between South and Middle Sister, a barren area that does not have a trail even today. "Surely no part of the mountains can be more rugged than we passed over," the men reported glumly. The second search party actually did find trees blazed with ax-marks by John Diamond the year before. Although the road was obviously not yet completed, hopes ran high that they would meet the roadbuilders soon. Besides, they had come so far, and it was so late in the year, that there was no turning back.

And so the vast wagon train rolled up into the forested Cascades, blind-ly hacking a route through the timber as they went. The men chopped and sawed trees low enough that the wagon axles could clear the stumps. It was hard, slow work, and the food supplies they had brought were gone. Hunters from the group managed to kill a bear and a few birds, but the meat didn't go far among more than a thousand hungry people. Deer and other game seemed nonexistent, no doubt frightened away by the mile-long caravan. Nor did the travelers know which plants in this unfamiliar Western forest might be edible and which were poisonous. One starving family shot a squirrel and promptly ate it raw, brains and all. A man who had earlier said he wouldn't sell his dog for a hundred dollars became so desperately hungry that he finally broke down, killed his pet, and mourn-fully ate it himself. His neighbors shunned him for years afterwards be-cause he had not shared in time of need.

The travelers inched across Emigrant Pass beside Summit Lake, throwing out gear along the way. Finally they abandoned their wagons altogether. On foot, they staggered down through the woods of Pioneer

Gulch to Indigo Springs on the Middle Fork Willamette River. There they devoured elderberries and a dead salmon they found by the river. Exhausted, sick, starving, and cold, they sent the strongest men ahead to bring help from the Willamette Valley.

On October 14, one of the men in an advance party wrote in his diary, "On this Night We Camped in the rain, & had a hard time to get our fire started, & McClure Was Sick, & discouraged, and Said 'Boys I don't think, I Shall ever be able to get into the Valley. But I want you to Save yourselves. Because While you are Stout enough to travel I think it would be wrong for you to perish, on my account.' I said, 'No, McClure, I'll Never leave you in these Woods, as long as there's a Button on your old Coat.'"

Andrew McClure and his friend stayed together by the river. Another traveler, Martin Blanding, was left to go on alone for help.

On October 16 a thirteen-year-old boy was watching cattle near his family's Lowell farm, fifteen miles from Eugene, when he noticed an emaciated man lying unconscious in a field. The boy roused the stranger from delirious sleep. The man mumbled that his name was Blanding. A wagon train, he said, was lost in the mountains. Would the settlers send food?

After the boy brought in Blanding, Lowell-area settlers debated whether the bedraggled stranger could be in his right mind. Who on earth would attempt to cross the vast, timbered Cascade Range without a road?

Indigo Springs.

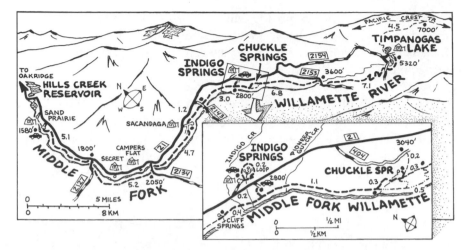

19. Middle Fork Willamette

HIKE LOCATION

Easy (to Indigo Springs)
0.2-mile loop
50 feet elevation gain

Moderate (to Chuckle Springs)
2.8 miles round trip
200 feet elevation gain

A wagon road passes giant springs at the Willamette River's head.

Getting There: From Interstate 5 just south of Eugene take Oakridge exit 188A and drive Willamette Highway 58 east for 37 miles. Beyond Oakridge 1.3 miles, turn south at a sign for Hills Creek Dam. After half a mile, turn right onto Road 21 and follow this paved route past Hills Creek Reservoir for a total of 28.7 miles. Between mileposts 28 and 29, turn left into Indigo Springs Campground. Go straight to a hiker parking spot.

Hiking Tips: The 0.2-mile loop path around Indigo Springs' mossy glen won't take you very long to hike. To see more of the area's scenery, try a more substantial 2.8-mile walk along the Middle Fork Willamette River to Chuckle Springs. To start, go 100 yards back to Road 21, turn left for 150 yards to a sign for the Middle Fork Trail, and turn right on a grassy spur road 100 feet to a trailhead on the right. Hike a connector path down 200 yards toward the river and turn left on the Middle Fork Trail. Hike 1.1 mile upstream, turn left at a "Middle Fork Trail" pointer, and keep left at junctions for 0.3 mile to Chuckle Springs. After admiring the spring's pool, return as you came.

Season: Open April through December.

They looked up at the forested mountains and shook their heads. Certainly a thousand Americans could not have committed such folly. But what other explanation could there be for the mysterious arrival of Mr. Blanding?

The settlers decided to send a rescue party just to be sure. When the rescuers rode up the Middle Fork Willamette's canyon they were astonished and appalled to find that the stranger had told the truth. They found Andrew McClure and his friend, and gave them potatoes and butter to help them recover their strength. Farther on, the rescuers found hundreds upon hundreds of starving people huddled beside smoky campfires. Everyone greeted them with joy and relief.

In the weeks that followed, the rescuers made many trips, bringing horses loaded with flour. A seventeen-year-old girl from the wagon train wrote that the rescuers would take no money. "This is the welcome of the settlers in the valley to the emigration," she reported that the rescuers said. "Put away your purses. We have been there. We know how it is ourselves."

The people who were sick, pregnant, or weak were helped onto horses for the last miles down into the Willamette Valley, while the rest of the travelers walked. By the time the snows of winter draped the mountains, more than a thousand people from the Lost Wagon Train had reached the Eugene area. Their numbers doubled the population of settlers in what became Lane County.

To sample the Lost Wagon Train's route—and to see a source of the Willamette River at the same time—drive a paved backroad from Oakridge upriver to the primitive but free Indigo Springs Campground. A quarter-mile trail from the parking area loops around a mossy glen where Indigo Springs spills out of the ground in half a dozen major fountains. Near the end of the loop you'll join the old wagon road, still clearly visible as ruts in the forest duff. To complete the loop, turn right. To the left, an overgrown portion of the old road heads uphill through Pioneer Gulch toward Emigrant Pass.

Although the track at Indigo Springs follows the general route of the Lost Wagon Train of 1853, the ruts you see are actually from later wagons. One of the Lost Wagon Train pioneers, Bynon Pengra, revived the idea of building a real road in 1864. By then the federal government was offering private roadbuilding companies three square miles of free land for every mile of road completed. Pengra convinced investors to chip in $250 apiece to form a company. They won a grant to build the Oregon Central Military Road from Eugene to Fort Boise on the Lost Wagon Train's route.

Pengra surveyed the route over the next two years together with W. H. Odell. On their travels they discovered Odell Lake and Pengra Pass (near today's Willamette Pass). Pengra himself realized that this more northerly Cascades crossing was better, but because his company's charter specified Emigrant Pass, he had to build there instead. And so, although the Oregon Central Military Road was completed in 1870 and was used for more than half a century, it was abandoned when the Southern Pacific Railroad opened the better route over Willamette Pass in 1929.

Today large sections of the old military road between Indigo Springs and Hills Creek Reservoir have been restored as a lovely riverside path called the Middle Fork Trail. For a longer hike from Indigo Springs, walk along the rushing, forty-foot-wide Middle Fork Willamette River as it tumbles through a forest of giant Douglas fir, western hemlock, red cedar, and alder. Along the path, Oregon grape, thimbleberry, yew, and vine maple sprout from a thick carpet of moss. It's a soothing rainforest garden in a forgotten corner of the Cascades—a delightful place for a Sunday hike, but a fearsome route for a wagon shortcut.

Scott Trail

If neither sleet nor snow can stop mail carriers, what happened to John Templeton Craig? He's the skiing postman who was found frozen beside his mail pouch in a shack atop McKenzie Pass in the winter of 1877. Mystery still shrouds the details of Craig's demise, but you can learn more about this stubborn pioneer by hiking the two wagon roads he helped blaze through the lava of this spectacularly scenic Cascade Range saddle.

Craig was one of fifty men hired by Captain Felix Scott to build a trail from Eugene over the Cascades in 1862. By then the rush of westward-bound Oregon Trail travelers had slowed. But because gold had just been discovered in Eastern Oregon, people were suddenly eager to go east instead. Scott's plan was to make a fortune selling Willamette Valley cattle to the wealthy, hungry miners east of the Cascades.

Scott took Craig and the rest of his roadbuilding crew up the McKenzie River valley, clearing a path for some seven hundred cattle, sixty oxen, and nine wagons. At Deadhorse Grade, where Highway 242 now switchbacks up the canyon headwall like a writhing snake, it took twenty-six oxen to pull each wagon up the slope.

When the roadbuilders neared McKenzie Pass it became obvious that the biggest obstacles ahead were lava and snow. The lowest route through the mountains at McKenzie Pass crosses miles of jagged lava rockfields. Craig favored chipping out a road through the lava. But Scott said no. Instead he headed a few miles south, skirting the lava fields to a high notch

North Sister from Four-In-One Cone along the Scott Trail.

he dubbed Scott Pass. Because Scott's route climbed a thousand feet higher on the shoulder of North Sister, it was steeper and crossed more snow. Believing that Scott had made a mistake, Craig vowed to return someday and open a lower route that crossed the broad lava fields. Years later, when he did just that, Scott's route was abandoned. Today it survives as the Scott Trail, one of the quieter paths in the Three Sisters Wilderness.

To hike the Scott Trail, park by the turnoff for Scott Lake, another landmark along Scott's early wagon road. From here, the path climbs several miles through lodgepole pine and mountain hemlock woods to a lava flow. Scott couldn't avoid this flow altogether, but he did choose the easiest crossing point possible. After just two hundred yards on the barren, blocky rocks, the path crosses a *lava island,* a small patch of forest completely surrounded by the basalt flow. After another hundred-yard lava crossing, Scott's route climbs gradually along the sandy fringe between the woods and the lava flow's rugged wall.

At the four-mile mark the trail enters a broad cinder barrens, with craggy North Sister looming to the right. To the left is a strange cinder pile called Four-In-One Cone—four small volcanoes that erupted so closely together along a fault line that their crater rims touch. A side trail here detours up to the rim of these four contiguous cinder cones for a top-of-the-world viewpoint. While you're up there, notice how the four volcanoes

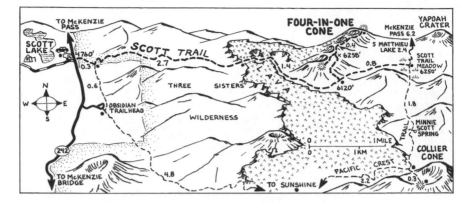

20. Scott Trail

HIKE LOCATION

Difficult
8.2 miles round trip
1400 feet elevation gain

Trace a pioneer trail to four cinder cones beside North Sister.

Getting There: From Eugene, drive east on Highway 126 past McKenzie Bridge four miles and turn right on Old McKenzie Highway 242 for 17 miles. West of McKenzie Pass 5.6 miles (between mileposts 71 and 72), turn north at the turn-off for Scott Lake and immediately turn right to the Scott Trail parking area. No special parking permit is required here, but you will have to fill out a free permit at the trailhead for entering the wilderness.

Hiking Tips: The trail starts at a registration box and then crosses the highway. After 0.2 mile pass a connector trail on the right to the Obsidian Trailhead. Go straight. The Scott Trail crosses a lava flow at the 2.7-mile mark and then climbs beside the flow's edge 1.4 miles to a cinder barrens. At a junction marked by a rock cairn, turn left on a trail that climbs up Four-In-One Cone to a saddle with a junction. Trails head left and right to viewpoints along the four cones' rims. To lunch in greener pastures, return to the cairn in the cinder barrens and continue east on the Scott Trail a relatively level 0.8 mile to a lupine meadow at the Pacific Crest Trail junction.

Season: Mid-July through October.

While You're in the Area: Take a picnic to the lovely walk-in campground at Scott Lake, just 1.5 miles down a gravel road opposite the trailhead. The lake's reflection of the Three Sisters is unsurpassed, and the water is often warm enough in summer for a swim. Remember to bring drinking water.

have spilled out four separate lava flows to the west. Cinder cones form when a bubble of magma rises to the Earth's surface. At the start of an eruption, cinders spew violently from the ground. Once the magma has released its volatile gases, the cinder cone's fireworks sputter out. Then a quieter basalt flow typically oozes from the base of the cone as the volcano's last gasp.

If you're just out for a day hike, you may want to turn back at Four-In-One Cone. For a longer hike you could follow the Scott Trail another mile to a delightful lupine meadow at the Pacific Crest Trail junction. From there Scott's route follows the Pacific Crest Trail left around Yapoah Crater to Scott Pass.

McKenzie Pass

But what about John Templeton Craig's other wagon road, and his mysterious death? After working for Scott, Craig spent the next fifteen years working for himself, championing his dream of a lower McKenzie Pass crossing. In 1871 he formed the McKenzie, Salt Springs, and Deschutes Wagon Road Company. He cut trees and laboriously chipped a roadbed out of the jagged lava. By the fall of 1872 he had opened his road, roughly along the route of present-day Highway 242. Tolls were two dollars for a wagon, one dollar for a horseback rider, ten cents for cattle, and a nickel per sheep.

Craig's wagon road over McKenzie Pass.

Craig's wagon road through the lava is still a marvel of pioneer engineering. To see his work, drive to the summit of McKenzie Pass. Beside the Dee Wright Memorial's stone lookout building you'll find the Lava River Trail, a half-mile paved loop path that visits a collapsed lava tube as well as a section of Craig's original roadbed. The county bought his road and eliminated the toll in 1898. The state took it over in 1917 and built the present highway, the first paved road across the Cascades.

Although Craig and later engineers had overcome the rugged lava, they didn't overcome the problem of winter snow. Even today, snowplows give up trying to clear the highway each year by about Thanksgiving. In winter, McKenzie Pass remains nearly as isolated as it was before the road was built. Twenty-two miles of winter-bound highway separate

21. McKenzie Pass

HIKE LOCATION

Easy (Lava River Trail)
0.5-mile loop
No elevation gain

Difficult (to Little Belknap)
5.2 miles round trip
1100 feet elevation gain

Visit a wagon road chipped out of lava atop Oregon's most scenic pass.

Getting There: From Eugene, drive east on Highway 126 past McKenzie Bridge four miles and turn right on the Old McKenzie Highway 242 for 23 miles to the McKenzie Pass summit.

Hiking Tips: From the parking pullout atop McKenzie Pass, first climb to the Dee Wright Memorial observatory's stone lookout. Then take the Lava River Trail's paved, 0.5-mile loop to see the old wagon roadbed.

If you'd like a longer hike in this lava landscape, drive half a mile west to milepost 77 and park at a hiker-symbol sign on the right. From here the Pacific Crest Trail climbs north through the lava 2.4 miles to a junction at a crest. Turn right on a 0.2-mile path to the summit of Little Belknap, a recent volcano with views of Cascade snowpeaks from Mt. Jefferson to Broken Top.

Season: Mid-July through October.

While You're in the Area: Visit the sites of Craig's two cabins. One was west of McKenzie Pass 2 miles, now marked by a roadside sign. The other was at Belknap Hot Springs (drive 23 miles west and turn right on Highway 126 for a mile). A resort there now keeps a 102-degree pool open year round.

the snow gates on the west and east sides of the pass. Drifts writhe across the buried lava fields. Frozen lakes sparkle with a dusting of snow. The great, ice-crusted crags of North Sister and Mt. Washington tower silently on either hand.

Craig believed so strongly in his road that he insisted the route could be kept open even in winter. He built cabins in McKenzie Bridge and at the pass itself. When a post office opened in Camp Polk, on the east side of the Cascades near Sisters, Craig bid for and won the contract to shuttle mail across the pass to the new station—all year round.

It was just after Christmas of 1877 when the fifty-six-year-old Craig shouldered his mailbag and set out from McKenzie Bridge, alone and on skis, never to return. Blizzards turned back a rescue effort six weeks later. A second search party discovered his frozen body wrapped in a quilt, on the cold ashes in his McKenzie Pass shack's fireplace. Had he failed to light a fire? Had he been unable to find firewood? Or had he been overcome with an illness on that wintry Cascade trip? Today a monument and sign mark Craig's grave, two miles west of the McKenzie Pass summit beside Highway 242, the route he pioneered.

An unusual skiing competition also commemorates the pioneer mailman's effort. Each year since the early 1930s, cross-country skiers assemble for the John Craig Memorial ski race at McKenzie Pass. During the event, usually on the first weekend in April, hundreds of skiers set off on the snow-buried highway, competing for speed to the top of pass. In the Craig tradition, some of the skiers carry letters. They are careful to protect their mail, stamped in the Sisters post office with a commemorative cancellation mark prized by collectors.

Craig may have succumbed to the snows of McKenzie Pass, but today the mail on his route goes through after all.

Santiam Wagon Road

The first automobile to cross North America—coughing and wheezing on dirt roads from New York to Portland's 1905 Lewis and Clark Exposition—crested the Cascade Range on the old Santiam Wagon Road between Sisters and Sweet Home. When the horseless Oldsmobile runabout sputtered down from the mountains, dragging a tree behind it on the steepest pitches as an emergency brake, the toll gate keeper studied the begoggled New York driver and charged him three cents, the going rate for hogs.

Today a nineteen-mile stretch of the old wagon road has been reopened as a trail. For a sample of the route's charms, try the short trail loop near House Rock Campground. The loop features a house-sized cave and a waterfall. It's a great place to take kids, and is close enough to the Willamette Valley for an afternoon outing.

The earliest trail up the South Santiam River canyon probably dates back at least 8000 years. That's the radiocarbon-dated age of a layer of campfire ash excavated from Cascadia Cave, a few miles downstream near Cascadia State Park. Artifacts found amid the ash reveal that the earliest travelers along the South Santiam hunted deer, elk, and rabbits, and used hand-held stones to grind nuts and seeds

In 1859 Andrew Wiley led a group of Lebanon pioneers up the South Santiam River to scout a more official route. They struggled up the forested canyon past House Rock, expecting to find a pass across the Cascade Range. But the South Santiam River springs from foothills fifteen miles west of the Cascade summit. And so when the trailblazers reached the river's head at Tombstone Pass, they stopped to argue. The pass they had found obviously did not overlook Central Oregon. Most of the men thought they were lost and should turn back. Wiley climbed a tall tree to reconnoiter. From there he could see east to the peaks of the High Cascades—and the saddle they had really wanted to find, Santiam Pass. With that encouragement, the group trekked onward.

The Lebanon-based entrepreneurs did not actually start building the road until 1864, when they founded the Willamette Valley and Cascade Mountain Road Company five years later. Their roadbuilding crews got unexpected help from the Army. Indians had killed two soldiers in East-

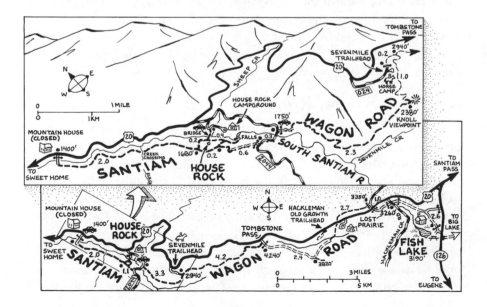

ern Oregon that spring, and reinforcements had been ordered east from the Willamette Valley. Forty soldiers marched up the half-completed road, looking for a shortcut. They helped build the road across the pass, and then built Camp Polk near present-day Sisters.

Because tolls didn't pay the road's expenses at first, the company was teetering on the brink of bankruptcy by 1866. Just in time, the entrepreneurs hit on a new funding source. The federal government had begun offering land grants to improve roads in Oregon, particularly for military use. The company quickly reorganized as the Willamette Valley and Cascade Mountain Military Road. They applied for a checkerboard of alternating square miles along a route from the Willamette Valley all

---

22. Santiam Wagon Road

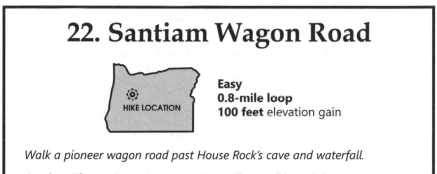

HIKE LOCATION

Easy
0.8-mile loop
100 feet elevation gain

Walk a pioneer wagon road past House Rock's cave and waterfall.

Getting There: From Interstate 5 at Albany, drive Highway 20 east 26 miles to Sweet Home. Then continue east 25 miles to a "House Rock Campground" pointer between mileposts 53 and 54. Here, turn right on gravel Latiwi Creek Road 2044 for 0.2 mile and then turn right again at a campground entrance sign for another 0.2 mile to the hiking trail parking lot beside the river.

Hiking Tips: Walk to the right 100 yards, cross a footbridge across the South Santiam River, and turn left to start the loop. Right away you'll pass House Rock. Continue upriver on the loop 0.2 mile and detour briefly left to House Rock Falls' 300-foot cascade. Then climb to a junction and turn right on the actual roadbed of the Santiam Wagon Road. After 0.2 mile on this wide trail, turn right to complete the loop.

Season: Open all year.

While You're in the Area: Cascadia State Park (12 miles west on Highway 20, between mileposts 41 and 42) preserves the site of an 1895 soda springs spa and resort popular with Santiam Wagon Road travelers. Today the park has picnic areas, a 0.7-mile waterfall trail, and a bedrock riverbank that's great for wading on hot summer days. Other trails in the area visit the Iron Mountain lookout site (Hike #48), and Santiam Pass (Hike #31).

the way to Idaho. Altogether, the land grant covered a staggering 861,512 acres — an area larger than Rhode Island.

A later investigation exposed how little work the company actually did in exchange for the huge land grant. Across Eastern Oregon, the company merely sent one wagon and a few men on horseback over the route. The "road builders" covered ten to fifteen miles a day, occasionally blazing trees or breaking down tall sagebrush bushes. The faint route they left across Eastern Oregon, with virtually no grade work and several impassable fords, was promptly ignored by travelers. But the company turned a profit by selling land, sometimes for as little as ten cents an acre.

Only the road segment between Albany and Sisters was maintained for regular use. Riders with good horses could usually make the trip across the Cascades in four days, stopping each night at roadhouses where hay,

Sign on the reopened wagon road.

a bed, and a meal cost twenty-five cents each. The Mountain House, a closed roadside store two miles west of House Rock, was the successor of one early roadhouse. The next inn was twenty miles east at Fish Lake.

The remote road between those inns saw its share of tragedies over the years. Near Iron Mountain, an eighteen-year-old traveler named James McKnight accidentally shot himself with his own hunting rifle.

His gravesite gave Tombstone Prairie and Tombstone Pass their names. Farther east, beside the trail at Fish Lake, a moss-covered rockpile marks the grave of nineteen-year-old Charity Ann Noble, who died in childbirth in an October 18, 1875 blizzard. No one knows why the unfortunate young woman was traveling this mountain road so far from help.

The Santiam Wagon Road remained the most heavily used link across the Cascades until 1917, when the state paved a highway across McKenzie Pass. By 1925 the Santiam Wagon Road was sold to the government, and in 1939 the state replaced it with Highway 20.

The hike near House Rock Campground starts with a footbridge across the South Santiam River. Turn left at a junction on the far shore and you'll promptly pass House Rock, a boulder so large that entire pioneer families could camp beneath its overhang to weather storms. The forest here is a jungle of moss-draped bigleaf maples, delicate maidenhair ferns, and six-foot-thick Douglas firs.

Continue upriver to find a side trail to House Rock Falls, a frothing thirty-foot cascade. Return from the falls and head uphill to join the actual roadbed of the Santiam Wagon Road, now a broad trail. For the loop, turn right on the old wagon road 0.2 mile, and then turn right again to descend to the footbridge back to your car.

If instead of returning to your car you were to follow the Santiam Wagon Road east, you would climb up to Sevenmile Hill, a treacherous grade that nearly killed the mayor of Eugene.

The mayor had driven his car up the Santiam Wagon Road in the summer of 1924 to inspect the Fish Lake area as a possible future water source for Eugene. On the return trip, brakes screeching, his car slipped over the edge of Sevenmile Hill's narrow track and rolled down the slope into the timber. The mayor was not seriously hurt, and his car was eventually winched back onto the road in operating condition. But the city of Eugene directed future searches for water supplies up the McKenzie River instead.

Reborn as a hiking trail, the perilous road to Sevenmile Hill has become a wild retreat where the river and the wind hush in the woods. It's a spot where time seems to have stood still.

Wolf Creek

Time has not stood still on the old wagon route through Southern Oregon to California. The cement lanes of Interstate 5 have buried the wagon ruts of pioneers on most of this busy corridor. But the old wayside landmarks remain, and if you're looking for an excuse to stretch your legs on a long freeway trip, there's really nothing better than a quick hike up Jack London Peak near the historic Wolf Creek stagecoach inn, or a climb to Pilot Rock's panoramic crag atop the Siskiyou crest.

Jesse and Lindsay Applegate scouted this southern alternative to the Oregon Trail in 1846. They also brought the first wagon train over the route. But their trail was so rugged that only one of the hundred wagons in the Applegates' train survived the trip intact.

The two brothers had originally come to the Willamette Valley in 1843 on the usual Oregon Trail route. Each had lost a son in the Columbia River rapids near the trip's end. They spent their first Oregon winter in the abandoned buildings of the Methodists' Willamette Mission, plotting how they might commemorate their sons' deaths by finding a better route to Oregon. In the spring of 1846, after Sam Barlow's bedraggled followers had recounted the horrors of their Mt. Hood crossing, the Applegates resolved to take action. They recruited a few roadbuilders and struck off on horseback, determined to blaze their way back as far as Idaho. Their goal was to find a shortcut that would avoid both the Columbia River rapids and the High Cascade peaks.

The Applegate Trail they laid out across Southern Oregon and Nevada skipped the renowned hazards of the Oregon Trail, but it stumbled into several new ones. For example, the only route the brothers could find through the hills near Wolf Creek plunged down a rocky canyon creekbed. And although their route east of the Ashland area sailed across the Cascades smoothly, it required crossing the baking wastes of Nevada's Black Rock Desert.

When the Applegate roadbuilding party reached Idaho's Fort Hall in early August of 1846, they convinced many of the Oregon Trail travelers there to turn their wagons south onto the new route. Of those who

The Wolf Creek Tavern.

followed the pathfinders, dozens died from thirst, sickness, and Indian attacks. By the time the wagon train reached Wolf Creek, winter rainstorms left the canyons awash. The creekbed route had become a hellish gauntlet of boulders and mud. Broken wagons and discarded belongings littered the gulch like curses.

Those who survived denounced the Applegates' trail, hoping it would never be used again. But two years later, in 1848, gold was discovered in California. Suddenly half the male population of Oregon rushed south to go mining. Nearly all of them took the Applegate Trail as far as the Ashland area. Then they struck off across the Siskiyous, using a skyline knob called Pilot Rock to "pilot" them to the best pass.

By 1860, road conditions had improved enough that daily stagecoach service opened on the route to California. Even packed with mailbags and sixteen passengers, the coaches could make the 642-mile run from Portland to Oroville (the railroad terminus for Sacramento) in just six days, although the trip often took longer in winter's mud. Relay stations ten miles apart kept fresh horses at the ready, so a new team could be harnessed up and on the road within sixty seconds. The entire operation required five hundred horses, twenty-eight coaches, and thirty-five drivers.

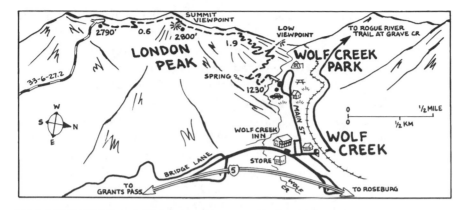

23. Wolf Creek's London Peak

HIKE LOCATION

Easy (from upper trailhead)
1.2 miles round trip
30 feet elevation gain

Difficult (from lower trailhead)
3.8 miles round trip
1570 feet elevation gain

A viewpoint overlooks Wolf Creek's historic stagecoach inn.

Getting There: Take Interstate 5 north of Grants Pass 18 miles (or south of Roseburg 48 miles) to Wolf Creek exit 76, and drive half a mile to the historic Wolf Creek Tavern. To find the easy trail to London Peak, drive 0.5 mile toward Grants Pass to the Interstate 5 on-ramp. Just before the freeway, turn right onto paved Bridge Lane for 2.1 miles. Beyond a small hill's crest, turn right on gravel Road 33-6-26 for 0.8 mile to a road cut. Then turn right on Road 33-6-27.2 for 1.7 miles, keeping uphill to a large gravel parking lot.

If you'd prefer the more athletic route to London Peak, start from the Wolf Creek Tavern and drive 100 feet into town to a "Wolf Creek Park" pointer. Turn left on Main Street for 0.4 mile to the park, and keep left for 200 yards to a large paved parking lot and creekside picnic area on the left.

Hiking Tips: For the difficult hike from Wolf Creek Park, wade the creek to find a steep, faint trail that's crowded with triple-leafletted poison oak. After climbing half a mile ignore a side trail to the right to a disappointing lower viewpoint. The main trail zooms up the ridge steeply another 1.4 miles to the more satisfying summit lookout point.

Season: Open all year.

While You're in the Area: Drive 5 miles south on Interstate 5 to Sunny Valley exit 71 to see the Applegate Trail Interpretive Center, in an 1860 hotel replica.

The most famous of the route's stagecoach drivers, Charlie Parkhurst, surprised everyone after his death. "One-Eyed Charlie," as he was called by his many friends, had served thirty years as a tobacco-chewing, fast-riding driver who had boldly foiled stagecoach robbers and had never missed work—except to sleep off hangovers from his hard-drinking monthly payday binges. But when One-Eyed Charlie died in 1879, the coroner discovered that he had actually been Charlotte Parkhurst all along. Charlotte had not only been among the best of the West's stagecoach drivers, but she had also been the first woman in the United States to vote.

The Wolf Creek Tavern, a white clapboard inn built in 1883, is typical of the hostelries that once fed weary travelers on stagecoach lines. The Oregon State Parks acquired the building in 1975, restored it, and reopened it to the public. Park employees now operate the ancient inn's reasonably priced restaurant and eight guest rooms. There's no charge to look around and see the upstairs room where author Jack London penned a short story on a trip through Oregon. London Peak, behind the historic inn, was named to honor the famous writer's stopover.

After visiting the Wolf Creek Tavern, hike up London Peak for a bird's-eye view of the old stagecoach route—and the twin ribbons of Interstate 5. Two paths lead to the summit viewpoint. The short upper trail is smooth enough even for wheelchairs. The tougher, lower route climbs nearly two miles at a heart-thumping pitch. Both are lined with grand old Douglas firs and gnarled, red-trunked madrone trees that date from the days of the Applegates' tortuous 1846 passage through the canyon below.

Pilot Rock

Pioneers once looked to Pilot Rock to find the easiest pass across the Siskiyous from California to Oregon. Today Interstate 5 misses this mountaintop Gibraltar by a few miles, but the landmark's sweeping viewpoints and dramatic cliffs are just a short hike away. The Pacific Crest Trail skirts the base of the crag. From there, agile hikers can tackle a very steep scramble route to the top.

Geologically, Pilot Rock is a remnant of a thirty-million-year-old lava flow. The lava here is called *columnar basalt* because it has cracked into scenic stripes. Whenever basalt lava cools slowly enough, it fractures into hexagonal pillars perpendicular to the cooling surface. The sheer cliffs on Pilot Rock's south and west faces are composed entirely of these six-sided stone columns. It's a popular practice spot for serious rock climbers.

The area also has a history as a wild hideout. Oregon's last grizzly bear, Old Reelfoot, was felled near the base of Pilot Rock in 1891. The legendary grizzly's eight-foot carcass was stuffed and displayed at the San Francisco Columbian Exposition of 1892.

The wilds near Pilot Rock did a better job of concealing a trio of train robbers in 1923. The D'Autremont brothers—twins Ray and Roy and their younger brother Hugh—had planned to rob a mail car with a valuable payroll shipment. They hijacked the train between tunnels at the Siskiyou summit on the Oregon-California border. The next step was to blow open the mail car's door to get the cash inside.

Trouble began when the brothers found the mail car staffed with a clerk who refused to leave. They set their suitcase full of dynamite by the door anyway. But they had miscalculated on the size of the charge. The resulting explosion destroyed the car and killed the clerk. With the loot gone and the whistle of an approaching train growing louder, the brothers decided to focus on escape. They coldly shot the train's engineer and the fireman, the only people who had seen them. The D'Autremonts discarded an extra pair of overalls they had brought and a knapsack they had planned to use for carrying the cash. Then they dipped their shoes in creosote and retreated into the forest, covering their tracks with pepper to throw bloodhounds off the scent.

Pilot Rock.

News of the murders outraged the nation. Sheriff and police departments from two states joined federal investigators combing the jungly woods for the gunmen. But the D'Autremonts had concealed themselves so well, underneath a fallen old-growth log in a gully below Pilot Rock, that the searchers walked right by.

After ten days, Ray D'Autremont boldly hopped a freight train into Ashland to buy supplies. When he opened a newspaper in the depot cafe, he was surprised to see his name in the headlines. Investigators had found a crumpled money order receipt from Eugene in the discarded overalls, and had traced it to the D'Autremonts. Four million wanted posters in seven languages had already been distributed from Canada to Latin America and from Europe to the Orient. But the poster's picture of the D'Autremonts was blurry. Ray slipped back to tell his brothers that they would need to split up and assume new identities.

The D'Autremonts took new names, settled down, and found jobs. The two elder brothers became steelworkers in Ohio. Ray married a pretty young wife. They were not suspected as murderers until four years later, when their younger brother Hugh was discovered as an Army private in the Philippines during a routine fingerprint check. The three brothers were soon sentenced to prison in Oregon. Hugh won parole in 1959, but died of cancer within a year. Ray was released on good behavior in 1961. Roy died in the Oregon State Mental Hospital in 1985, hopelessly insane.

Today, the old growth forest where the D'Autremont brothers hid so successfully has mostly given way to younger woods. When you hike from the parking area at an old quarry, you'll amble past small incense cedars, Jeffrey pines, and blue elderberry bushes. After 0.8 mile, turn left on the Pacific Crest Trail, and then keep right toward Pilot Rock. Wildflowers along this rocky, braided route include fuzzy mint, yellow Oregon grape, gooseberry, wild rose, and strawberry.

If you're just out for a moderate hike, declare victory at the base of Pilot Rock's cliffs, where the view opens up across California's Shasta Valley to the colossal double-topped cone of 14,162-foot-tall Mt. Shasta. Only confident adventurers with rock-scrambling experience should continue the final few feet up to Pilot Rock's summit, and only with the greatest caution. From the top, the view of Mt. Shasta steals the show. Close by to the west is Mt. Ashland, with the white dot of a radar dome on top. If you face north you'll see Mt. McLoughlin's cone guarding the horizon while Interstate 5 snakes between Ashland and Emigrant Lake.

Emigrant Lake, in the valley below Pilot Rock, was named by the 1846 Applegate Trail wagon train. Why didn't they call it *Immigrant* Lake instead? At that time, the Oregon Country was still jointly occupied by Britain, and did not officially belong to any nation. On their difficult trip west, the wagon trail pioneers had left the protection and comforts of the United States far behind. They were emigrants into the unknown.

24. Pilot Rock

HIKE LOCATION

Moderate (to base of rock)
2.8 miles round trip
1010 feet elevation gain

Hike the Pacific Crest Trail to a basalt landmark overlooking two states.

Getting There: Drive 8 miles south of Ashland on Interstate 5, take Mt. Ashland exit 6, and follow a "Mt. Ashland" pointer onto old Highway 99, paralleling the freeway south. After 0.7 mile go straight under the freeway, following the old highway another 1.2 miles. Beyond the Siskiyou summit 0.4 mile turn left onto Pilot Rock Road 40-2E-33. After 1 mile on this bumpy one-lane gravel road, ignore a Pacific Crest Trail crossing. After another mile, pull into a huge parking area in an old quarry on the right.

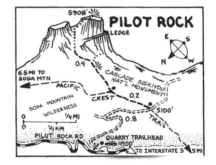

Hiking Tips: The trail from the quarry begins as an old roadbed blocked by boulders. After 0.8 mile the Pacific Crest Trail crosses the roadbed. Turn left on the PCT for 300 yards and then fork to the right on a wide, unmarked path toward Pilot Rock. Most hikers should turn back at the base of the cliffs.

If you're ready for a scramble, head left up a dusty scree chute along the cliff's base. After another 100 yards, you may be tempted to follow a ledge angling up to the right—but that slippery route deadends at a cliff. Instead go straight up a very steep chute, using hands and feet to climb past a tricky spot. Then continue cautiously to the summit's 360-degree view.

Season: Open late May through November.

While You're in the Area: Stop in Ashland to visit the looping pathways and swan ponds of Lithia Park. Site of a 1852 sawmill that cut boards for Southern Oregon's newly discovered gold mines, the park was landscaped in 1908 by the architect who laid out San Francisco's Golden Gate Park. Since 1935, Ashland's Shakespearean Festival has staged plays adjacent to the park, infusing the town with an Elizabethan ambiance. Start your exploration at downtown's triangular Plaza, where a fountain serves up Lithia water from a naturally bubbly spring full of zingy minerals.

CHAPTER VI

Gold!

Portlanders thought it odd when a large ship sailed into their up-and-coming port in late July, 1848, with nothing to sell. The *Honolulu* had no cargo at all. Stranger still, her captain went from store to store, ordering every pick and shovel in town. Only then did he reveal that he would pay for all his purchases with a small bag of what looked like wheat. But it wasn't wheat. It was gold dust. Gold had just been discovered in the creeks of California, he announced, and any man with a shovel could earn a hundred dollars a day.

The news turned Oregon upside down. From nearly every farm and town, the able-bodied men rushed south to seek their fortunes. Meanwhile the men's wives and children were left behind to run Oregon's fledgling farms. These plucky, homebound pioneers made substantial fortunes of their own by raising crops. Prices for grain and livestock tripled overnight. By 1849, more than fifty ships had taken Oregon produce south to sell in San Francisco. One captain gloated when he sold several tons of eggs to a passenger at the outrageous price of thirty cents a dozen—before the ship had even reached California. But the captain soon regretted his bargain when the cargo resold in Sacramento for a dollar *per egg*.

Before 1848, currency had been almost unknown in Oregon. Stores had operated by barter, with wheat exchanged at a dollar a bushel. In a single year, nearly three million dollars of gold dust avalanched into Oregon's economy. Suddenly every businessman needed a scale to weigh gold dust. In desperation, the provisional government began stamping the gold dust into "beaver money," five- and ten-dollar slugs of crude gold marked with a beaver symbol. When Oregon became a territory in 1849, the new governor denounced the impromptu coinage as unconstitutional. But the local beaver mint just switched to private ownership and kept stamping.

Meanwhile, California's forty-niners began spreading north in search of fresh strikes. They founded bustling boomtowns, but because their

Gold miner's cabin on Briggs Creek.

finds were in remote mountain areas, the sites have largely been bypassed by civilization ever since. Today the best way to see the relics of the gold rush is the same way most miners arrived: on foot.

The featured hikes investigate three different kinds of gold mining operations. The earliest and simplest mines in Oregon were *placer claims,* where miners simply washed gold dust from creek beds with a pan or a sluice box. Later *hydraulic mines* washed away entire hillsides with giant hoses to sort out the gold dust. The third and most expensive mining method, *hard rock mining,* involved tunneling into the rock, blasting loose the ore, and hauling it out to a gold mill for refining.

Start your hiking tour in the Klamath Mountains of Southern Oregon, where flakes first sparkled from gold pans on tributaries of the Rogue River. Take a trail along Briggs Creek to relive the early days of placer mining, with prospectors' shacks, active claims, and a vanished boomtown. Then take a quick stroll around the Gin Lin Trail to see the work of Oregon's Chinese miners—and the second stage of gold mining, hydraulics. Finally, tour more recent gold discoveries by trying a trail in Eastern Oregon.

Briggs Creek

The first documented gold strike in Oregon was on Josephine Creek, near present-day Cave Junction, in 1850. But a much bigger find came in December, 1851, when two freight packers on the Applegates' trail to

California stopped to try their luck in Jackson Creek, west of present-day Medford. The boomtown of Jacksonville sprang up almost overnight, and was soon the largest city in Oregon.

Jacksonville was also the hungriest city in Oregon. Food was scarce because the nearest farming settlements were more than a hundred miles away. In the winter of 1852-53, flour prices soared to a dollar a pound. Salt

Briggs Creek.

traded even with gold by weight. In fact, gold was so abundant that the Jacksonville bank became the first in the country to charge its depositors interest for storing their money, instead of vice versa. The nearest seaport, Port Orford, was useless as a supply point because there still was no trail from that town up the Rogue River. Supplies had to be shipped from San Francisco to Scottsburg on the Umpqua River, and then hauled south on the old Applegate Trail at fantastic expense. Nonetheless, miners continued to pour in, combing the hills for still more strikes.

One of these prospectors was David Briggs, a stooped old-timer with a bare chin and a massive mustache. West of what is now Grants Pass, he found a pocket of gold nuggets so rich that he dug up $32,000 in two weeks from a single ten-foot trench. Instantly the town of Briggs sprouted in a meadow beside Briggs Creek.

Today a trail from the site of Briggs' ghost town follows a mountain stream past old mines, a flume ditch, and an abandoned mining shack. And yet this is not just a path for history buffs. The valley's old-growth forest and lovely creekside scenery have survived the area's rough-and-tumble gold rush era surprisingly well.

Start at Sam Brown Campground, a half hour's drive from Grants Pass. The meadow here is all that remains of Briggs, a town that once boasted a hotel, barber shop, brothel, and bar. A gravesite near the picnic shelters commemorates one of the first black men in Southern Oregon, a barkeeper named Sam Brown. The white citizens of Briggs responded to this racial diversity with murder. They shot Brown on a trumped-up charge of allegedly "messing with miners' wives." No trial or inquiry followed.

25. Briggs Creek

HIKE LOCATION

Moderate (to ford)
4.8 miles round trip
200 feet elevation loss

Difficult (to cabin)
7.8 miles round trip
600 feet elevation loss

Hike along a woodsy creek from a ghost town site.

Getting There: From Interstate 5 just north of Grants Pass, take Merlin exit 61, follow signs 3.6 miles to Merlin, continue straight 8.5 miles toward Galice, and then turn left onto paved, one-lane Taylor Creek Road for 13.4 miles. A mile after Big Pine Campground, turn right on Road 2512 for 0.3 mile. Then turn left into the Sam Brown Campground entrance and keep left for 200 yards. Just before 2 picnic shelters, pull into a large trailhead parking lot on the right. A Northwest Forest Pass is required here. It costs $5 per car per day or $30 per season, and is available at outdoor stores and Forest Service offices—notably the Grants Pass ranger station and the Rand information center just north of Galice.

Hiking Tips: After hiking 0.4 mile you'll have to hop across Dutchy Creek. In another 0.3 mile, join dirt Road 017 and follow it left for 600 yards. When the path resumes, it briefly crosses two old clearcuts before launching into uncut woods. At the 2.4-mile mark the trail fords Briggs Creek, a possible turnaround point. On the far shore, the trail continues 1.3 miles before descending to another ford of Briggs Creek, near a dilapidated shake cabin.

Season: The trail is open all year, but the ford is impassable in high water.

While You're in the Area: Visit the Wolf Creek Tavern (see Hike #23) or the Rogue River Trail (Hike #29).

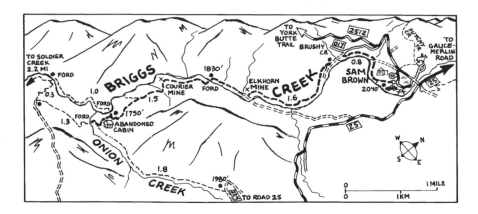

From the parking area, the trail sets off through creekside Douglas firs and big ponderosa pines. In early summer expect a carpet of inside-out flowers (delicate white blooms dangling from six-inch stalks) and tiny six- or seven-pointed white starflowers. Also notice pathfinder plant, a plant that won its name in pioneer days. The plant's leaves are arrow shaped, with bright silver undersides. A careless off-trail traveler will often kick over the plant's leaves in passing. The result is a trail of silver arrows pointing out the route the tenderfoot took.

If you meet other hikers on this trail, they're likely to be gold miners. Much of Briggs Creek and its tributary Onion Creek are covered by active placer mining claims, so outsiders aren't allowed to dip in a pan just anywhere. But even the claim holders are not likely to strike it rich anymore. Full-time mining rarely nets more than a few hundred dollars a month here.

After two miles you'll pass a campsite with rusty hydraulic mining equipment marking the Elkhorn Mine. Just beyond, the trail fords Briggs Creek—a good turnaround spot if you don't want to take off your boots. The creek is cold, thirty feet wide, and calf-deep even in summer. After winter rainstorms, it's too deep to wade at all.

If you do cross the creek, you'll find the trail continues, climbing gradually through drier woods of tanoak and madrone. After a little more than a mile it drops steeply past an abandoned flume ditch and several

Hydraulic gold mining, circa 1875.

huge sugarpine trees to a dilapidated one-room shake cabin—a good goal for a long hike. The mossy creekbank here, overhung with bigleaf maples, makes a nice lunch spot.

This is also a good place to contemplate why these mountains have gold at all. The Klamath Mountains actually began at least 300 million years ago as a chain of volcanic islands in the Pacific Ocean, similar to Hawaii or Japan. Because the earth's crust is made of several dozen shifting plates that float around on the molten rock of the planet's interior, the old Klamath islands were gradually "rafted" to one side of the ocean. About a hundred million years ago they "docked" against the advancing North American plate. It wasn't a smooth landing. The old islands crumpled against Oregon, buckling up layers of rock from the interior of the planet. Gold is one of the heaviest elements, and by rights should not be found on the surface at all. But here, where the land has been kneaded like bread dough, the crust is seeded with traces of the heavy metal.

Mostly, the traces of gold aren't concentrated enough to make mining pay. Placer miners let streams do the preliminary sorting for them. Spring floods quarry out the rock and send it down the creeks. The gold is so heavy that it catches in the bedrock's chinks and crevices. Pockets of gold-bearing black sand settle out behind stumps or boulders. The placer miners along Briggs Creek have simply staked claims to the creekbed. They clean the gold out of the cracks after floods and wash loose old black sand deposits.

When the easy placer gold is gone, miners sometimes try larger scale mining methods. To see an example, hike through the hydraulic gold mine of a Chinese entrepreneur, Gin Lin.

Gin Lin Trail

Chinese nationals were not allowed to own claims in the heyday of Southern Oregon's 1850s gold rush. At a time when daily earnings for white miners ran as high as five or ten dollars, laws limited the Chinese to work as hired laborers, usually for twenty-five cents a day. After the easy gold had been panned out of the Applegate River country, however, the laws loosened. By then American miners were eager to sell their worn-out claims to whomever they chose. And men like Gin Lin—a Chinese pioneer who had spent years as a crew boss—realized that hard work and ingenuity might make the whites' "worthless" claims profitable after all.

A three-quarter-mile path explores the mining claim that Gin Lin bought in 1881. The trail loops through a young forest on a slope overlooking the upper Applegate River south of Jacksonville. Hydraulic mining has turned the hillside here inside out.

With the hydraulic mining system, water from a creek or flume was funneled downhill through *penstocks*—riveted iron pipes—to build pressure. Then it was blasted out through *giants*, brass nozzles that look like huge firehoses. The water jets could move boulders the size of wagons. They also could strip eight hundred cubic yards of earth a day. The resulting slurry of dirt and sand was run through long wooden sluice boxes, where riffles, or slats, trapped the heavy gold flakes.

The Gin Lin Trail passes former water flumes, a cavernous pit excavated by Gin Lin's water jets, and vast tailing piles of cobbles tossed from

26. Gin Lin Trail

HIKE LOCATION

Easy
0.8-mile loop
200 feet elevation gain

Tour the hydraulic gold mine of a Chinese pioneer.

Getting There: From Interstate 5, take Medford exit 30, follow signs west 7 miles to Jacksonville, and continue straight on Highway 238 for 8 miles to the settlement of Ruch. (If you're coming from Grants Pass, follow signs south to Murphy and continue straight on Highway 238 to Ruch, between mileposts 25 and 26.) In Ruch, turn south at an "Upper Applegate" pointer for 9 miles. Beyond the Applegate Ranger Station 2.2 miles, fork to the right on paved Palmer Creek Road. After 0.8 mile pull into the trailhead parking area on the right.

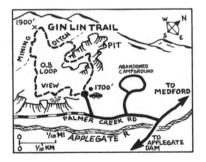

Hiking Tips: Pick up a brochure at the trailhead and hike the nature trail loop clockwise.

Season: Open all year.

While You're in the Area: Don't miss Jacksonville, an amazingly well preserved frontier town with more than 80 designated historic buildings. The Beekman Bank (open free 9am-4:30pm daily in summer) at 470 East California St. preserves a turn-of-the-century gold assaying office and Wells Fargo depot.

the sluice boxes. A young forest of Douglas fir, ponderosa pine, madrone, and manzanita is struggling to grow over the devastation left more than a century ago.

Jacksonville's white miners scoffed when Gin Lin bought this claim, but he surprised and angered them by turning a substantial profit. The success of Chinese men like Gin Lin made locals so jealous that they harassed the area's Chinese population with discriminatory taxes and calls for deportation. On one occasion a drunken white miner shot a Chinese man on the streets of Jacksonville. The killer wasn't tried for murder. He was merely fined for firing a gun inside the city limits.

Despite the hostile climate, Gin Lin prospered. Nearly every year he could afford to send to China for a new wife. Finally, after he had banked more than a million dollars in Jacksonville, he withdrew every penny and sailed triumphantly back to China.

Gin Lin's fate after his return to China is not well documented. In Jacksonville, however, the story soon spread that Gin Lin had hardly stepped off the boat at the Shanghai docks when he was robbed of all his earnings and murdered by waterfront thugs.

North Fork John Day

Oregon's gold rush to the Klamath Mountains had been launched by California '49ers. The state's second great gold rush, to Eastern Oregon's Blue Mountains, began with a legend about a blue bucket. In July of 1861, when Portland was abuzz with word of newly discovered gold in Idaho, a drunken old man named I. L. Adams stood on Front Street telling the tale to anyone who would listen. The strike in Idaho was nothing, he said, compared to the Blue Bucket Mine he could find in Eastern Oregon. A crowd gradually gathered, listening to his story with growing interest.

Adams told his listeners that the Blue Bucket Mine had been found — and then lost — while he was on Stephen Meek's Lost Wagon Train of 1845. Wandering without landmarks across the arid mountains of Southeast Oregon in search of an Oregon Trail shortcut, the thirsty, exhausted pioneers had discovered a creek that flowed southwest. They had camped to drink their fill. Some of the women had done laundry while the children played in the creek, gathering pretty yellow pebbles in one of the wagon's blue buckets. That night by the campfire one of the men had hammered a yellow pebble flat on a wagon tire. But in 1845 no one knew that the West had gold, so the rocks had been discarded as useless weight. Hungry, sick, and still desperately lost, the pioneers had moved on the next day. Adams boasted that he could go back and find the exact spot.

Within days a group of fifty Portland men had hired Adams as a guide to locate the creek of golden pebbles. The troop took a steamboat to The Dalles and rode cross-country up the Deschutes River into the high desert. They trekked across sagebrush flats shimmering with heat. When it became obvious that Adams could not recognize any of the route's landmarks, the men turned on him angrily. They forced him to sign a statement that he had never been on the Lost Wagon Train at all, and that he had lied about the blue bucket of gold. Then they drove him out into the desert without a horse or a gun. Adams, the garrulous old-timer who had enticed so many people with his tale, was never seen again.

Most of Adams' disgruntled followers immediately returned to Portland. But twenty-two of the men decided to head for the gold mines of Idaho instead, taking a shortcut across the Blue Mountains toward Walla Walla. Along the way they dipped their gold pans in countless creeks without luck. And then on October 23, in a gulch southwest of present-day Baker City, Henry Griffin dug a small hole down to bedrock, washed out a panful of sand, and found a dollar's worth of gold flakes sparkling up at him. The next pan was just as rich, and the one after that. It wasn't the Blue Bucket Mine of legend, but it would do.

With snowstorms looming, the twenty-two men quickly staked out claims in what they called Griffin Gulch. Then eighteen of them returned to Portland for the winter. The remaining four men built a small log cabin to guard their find. The winter of 1861-62 blasted the cabin with relentless blizzards. Finally, when their food was nearly gone, two of the men staggered a hundred miles north to Walla Walla to trade a pouch of gold dust for supplies.

The merchants in Walla Walla examined the gold flakes with intense curiosity. Could the gold really have come from Oregon, and not Idaho? A quick-thinking merchant from the rival town of The Dalles bought the pouch of Eastern Oregon gold. He promptly put the gold on display in Portland, hoping to boost the fortunes of his supply business in The Dalles. Sure enough, within months five thousand men had flocked to Griffin Gulch, using The Dalles and not Walla Walla as their supply point. By May, the newcomers had built the city of Auburn, a mile-long main street with seven hundred cabins and countless tents. By June, Auburn was not only the largest city in Oregon, it was also the seat of a new county called Baker.

Today a quiet highway loop from Baker City tours the Blue Mountains' gold country. Take the drive and stop along the way to stretch your legs with a hike along the North Fork John Day River to a log cabin at a rustic

Sumpter's planked Main Street before the 1917 fire.

gold mining claim.

Start your tour in Baker City, the town that replaced Auburn as county seat in 1868. Auburn vanished when its gold was gone, but Baker City, just seven miles to the northeast, thrived because of its location on the Oregon Trail and Powder River. Drive south on Main Street past the cast-iron facades and false fronts of the picturesque old downtown. Then continue on what becomes Highway 7 to Sumpter, the self-proclaimed "Liveliest Ghost Town in Oregon."

Sumpter was founded by three Confederate army deserters from South Carolina. They panned a little placer gold here in 1862, built a log cabin, and named the settlement to honor their home state's victory at Fort Sumter. Because most of the area's gold was locked in solid rock, however, the town grew slowly.

Things changed in 1896. That year the twenty-seven-mile Sumpter Valley Railroad connected this sleepy mining camp to the transcontinental train line in Baker City. Suddenly it became profitable to haul ore from Sumpter's hard rock mines. Railcars stacked with ponderosa pine logs rolled down the line, too. By 1903 the town had boomed to 3500, with fifteen saloons, three newspapers, and a high-class opera house where "sheepmen" were banned.

Because Sumpter's forests were logged to feed the railroad, the run

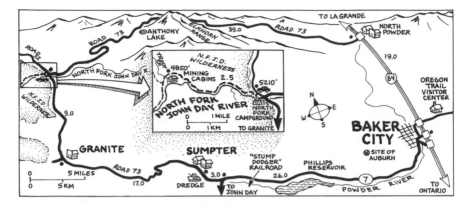

27. North Fork John Day

HIKE LOCATION

Moderate
5 miles round trip
300 feet elevation **loss**

Hike along a wilderness river to a gold mining cabin.

Getting There: Drive to the trailhead on a paved, 106-mile loop from Baker City. From downtown, drive south on Main Street (which becomes Highway 7) for 23 miles to the restored Sumpter Valley Railway's McEwen Station, on the left. Steam trains leave here for Sumpter at 10am and 1:15pm on weekends and holidays from Memorial Day weekend through September. Expect to pay $17.50 per adult for the hour-and-a-half round trip. Then drive onward 5 miles to Sumpter, continue straight on Road 73 another 17 miles to Granite, and continue 9 miles farther to a bridge and an X-shaped road junction. Turn left through the North Fork John Day Campground to the trailhead beside tent campsite #16. After the hike, complete the driving loop by heading west on Road 73 for 35 miles to North Powder. Then take Interstate 84 south to Baker City.

Hiking Tips: From the campground, cross Trail Creek and follow the North Fork John Day River Trail downstream 2.5 miles. Just before the Trout Creek footbridge, look for the "Bigfoot Hilton" cabin to the left—a good turnaround point. Backpackers can continue downstream, following the North Fork John Day River Trail a total of 25 miles through a deep wilderness canyon.

Season: Snow blocks the trail and the loop drive December through March.

While You're in the Area: Visit the Oregon Trail Interpretive Center (see Hike #17), 6 miles east of Baker City.

became known as the "Stump Dodger." As you drive to Sumpter you'll pass five miles of narrow-gauge track laid on the old route by history buffs in the 1970s. On summer weekends, steam locomotives now pull passenger cars along the track for tourists.

Sumpter's boom years had already passed on August 13, 1917, when fire broke out in the kitchen of the town's Capital Hotel. Flames quickly spread to neighboring buildings, boardwalks, and even the planked Main Street itself. When the town's water supply failed, firemen dynamited buildings in an attempt to stop the conflagration. But all of downtown Sumpter was lost, and the city never recovered. Today a population of more than 200 enlivens this "ghost town," although the number drops during the cold winters. You'll find an antique shop, cafe, and folksy general store with a small museum display in back. The only relic of the great fire is an iron vault door in an overgrown lot, on the site of the town's original bank.

Surprisingly, the largest structure in this land-locked ghost town is a ship. In a gravel pond beside Sumpter's Main Street rests the ungainly hulk of a 1200-ton, sixty-foot-tall gold dredge. Until it was abandoned in 1954, the dredge's eighty-foot chain of giant buckets, powered by an electric motor, scooped up dirt and gravel twenty feet deep from in front of the ship. Inside the

The Sumpter dredge dug a lake for gold.

ship, shaking and sorting machines winnowed out about $20,000 of gold a month. The remaining rocks and debris were dumped out the back the ship. Meanwhile, pumps poured enough water into the pit beneath the ship to keep it afloat. And so the ship slowly ate its way back and forth across the valley floor, digging its own sailing channel.

Sumpter's first two dredges were brought here from California in 1913. Operating day and night, they churned most of the lower Sumpter Valley to a wasteland of gravel tailings. Today, short hiking trails from the dredge tour the former moonscape, which is recovering as habitat for plants and birds. Especially during the Depression, farmers were tempted to lease acreage to the gold dredgers in exchange for ten percent of the recovered gold, although they knew their pastures would be ruined. One of the two original dredges burned. The other was dismantled in 1935 to construct the ship you see in Sumpter today, now restored as the centerpiece of a state heritage park.

After touring Sumpter, drive on to the even smaller mining boomtown of Granite, on a grassy hillside surrounded by pines. Because gold was discovered here on Independence Day in 1862, the town's original name was Independence. But when the settlers applied for a post office under that name in 1878, authorities objected that Oregon already had a city called Independence. The governor resolved the standoff by dubbing the town Granite instead.

By the early 1960s, Granite's population had dwindled to just three. Then the mayor hanged himself and "Cliff the Prospector" left to hunt gold on Ten Cent Creek. That left Ote Ford as sole citizen and mayor of the smallest incorporated city in the world. Since then the population has sky-rocketed to thirty—at least in summer. Start your visit at the town's gen-

Granite's city hall.

eral store/gas station/cafe and walk up the dusty streets past the weathered wooden ruins of the town's mercantile, a derelict Wells Fargo freight office, and a two-story dance hall. The old city hall leans a bit. Its bell tower recalls the building's original use as a schoolhouse.

To try a hike through the gold mining country, drive nine miles up the road from Granite to a campground in a bend of the North Fork John Day River. The area here looks as though it has been damaged by floods, and that's almost true. Hydraulic mining washed the riverbank gravels through sluices a hundred years ago, and the wounds are still raw. As you follow the nearly level North Fork John Day River Trail downstream, however, you'll hike into a designated Wilderness Area that hasn't changed much since the first prospectors visited. The river rushes down a canyon forested with Douglas fir and larch. In early summer, look for wild strawberries and huckleberries. In autumn the woods glow with the bright leaves of golden currant bushes.

The Wilderness here also shelters the largest share of the Blue Mountains' 52,000 elk and 150,000 mule deer. Each fall, 800-pound elk bulls with five-foot-wide antlers bugle challenges to rival males. Twice as large as

The "Bigfoot Hilton," a miner's cabin in the North Fork John Day Wilderness, in 1990.

mule deer, elk bulls assemble harems of as many as sixty cows during the August-to-October mating season. In those months, listen at dawn and dusk for the bull's bugle, a weirdly musical snort that rises to a clarinet-like whistle and ends with several low grunts.

Every mile or so along the trail you'll pass the ruin of a gold miner's shack. Watch for tobacco tins or baby food jars nailed to tree trunks along the way. These have been left by prospectors to hold claim registration papers. No new claims have been permitted since the area was designated Wilderness in 1984.

After two and a half miles, just before a footbridge over Trout Creek, look for the ruin of the Home Mine's log cabin to the left. Also known as the "Bigfoot Hilton" because it was open as an emergency shelter, this derelict, publicly owned shack makes a good turnaround point for a day hike. Backpackers can continue downstream through the canyonlands for days on the twenty-five-mile North Fork John Day River Trail, reliving the treks of the Blue Mountains' early prospectors.

Don't try to pan for gold, however, because many of the private claims are still in use. Oregon's gold boom may have faded more than a century ago, but for some the heady rush is not yet entirely over.

CHAPTER VII

Trails of Tears

Lewis and Clark survived their expedition to Oregon only with the help of the native tribes. The settlers who followed to the farmlands of the Willamette Valley also generally lived in peace with the sparse native population there. But when miners began ransacking Oregon's far corners for gold, the frontier erupted in war. Inevitably, the outgunned and outnumbered natives lost the wars and their land. Along the way, however, they won a few stirring victories.

Today you can hike through the battle zones where Oregon's tribes briefly stymied the newcomers. Start at Lower Table Rock, a natural fortress near Medford where the Takelma tribe once held the U.S. Army at bay. Then hike the Rogue River Trail, where the Takelmas countered a military trap by springing a trap of their own. Finally, follow Chief Joseph's footsteps through Hells Canyon, where the Nez Perce set out on what would become a heroic flight for freedom.

Lower Table Rock

From a trailside viewpoint on the perilous edge of this mesa, the Rogue River seems to writhe like a great green snake across suburban Medford's orchards, ranches, and gravel pit ponds. The distant white cone of Mt. McLoughlin gleams from the horizon. Turkey vultures soar on updrafts from the plateau's cliffs.

Thanks to the intense efforts of public-spirited conservationists, Lower Table Rock has become a haven for hikers — and for endangered wildflower species. But as you hike up the trail through the chaparral and flowers, you'll also be tracing the steps of the Takelma warriors who retreated here to find a stronghold against white invaders.

The native population in Southern Oregon was more diverse than anywhere else in North America. Neighboring tribes here spoke five entirely different languages, as unlike each other as Icelandic and Chinese.

Nonetheless, early French-Canadian trappers who passed through the area simply called all the locals *coquins* ("rogues"), a disparaging term that gave the Rogue River its name. Later travelers did not bother to distinguish the region's various tribes either, lumping them together as Rogue River Indians. "Use your pleasure in spilling blood," a government agent advised travelers on the trail between Oregon and California in 1847. "Were I traveling with you, from this on to the first sight of the Sacramento Valley my only communication with these treacherous, untamable rascals would be through my rifle."

Most of this violence was directed at the Takelma tribe. In their own language, *Takelma* means "those who live along the river," and the river they lived along was the Rogue, in the valley between present-day Ashland and Grants Pass. The Takelmas responded to the belligerent white travelers by demanding payment in goods for passage across their lands. In the summer of 1851, the U.S. Army sent a survey patrol to "clear the road" of hostile Indians between Oregon and California. The Takelmas spotted the troops first and shot one soldier from his saddle. The Army called for reinforcements. The new troops didn't attack the warriors. Instead they simply took thirty Takelma women and children hostage. The Takelmas quickly agreed to peace, and the hostages were released.

That tenuous peace agreement took a blow five months later, when two packers discovered gold in a creek at Jacksonville. Suddenly thousands of miners swarmed into Southern Oregon, churning up the salmon streams and shooting deer for food. With game scarce, the hungry Takelmas suffered miserably during the cold winter of 1852-53. When two Takelma men tried to exchange gold for food in a town they were summarily shot, on the assumption that their gold must have been stolen from white miners.

The winds of war picked up speed the next summer. On August 3, 1853, a settler was found dead from hatchet wounds in a cabin on Bear Creek, south of present-day Medford. Two days later a packer was ambushed at dusk and fatally wounded on the outskirts of Jacksonville. Jacksonville townspeople didn't know who was responsible for the attacks. But by August 6, an angry mob of miners called for revenge against all the Rogue River Indians. The mob hanged two Shasta tribesmen who happened to be in Jacksonville from California. One outraged witness, Benjamin Dowell, recalled that when a family of settlers arrived in town with a seven-year-old Takelma boy, the crowd chanted, "Hang him! Hang him! Exterminate the whole Indian race! When he is old he will kill you!" Despite Dowell's pleas, the mob hanged the boy in a street tree. Dowell himself was threatened as an Indian sympathizer and had to flee for his life. A few days later, a group of volunteers arrived from Crescent City under a homemade banner that read, "Extermination!"

Buoyed by the Crescent City recruits, the mob in Jacksonville formed a ragtag militia of twenty-two men and sallied forth to wage war. The Takelmas, however, were ready. They ambushed the volunteers on August 17, killing two men and capturing eighteen horses loaded with guns and ammunition. That same day, Takelmas attacked settlers and travelers throughout the Rogue Valley, killing six.

The U.S. Army agreed to join forces with the volunteers on August 21. Under the command of Joe Lane they fought a bloody but indecisive battle with the Takelmas in the hills north of the Table Rocks. Lane himself took a rifle ball through his shoulder. Before the Army could regroup for another attack, seven hundred Takelmas slipped away and climbed a narrow trail up past the cliffs ringing Lower Table Rock.

To the soldiers left on the plains below, this horseshoe-shaped mesa must have looked as unassailable as an island in the sky. The tribes' rifles bristled from the rimrock. Days passed as the Army men debated how to dislodge the Takelmas from Lower Table Rock. A frontal attack on the cliffs was obviously hopeless, and a siege might take months. Finally Joe Lane decided he would try diplomacy. On September 10 he rebandaged his wounded shoulder, recruited an intrepid interpreter, left his weapons behind, and walked up toward Lower Table Rock under a flag of truce. Few men thought he would come back alive.

Today as you hike the trail, the wildflowers along the way make it easy to forget, for a time at least, the tension of Joe Lane's daring 1853 walk. Most of Lower Table Rock was dedicated as a nature preserve in 1979 by The Nature Conservancy, the public-spirited non-profit organization that built the modern trail. In spring the scrub oak grassland here is ablaze with blooms. In April you'll see blue camas and pink fawn lilies. In May look for pink, four-petaled clarkias (alias "farewell to spring"), California blue-eyed grass (with six small petals), and elegant brodiaea (with six long purple petals). By June, orange paintbrush and purple crown brodiaea are blooming too. Listen for the musical warble of redwing blackbirds and the squawks of ring-necked pheasants.

While you're climbing, you'll have a nice view across the plain to Upper Table Rock, an almost identical U-shaped mesa a few miles east. Geologists puzzled for years over the origin of these two peculiar plateaus, marooned in the midst of the Rogue River's plain. Both mesas are capped with 125-foot-thick lava flows, but where did the lava come from, and how did it end up so high? Some geologists believe the mesas are remnants of

Lower Table Rock.

an ancient Rogue River channel. An andesite lava flow snaked down the Rogue River Valley 9.6 million years ago from vents in the Cascade foothills, filling the original channel from wall to wall. The river was forced to move elsewhere. Since then, erosion has worn away the softer surrounding rock, leaving the hard andesite perched 800 feet above the plain. Perhaps the mesas are shaped like horseshoes because they were originally U-shaped bends in the winding river channel. At Lower Table Rock, a valley has become a mountain—a trick known to geologists as *inverse topography.*

A good place to return to Joe Lane's 1853 drama is where the path suddenly crests at the plateau. When Lane reached this summit he was surrounded by seven hundred wary Takelmas. The warriors wore stripes of white war paint on their foreheads, a decoration betokening the grizzly bear. Men and women alike wore bones, shells, and leather straps through their pierced noses and ears. The tribe took Lane under heavy guard to a parley site overlooking the valley to the south.

As you hike across the plateau to this viewpoint today you'll walk the length of an abandoned, grassy airstrip. Look alongside the old runway for *vernal pools*—ponds that dry up by May, leaving a haze of flowers. Some of the blooms are dwarf meadowfoam, a rare subspecies that exists

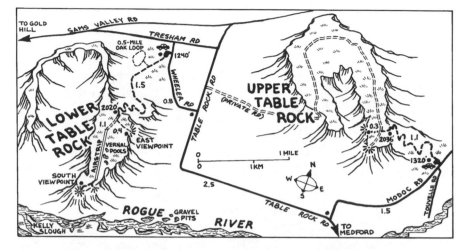

28. Lower Table Rock

HIKE LOCATION

Moderate
5.2 miles round trip
780 feet elevation gain

Climb a Rogue Valley mesa that once served as a Takelma fortress.

Getting There: From Interstate 5 just north of Medford, take Central Point exit 33, drive east on Biddle Road 1 mile, turn left on Table Rock Road 7.7 miles to the "10" milepost marker, and turn left on Wheeler Road 0.8 mile to a parking area on the left.

Hiking Tips: Note that dogs, horses, fires, and flower picking are banned in this nature preserve. Also beware of poison oak alongside the trail. From the parking area, the path climbs 1.5 miles, suddenly crests at the plateau, and becomes an old road. The quickest route to a viewpoint is to walk the road 200 yards and fork left on a trail that deadends in 0.3 mile at a 200-foot cliff. For the better view, however, hike back to the road and follow it a mile across the mesa to a cliff overlooking the Rogue River.

Season: The trail is open all year, but it's slippery in winter and mercilessly hot in summer. Visit in spring to catch the best flower displays.

While You're in the Area: Another nearby mesa, Upper Table Rock, has a trail that's slightly shorter and easier. To find its trailhead, drive back toward Medford on Table Rock Road 2.5 miles and turn left on Modoc Road for 1.5 miles to a parking lot on the left, just opposite an electric substation. This path climbs 1.1 mile to the mesa's top, where viewpoints are easy to find.

only on the Table Rocks. At the airstrip's end, continue right on a path to the cliff-edged parley point, towering above the Rogue River.

Here Joe Lane looked down to see his Army dragoons drawn up on the plain below, hopelessly out of reach. Through his interpreter he began negotiating with the Takelma leaders. He seemed to be making progress toward a settlement when a naked warrior dashed into the encampment with news that miners on the Applegate River had tied a Dakubetede man to a tree and killed him. Suddenly the Takelmas grabbed their weapons and began clamoring to tie Joe Lane to a tree and kill him in revenge.

Through his interpreter, Lane gave a speech that saved his life. He promised to find the guilty miners and punish them. He pointed to the Army troops below and said if the Takelmas killed him, more soldiers would come to attack the tribe. He offered to set aside Lower Table Rock and the lands to the north as a reservation. He promised to build an Army fort nearby to protect the tribe from white vigilantes.

The Takelma leaders calmed their warriors, listened to the sobering words of this courageous white man, and before the day was out, agreed to peace on Lane's terms.

Joe Lane became a hero among both the Oregon tribes and the white settlers. The Table Rock Reservation was ratified as promised. The Army built Fort Lane across the river from Lower Table Rock as agreed, reassuring both the tribe and the settlers. The fort's 19-acre site became a state park in 2008, with visitor facilities planned. Catapulted by his fame, Joe Lane became the namesake for a new Oregon county and later was nominated for Vice President—a bid that probably would have succeeded had he not been running against the ticket of an Illinois lawyer named Lincoln.

For a time, it seemed Southern Oregon's Indian wars were over. But a second, grimmer round of battles lay just ahead. The next battleground would be downstream, where the wilderness Rogue River Trail now runs.

Rogue River

Deep in the Wild Rogue Wilderness, a spectacular riverside trail has been blasted out of sheer rock cliffs. Hundreds of feet below, kayaks and rafts drift through green-pooled chasms toward the roar of whitewater.

In other places along the river trail's route, the path ducks into forested side canyons with waterfalls. Sometimes the trail emerges at grassy river bars with ancient ranch cabins and gnarled oaks. Everywhere hikers share this wilderness with the plentiful wildlife drawn by the river—kingfishers, black bears, deer, and eagles.

This wilderness portion of the Rogue's canyon looks much as it did in

1856, when the tribes of Southern Oregon retreated here for their last great battle against the white intruders. The modern Rogue River Trail stretches for forty miles through the canyon, but the battleground is near the western trailhead at Illahe, so hikers can easily visit the site and still have time for a day hike that samples the canyon's scenic charms.

The seeds for the Rogue River battle had unwittingly been planted

The Rogue River.

in 1853, when the Takelma tribe agreed to Joe Lane's peace treaty at Lower Table Rock. That treaty stripped the Takelmas of their firearms, a precaution the Army believed would prevent another war. But without guns, the tribe could not feed itself. Overhunting by the white newcomers had left the local deer so scarce that hunting with arrows was all but hopeless. Twenty percent of the Takelmas on the Table Rock Reservation died of starvation in the winter of 1853-54. Still the tribe stayed put, trusting the treaty.

The local gold miners weren't as patient. In the hot summer of 1855, after creeks had run dry and mine operators had laid off hundreds of men for lack of sluice water, unemployed miners gathered in Jacksonville to grumble about their problems. When word arrived that two travelers had been robbed and killed on the Siskiyou pass, perhaps by Indians, the miners' pent-up frustrations suddenly focused on the nearby Indian reservation. At a meeting the miners called for the complete extermination of the Rogue River tribes. A heavily armed group of volunteers rode out to do battle, carefully bypassing the Army outpost at Fort Lane to reach the reservation. The vigilantes charged into a sleeping Takelma encampment in the pre-dawn darkness, guns blazing. When the sun rose and the miners' gunsmoke cleared, twenty-three Takelma tribespeople lay dead.

Half of the surviving Takelmas hurried to Fort Lane for Army protection against the vigilantes. The other half fled downriver toward the relative safety of the Rogue River's remote lower canyon. Along the way, angry warriors killed several settlers. The second round of the Rogue

River Wars had begun.

The 614 Takelmas who had trusted the Army to protect them in Fort Lane were held there, essentially as prisoners of war. That winter the Army marched them north 260 miles on a grueling "Trail of Tears" to the newly created Grande Ronde Reservation in the distant Northwest Oregon Coast Range. Many Takelmas died on the trek. None was ever allowed to return to the tribe's Rogue River home, and the Table Rock Reservation was abolished.

Meanwhile, word of the Army's betrayal spread throughout the Southern Oregon tribes. The Tututnis on the coast, still angry about their treatment by Captain Tichenor's settlers at Port Orford, decided the time had come to wipe out the white intruders once and for all. On February 22, 1856, when virtually all the soldiers of the Southern Oregon Coast were at a Washington's Birthday dance in the town of Gold Beach, the Tututnis attacked. They burned Gold Beach and most of the settlers' cabins. They killed 23 people, nearly all of them soldiers. One of the dead was the feared federal Indian agent, Ben Wright.

The Army sent fresh troops to reclaim the Southern Oregon Coast settlements, driving the Tututnis inland to the Rogue River canyonlands. There the Tututnis joined the remaining free Takelmas. Together, the two tribes discussed their few options. They had already tried submitting, fighting, and retreating. Nothing had worked to stop the white invaders.

In May the new leader of the Army troops, Captain Smith, called on the tribes to negotiate. Smith marched up the Rogue River from Gold Beach with three companies of fresh soldiers. He waited at Oak Flat, hoping that the Indian leaders would agree to meet with him there.

Today a roadside sign near Agness marks the spot, about two miles from the confluence of the Rogue and Illinois rivers. The tribal leaders approached the parley site warily. Would this be a good-faith peace negotiation of the Joe Lane variety, they wondered, or would it be a trap like the attacks of the Jacksonville volunteers?

Captain Smith did his best to calm the tribal leaders' suspicions. He offered complete amnesty. If the tribes agreed to be relocated to a new, large Siletz Indian Reservation on the Northern Oregon Coast, he promised the government would provide them with free blankets, food, clothing, housing, plows, seeds, and education. The tribes could learn to provide for themselves as farmers, just like the white men.

The leaders considered Smith's offer. One of them, Tyee John, said he saw no reason to leave their homeland at all. He asked if there were an alternative. Captain Smith shook his head. Any tribespeople who remained would be labeled "wild Indians." They would be beyond the protection of the law. Independent bounty hunters would be allowed to track them down and bring them to the reservation by force.

One by one, the tribal leaders somberly agreed to Smith's terms. They said they would assemble their people for surrender on May 26 near Illahe, at the Rogue River's Big Bend. Only Tyee John refused, and stormed angrily away from the meeting.

After the Oak Flat parley, the Army soldiers marched up past Illahe to wait for the tribes' surrender at Big Bend. The route they followed is much the same as the route people now drive to the Rogue River Trailhead. At the trailhead itself, the parking area looks out across Big Bend's broad pasture. Purple wild onions and white yarrow wildflowers still bloom here in late May, and the wild grass is green, though dry stalks portend the hot summer days ahead. Crickets chirp and black crows caw. The Army troops camped in the field here, waiting.

Only two Indians arrived on May 26, 1856, the day appointed for the surrender. They were women who had swum the Rogue River to bring a furtive warning to the Army troops. They said that the Takelmas and Tututnis had been peacefully walking toward the surrender site when the Jacksonville vigilantes attacked. Taken by surprise, many of the tribespeople had died in a gun battle. Most of the survivors had joined Tyee John, who claimed the vigilantes' attack was proof that the Army had lied about the promise of amnesty. The two Indian women said Tyee John planned to attack the Army troops in revenge.

Captain Smith ordered his men to move to a higher, more defensible position. As you hike along the start of the Rogue River Trail you'll be walking through the position Smith chose. Today the slope is forested with Douglas fir and bigleaf maple, with occasional blackberry patches

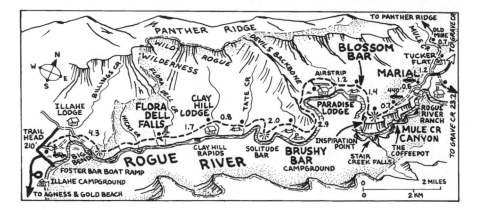

and gnarled apple trees. In 1856 this was a grassy hillside with a clear view overlooking Big Bend's field.

On the morning of May 27, a cluster of unarmed Indian men quietly crossed the field as if to surrender. They lingered a while, getting a good

29. Rogue River

Moderate (to Flora Dell Falls)
8.6 miles round trip
600 feet elevation gain

HIKE LOCATION

Cross Oregon's bloodiest battlefield to a riverside waterfall.

Getting There: Turn off Highway 101 at the south end of the Gold Beach bridge and follow Jerrys Flat Road (which becomes Road 33) up the Rogue River 32 miles. Just after crossing a river bridge, fork to the right at a sign for Illahe and follow a one-lane, paved road 3.5 miles to the trailhead spur on the right.

Hiking Tips: The path skirts Big Bend Pasture for half a mile through the woods, crosses some fields and a dirt road, and then contours along a wooded slope above the river. In its first 4.3 miles, the path bridges 5 streams (Billings, Buster, Dans, Hicks, and Flea creeks) before reaching Flora Dell Creek and the trailside waterfall. Beware of lush poison oak along the path from the falls down to the Rogue River's bank

If you'd like to stay overnight, hike onward 1.7 miles to Clay Hill Lodge. Book well in advance at 503-859-3772. For a backpacking campsite, either continue 0.8 mile to Tate Creek or hike an additional 2 miles through Solitude Bar's scenic gorge to Brushy Bar, a forested plain with a large, official campground. Beyond Brushy Bar the trail continues 2.9 miles to Paradise Lodge (place reservations at 888-667-6483), another 3.3 miles to Marial, and another 25 miles to trail's end at the Grave Creek Bridge near Galice. Expect to pay $130-165 per person per night at commercial lodges on the Rogue River Trail, but meals are included.

Season: The Rogue River Trail is open all year, but avoid the rains of mid-winter and the blazing heat of late summer.

While You're in the Area: Jet boats from Gold Beach ascend the Rogue River as far as Paradise Lodge, where some stop for a buffet lunch. The 64- to 104-mile tours cost $50 to $95 and leave Gold Beach at about 8:30am from May to October (and also at 2:30pm from July to September). Jerry's Rogue Jets (800-451-3645), dock downstream from the bridge's south end, beside a free museum of Rogue River memorabilia.

look at the Army troops' defenses, and then ambled off into the nearby woods.

Suddenly one of the Army's sentinels fell. There was a puff of powder and a rifle crack. Without orders, the white soldiers began frantically digging rifle pits with bayonets and tin plates. The warriors of the combined tribes charged, firing arrows and bullets. The troops drove them back with withering rifle fire. But the warriors charged again and again all that day. After a sleepless night the soldiers counted eleven of their number dead and sixteen wounded. The wounded men moaned for water, but the supply of water was gone.

Between charges, the tribes taunted the soldiers in a mixture of English and Chinook jargon, the trade language of the Oregon frontier. "Mika hias ticka chuck (you sure would like some water)," the warriors called out. "One more sun no water, no muckamuck (food), no soldier. All dead."

Captain Smith bellowed back that they would all hang.

Tyee John made a cedar-bark noose and waved it, yelling, "Oh, Captain Smith! If you promise to go on the reservation and not travel around the country, I will not hang you! See this rope? It is for you, because you do not want to stay on a reservation where you can have plenty of plows and wagons and plenty to eat, and white men to teach you."

Sensing victory, the tribes drew up ranks for a final charge to wipe out the whites.

At that moment a column of seventy-five additional soldiers came into sight, marching up the river trail from Gold Beach. Captain Smith's men jumped from their shallow pits and charged down the hillside. Caught in the soldiers' crossfire, the tribespeople ran for the river. Many were shot at the bank or in the water. The battle was over.

In the month that followed, the Army rounded up more than 1400 Indians from Southwest Oregon, including tribes that were not involved in the war. A steamship took 1192 captives from Port Orford to the Siletz Reservation. Another 215 were forced to walk 150 miles to the reservation on the perilous coastal path that passed Cape Perpetua. Tyee John and his son were sent to the Presidio, a military detention center in San Francisco.

As Captain Smith had warned, the area's remaining Indians were declared fair game for bounty hunters. The most avid of these hunters was William Tichenor, the speculator who had founded Port Orford. He spent seven months collecting 152 "wild Indians" — mostly elderly people and isolated families who had been overlooked or left behind. When Tichenor began marching them north toward the reservation to collect his bounty, however, vigilantes with rifles attacked the group. Tichenor was furious that so many of his captives were killed before he could be paid. And he knew he couldn't find replacements. By February of 1857, Southwest Oregon was virtually devoid of native tribespeople.

Today as you hike the Rogue River Trail at Big Bend, you'll find few indications that this was the bloodiest and most important battlefield in Oregon history. Locals used to claim that they could point out the shallow trenches where Captain Smith's men cowered, but time has smoothed over evidence of the Takelmas' final battle.

After contemplating the battlefield, hike onward to see the country the tribes fought so hard to keep. After about a mile you'll cross the Wild Rogue Wilderness boundary and reach a viewpoint above a riverbend. The canyon twists between hillsides of red-barked madrone trees. Whitewater brawls past gravel islands below.

Jet-powered mail boats now also brawl past this viewpoint several times a day, ferrying sightseers up from Gold Beach. The mail boats trace their lineage to 1895, when a stout-hearted pioneer volunteered to carry mail to Gold Beach in his skiff. The ranchers and miners who had settled this remote canyon doubted his little boat would survive the whitewater, but they gave

Rogue riverbank at Flora Dell Creek.

him a few letters anyway. To their astonishment, the mailman returned in less than a week. It had taken him a single day to ride the river down to Gold Beach. After dropping off the mail there, he had managed to pole the skiff back up through the river's raging rapids in just three days. Even more surprising, he continued making the arduous round-trip every week for decades. Somehow the tradition of this heroic postman has evolved into a fleet of fifty-passenger jet boats, whisking tourists into the wilderness at a roar.

If you have the time, hike on a couple miles to Flora Dell Creek. Here a twenty-foot waterfall showers into a small mossy pool beside the trail. It's a wonderful place for a cool swim on a hot day. And don't be afraid because of the nearby sign: "Hathaway Jones Died Here Sept. 20, 1937." Jones didn't drown. He was a lanky, good-natured trail packer who hit his head when he was thrown from his saddle at the age of sixty-seven.

Hathaway Jones had been the most popular storyteller of the entire Rogue River area, despite a harelip that left him with a severe speech impediment. According to one of Jones' tales, he once pushed a boulder from the Rogue River Trail in order to watch it roll down the canyonside. The giant rock rumbled downhill so fast that it crossed the canyon bottom and went a long ways up the opposite slope. When it started rolling back at him, Jones jumped on his horse and rode for safety. He didn't come back to that part of the trail for several years. When he finally did, he heard a faint rattling. It was the boulder, now worn down to the size of a marble, still rolling back and forth across the canyon in the groove it had carved.

Fifty yards before Flora Dell Creek, a side trail descends to the bedrock bank of the deep, green Rogue River. Most day hikers turn back here. It's the best riverbank access for miles—a perfect spot to dry off after a swim, or to eat lunch while watching drift boats and jet boats pass.

As you walk back along the river trail toward the ancient battlefield, you might wonder what became of the Takelmas who lost this land. In fact, their culture crumbled within a single generation on the rainy reservations of the Northern Oregon Coast Range. The Takelmas were mixed with strangers who spoke a dozen different languages. Food, housing, and health care were scandalously inadequate. Disease swept through the crowded tribes. Because the Takelmas believed that a shaman doctor should die if his or her patient succumbs, their losses were multiplied.

More than one thousand Takelmas had been brought to the northern reservations. By 1884, only twenty-seven were still alive. From his prison tent in San Francisco, Tyee John said of the white usurpers, "It is not your wars, but your peace that kills my people."

Hells Canyon

A thousand feet deeper than the Grand Canyon, the gigantic gorge between Oregon and Idaho looks like the end of the world—the ragged edge of a broken planet. Above the roiling whitewater of the Snake River, a dozen layers of basalt rimrock stack more than a mile into the sky. Prickly pear cactus and red sumac bushes cling to treeless slopes between the terraces. As the day's shimmering heat fades in the crumpled badlands of Hells Canyon, sharp black shadows creep into Idaho.

This starkly beautiful land was once home to one of the West's most powerful and peaceful tribes, the Nez Perce. When the U.S. government forced them to leave Oregon in 1877, the legendary Chief Joseph led his people through this chasm, crossing the Snake River at flood stage in early summer. Their grim march began what would become a historic flight for freedom. Today hikers can trace the tribe's footsteps through Hells Canyon on the Nee-Me-Poo Trail.

To some visitors, "Nee-Me-Poo" sounds like a fanciful name — but the word is actually authentic, while the name "Nez Perce" is not. To this day, the Nez Perce refer to themselves as the Nee-Me-Poo, or *nimipu,* a word that means "the real people" in their own language. The label *nez percé* is French for "pierced nose," and was based on hearsay from early French-Canadian voyageurs who thought, incorrectly, that the tribe wore ornaments in their noses.

An ancient tribal legend helps explain why the tribe considers themselves the "real people." According to the story, the trickster god Coyote created both Hells Canyon and the tribe.

In 1901, Se-cmo-wu was the last to remember Lewis and Clark's 1806 visit to Oregon.

In the time before human beings, when animal-spirits walked the earth, a voracious monster came down from the north eating everyone. Coyote dug Hells Canyon to try to keep the monster away, but it didn't help. The huge beast kept sucking up all the animals. Coyote managed to survive by tying himself to Oregon's Wallowa Mountains with a rope. The monster couldn't suck him up.

The monster was so impressed that he made friends with Coyote and let him walk safely down his huge throat. Once inside, Coyote tore out the monster's heart and freed the animals. Then he celebrated by cutting the monster's heart into four pieces and throwing them to the four directions. Where each piece landed, a race of people was born.

Then Fox told Coyote, "That was foolish. You forgot to create any people here in the middle of the world, at Hells Canyon."

After Coyote had thought about that a moment, he replied, "All I have left of the monster is his blood. I'll wash it off and let the drops fall here. They will become the *nimipu*. Like the drops of blood, they will be few in number, but strong and pure."

Lewis and Clark found the Nez Perce the friendliest of all the tribes they encountered. On their way back across the continent in 1806, the explorers lingered in a Nez Perce camp near present-day Lewiston from mid-May until early June, waiting for snow to melt from the mountain ranges ahead. Meriwether Lewis asked his Nez Perce hosts if it wouldn't be easier to return east simply by paddling up the Snake River. The Nez Perce shook their heads vehemently, warning him about Hells Canyon.

Lewis sent three scouts toward the canyon anyway, just to check. When the scouts returned, they described the gorge, according to Lewis' journal, as "one continued rapid about 150 yards wide it's banks are in most places solid and perpendicular rocks, which rise to a great hight; it's hills are mountains high."

Captain William Clark, meanwhile, had left more than just the usual trinkets and souvenirs with the Nez Perce. He had fathered a child.

Early visitors often reported that the Nez Perce seemed civilized and sophisticated. They were the only tribe in the far West that dared cross the Rocky Mountains to compete with the war-like Blackfeet in annual buffalo hunts. They were the first in the Northwest to own horses, and the only tribe that selectively bred their stock, creating the prized, dappled breed known as the Appaloosa.

Even their politics stood out. The Nez Perce had no single leader. Each of the tribe's dozen or so bands chose local chiefs, who met when necessary to resolve policy questions by consensus. The first Protestant missionary to the area marveled, "Probably there is no government upon earth where there is so much personal and political freedom, and at the same time so little anarchy. The day may be rued when this order and harmony shall be interrupted by any instrumentality whatever."

The tribe's order and harmony faltered slightly when the U.S. government demanded in 1855 that they choose a single leader to negotiate a treaty. The chiefs temporarily picked a man named Lawyer for the job. Lawyer was the chief of the Lapwai band in Idaho, and had been given his odd Christian name by the missionaries there. Lawyer signed a treaty that guaranteed the tribe formal ownership of virtually the entire Nez Perce homeland, from the Blue Mountains to the Rockies.

But five years later, in 1860, when a miner discovered gold on Idaho's Clearwater River, thousands of fortune-seekers began pouring into the

Hells Canyon.

reservation, illegally claiming land. In 1863 the government called all the chiefs to a conference. The government demanded that the reservation be shrunk to a tenth its size. The new reservation would include only the land of Lawyer's Lapwai band in Idaho. Although Lawyer no longer represented the entire tribe, he signed the treaty. The other chiefs left the conference proclaiming that they were not bound by the paper Lawyer had signed. They had not agreed to the smaller reservation, and thus did not need to leave their land. They became known as the non-treaty Nez Perce.

The largest of the non-treaty bands lived in Oregon's beautiful Wallowa Valley, between Hells Canyon and the snowpeaks of the Wallowa Mountains. The band's leader, known as Old Chief Joseph to the early missionaries, carefully marked the original reservation boundary around the Wallowa Valley with tall white poles to warn settlers away from the band's property.

On his deathbed in 1872 Old Chief Joseph called his son to his side and told him, "When I am gone, think of your country. You are chief of these people. Always remember that your father never sold his country. You must stop your ears whenever you are asked to sign a treaty selling your home. A few more years, and white men will be all around you. They have their eyes on this land. My son, never forget my dying words. This

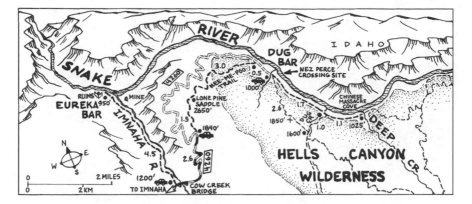

country holds your father's body. Never sell the bones of your father and mother."

After the death of Old Chief Joseph, his son assumed leadership of the Wallowa band, and became known to whites as the younger Chief Joseph. Among his own people, however, the young man's name was Hinmaton Lalaktit, "Thunder Rolling in the Mountains."

For five years, the young Chief Joseph fought for his land with words. Then, in 1877, the government issued an ultimatum: The non-treaty Nez Perce must all be on the small Idaho reservation by April 1, or they would be forcibly moved there by the U.S. Army. Chief Joseph sent a negotiator to try to work out an agreement. The Nez Perce emissary told the government officials, "The Great Chief made the world as it is, and as he wanted it, and he made a part of it for us to live upon. I do not see where you get the authority to say that we shall not live where he placed us."

The government threw the negotiator in jail and set a new deadline of June 14. This time there seemed no alternative. In late May of 1877, Chief Joseph sorrowfully gathered the four hundred people of the Wallowa band, rounded up their two thousand head of cattle and Appaloosa horses, and began the trek that would take them away from their Oregon homeland forever.

Today as you hike the portion of their route preserved as the Nee-Me-Poo Trail, you'll start by climbing an open, grassy slope. Bring binoculars to scan the canyon sides for big-eared mule deer, elk, mountain goats, and bighorn sheep. Because there are no forests here, the wildlife is often in plain sight. After about an hour you'll reach Lone Pine Saddle, a pass with the only tree for miles. Here you suddenly face the dizzying chasm of the Snake River's inner gorge.

In geologic terms, Hells Canyon is one of the newest large features on

30. Hells Canyon

HIKE LOCATION

Moderate
3 miles round-trip (Nee-Me-Poo Trail)
810 feet elevation gain

Difficult (to Deep Creek)
9.4 miles round-trip
1700 feet elevation gain

Trace Chief Joseph's steps through the Snake River's colossal gorge.

Getting There: From La Grande, follow Highway 82 for 65 miles to Enterprise, continue 5 miles to the middle of Joseph, and turn left for 30 paved miles to Imnaha. Turn left, following the Imnaha River Road 20 miles to the Nee-Me-Poo Trail sign on the right, 2.6 miles beyond the Cow Creek Bridge over the Imnaha River. Note that the final 14 miles of the Imnaha River Road are gravel and very slow. The Forest Service recommends the route only for high-clearance four-wheel-drive vehicles, but passenger cars do fine if they're not too low-slung—and if they're driven slowly.

To find the Dug Bar Trailhead, continue an additional 10 slow, winding, gravel miles to road's end at the Snake River. This road is so rough that high clearance is a necessity.

Hiking Tips: The start of the Nee-Me-Poo Trail has been confused by a profusion of cow paths, but keep angling uphill until you reach Lone Pine Saddle at the 1.5-mile mark, the recommended turnaround point. If you'd like another hike, return to your car, drive on to Dug Bar, and follow the Snake River Trail upstream 4.7 miles to Deep Creek.

Note that maximum group size in the Hells Canyon Wilderness is 8 people. Be sure to bring a hat and/or sunscreen. If you're backpacking, carry a backpacking stove because campfires are banned within a quarter mile of the Snake River. Also carry a filter pump for purifying water because few sources are trustworthy.

Season: The trails are open all year, but avoid mid-winter's icy winds and August's shadeless heat. If you intend to backpack to Hat Point, note that snow closes the trailhead there from about mid-November to early May.

While You're in the Area: For another walk in the area, try the 4.5-mile Imnaha River Trail. Blasted out of the cliffs of a gorge, the rough but nearly level path starts at the Cow Creek Bridge and follows the Imnaha River down to Eureka Bar, site of a 1902 gold mining boomtown.

For a scenic drive nearby, consider a side trip from the town of Imnaha up a 23-mile gravel road to Hat Point. A fire lookout tower on the Hells Canyon rim here overlooks the gorge and Idaho's snowy Seven Devils Mountains.

the Oregon landscape. This enormous chasm did not exist as recently as fifteen million years ago, when vast Columbia River Basalt flows inundated much of Eastern Oregon. For proof, notice that the rimrock cliffs on either side of the gorge match up perfectly. Erosion has ripped through the lava layers like a buzz saw.

After river erosion had cut through four thousand feet of Columbia River Basalt, it began exposing the older surface below. From Lone Pine Saddle you can see this older, light gray rock in the Snake's rugged inner gorge. The rock consists of jumbled sedimentary and volcanic strata from a Pacific Ocean island chain at least 200 million years old. The islands were scraped up into an ancient coastal range by the westward-moving continent of North America. Since then the continent has scraped up new coast ranges, leaving this old rock far inland.

The Snake's inner gorge fascinates geologists, but it has long been a horrific barrier for travelers. Try to imagine the four hundred people and two thousand head of livestock that Chief Joseph led over this trail to the riverbank at Dug Bar, hurrying to meet the army's June 14 deadline. White settlers rushed in after the tribe, claiming pastures and branding the Appaloosa horses that lagged behind. Ahead, the flooding Snake River roared through the gorge a hundred yards wide. Joseph ordered rafts built of hide bundles. He loaded the rafts with baggage and had the tribe's infirm or elder members sit on top. Then he ordered young men to swim the rafts across with the strongest horses. Women and children followed on horseback into the raging river. Finally the remaining horses and cattle were driven into the water to cross on their own. Many of the animals drowned, but miraculously, no human lives were lost.

After the tribe had regrouped and climbed the Idaho side of Hells Canyon, they stopped two miles short of the reservation for a "last council in freedom." Chief Joseph went back to check on their cattle. When he returned, he found the tribe preparing for war. Three young hotbloods, taunted by an old warrior, had murdered settlers in nearby cabins. The U.S. Army was already advancing. Hoping to avoid more bloodshed, Joseph managed to convince the tribe that they must first meet the troops with a white flag of surrender.

On June 17, 1877, a hundred cavalrymen and a detachment of Idaho volunteers marched into a box canyon near the present-day town of Whitebird, looking for the non-treaty Nez Perce. The soldiers stopped uncertainly when they found a group of warriors assembled for surrender. Then one of the Idaho volunteers raised his rifle and shot at the Indian holding the white flag. For the Nez Perce, this was the signal that there would be no peace. The well-prepared tribespeople opened fire from the rimrock on all sides of the canyon. In the rout that followed, the Nez Perce killed a third of the white soldiers while suffering no losses themselves.

Thus began the Nez Perce's historic flight toward permanent sanctuary in Canada. For three months Joseph led them on a zigzagging 3000-mile retreat across the Continental Divide, through Yellowstone National Park, and into the plains of Montana. As they went, they paid for all the supplies they obtained, harmed no noncombatants, and moved peaceably, except in brilliant defensive battles. Their conduct won sympathy across the nation. The people of Billings, Montana, welcomed them as heroes.

The final, crushing defeat came just thirty miles short of the Canadian border. In the surrender, as reported to the world by an alert young adjutant named C.E.S. Wood, Chief Joseph announced, "I am tired of fighting. Our chiefs are dead. The old men are all dead. The little children are freezing to death. Hear me, my chiefs. I am

Chief Joseph.

tired; my heart is sick and sad. From where the sun now stands, I will fight no more forever."

Even the army general who had pursued them was so moved by the tribe's valor and integrity that he urged the government to return the Nez Perce to their homeland. Pleas for mercy poured in from around the world, but to no avail. The captives were sent to a prison camp in Leavenworth, Kansas, and later to a reservation in Oklahoma, where many died of malaria. Among the dead was one of the oldest Nez Perce, the seventy-year-old son of explorer Captain William Clark.

After eight years in Oklahoma, the tribe's survivors were allowed to return to the Northwest, but never to Oregon. Chief Joseph lived out his years on the Colville Reservation of Eastern Washington. Not once was he permitted to see his beloved Wallowa homeland. He died in 1904 of what the reservation doctor termed simply "a broken heart."

Nearly a hundred years passed before Chief Joseph's descendants returned as landowners to the Wallowa country — but that is a later story. First hike onward along the Snake River a few miles to find out what has become of Hells Canyon in the meantime.

Two trails start at a primitive campground at the far end of Dug Bar. One path leads down along the riverbank a few hundred yards to a dead end at a sign commemorating the Nez Perce river crossing site. The other path sets off uphill past a corral.

Prickly pear cactus in Hells Canyon.

This is the start of the Snake River Trail, a very difficult route that often scrambles thousands of feet up and down to avoid riverside cliffs. The Hat Point trailhead at the far end is 47 miles away and requires a final, grueling, 6000-foot climb. But for a relatively easy sample, you can try just the first 4.7 miles to the mouth of Deep Creek.

Half a mile up the Snake River Trail you'll reach a sweeping viewpoint of the river. From here you can often watch small jet boats bouncing up through the perilous whitewater, bringing tourists from Lewiston for a quick look at Hells Canyon. You can also expect to see brightly colored rubber rafts of paddlers zipping downstream.

What you wouldn't expect is that a full-sized steamboat once ran this raging river too.

The 136-foot, 300-ton steamboat *Shoshone* had been built in Idaho in 1866, assembled from parts hauled overland by train and wagon. After sailing the upper Snake River for a few years, serving the Idaho City mines near Boise, the ship began losing money because the mines were dwindling. John Ainsworth, president of the Oregon Steam Navigation Company that owned the ship, wanted to bring her to Portland where she could be more useful. At first he considered dismantling the ship and transporting the pieces by wagon trail to the Columbia River. But the cost of such an effort would have been more than the ship was worth. And so in 1869 he ordered the pilot to run the *Shoshone* downstream through Hells

Canyon or "wreck her in the attempt."

The *Shoshone's* crew dutifully steamed downriver. At the top of Copper Ledge Falls, however, the pilot stopped to reconnoiter. After inspecting this terrifying cataract, where the Snake drops eighteen feet in a hundred yards, the pilot moored the boat in place. Then he and most of the crew climbed out of Hells Canyon on foot, never to return. Only two caretakers stayed behind to watch the ship.

Ainsworth was furious. Six months passed before he could find a pilot and crew daring enough to hike back into the depths of Hells Canyon and try again. The new pilot was Sebastian Miller, and Ainsworth's instructions to him were explicit: Run Copper Ledge Falls or burn the boat in place.

After the long hike down to the ship, Miller set about packing its hold with cordwood so it would be more likely to stay afloat. Then he ordered the crew to cast off the mooring lines. The swirling current grabbed the 136-foot ship and spun it like a toy at the head of the falls' narrow chute. The paddlewheel flailed in the air and then splintered against the whitewater. The ship smashed against the chasm's cliffs, ripping eight feet off its bow. But the *Shoshone* bobbed out from the cataract upright. Miller quickly spun the wheel and managed to beach her before she could sink.

Inspecting the damage, Miller realized it would be safest to burn the boat after all. But then he'd have to hike back out of Hells Canyon. And so, after making emergency repairs for several days, the stalwart Miller ordered the crew to fire up the *Shoshone's* boilers and push off again. The paddlewheel limped and the prow was missing, but Miller drove the ship through one whitewater drop after another. Finally he shot her through Mountain Sheep Rapids, where the Snake River stands on edge in a canyon just sixty feet from wall to wall. Cliffs flashed past within inches of the ship railings on either hand.

When Miller steamed the battered *Shoshone* into the port of Lewiston, townspeople gaped as if at a ghost. Wreckage of the ship's bow and nameplate had beaten him to town by four days. Newspapers had already reported the ship lost and the crew dead.

As you hike along the Snake River to Deep Creek, it may be difficult to picture a 300-ton steamboat sailing past. It's even harder to imagine the mass murder of gold miners that took place on the sandy bar where Deep Creek spills into the Snake.

Hells Canyon doesn't have much gold, but thirty-two determined Chinese placer miners set up camp on the remote beach by Deep Creek in 1886 to sift nearly microscopic grains of gold from the sand. The next year, rumors began spreading that the Chinese had struck it rich—that they had already filled seventeen vials with gold dust. Seven Idaho cowhands swore a secret oath to get the Chinese gold. They rode down to the Deep Creek camp and shot every one of the thirty-two miners mercilessly in the head. Then the murderers buried what gold they could find, plotting to come back for the loot when the fuss blew over.

Before the cowhands rode away from the bloody camp they dumped more than two dozen of the bodies in the river, thinking that this would help conceal their crime. The strategy backfired. Within days, corpses began washing ashore near Lewiston at what became known as Dead Man's Eddy. Word quickly spread. The investigation that followed sparked an international furor. Newspapers bannered the mass murder as the crime of the century. The Chinese ambassador demanded, and received, an unprecedented $275,000 settlement from the U.S. government.

Meanwhile the cowhands still eluded suspicion. They chose one of their number to fetch the buried gold. He never came back. Perhaps he kept the gold for himself. Perhaps he was followed and killed by some of the others. Before long, six of the cowhands had vanished. The seventh complained in public that he had been cheated, and as a result became the only one of the seven brought to justice for his role in the murders.

But what about the missing gold? Years later, in 1902, a prospector reopened that mystery by discovering a Chinese vial with $700 of gold dust

Abandoned homestead near Deep Creek on the Snake River Trail.

at the Deep Creek camp. Did none of the murderers actually make it back to Deep Creek for the gold? Was this the Chinese miners' entire wealth? Or is more gold still hidden here?

Today at Chinese Massacre Cove the hardest questions remained unanswered. You can visit the ruins of a crude rock shelter where the thirty-two immigrants lived. Chinese numerals still mark the wall, but who can say what they tallied? Mystery and tragedy linger here like uneasy ghosts.

Backpackers who continue beyond Deep Creek on the increasingly rugged Snake River Trail will encounter other ghosts as well. Between 1910 and 1930, optimistic homesteaders built hardscrabble ranches throughout Hells Canyon. The weather proved too severe for farming, and there was no easy way to take crops to market. Today the trail passes the gray plank ruins of abandoned buildings every few miles, with rusting farm machinery and children's toys strewn amongst the weeds. The Forest Service has gradually acquired nearly all of the old ranches. One of these, the Kirkwood Ranch on the Idaho shore, has been restored as a museum visitable only by trail or by boat. The failed farms along Hells Canyon's trails stand as evidence that this land was perhaps best suited to the nomadic ways of the Nez Perce all along.

The long drive back from your hike in Hells Canyon gives time to contemplate more recent twists in the fortunes of the Nez Perce. Turn left in the town of Joseph for a side trip to the gravesite of Chief Joseph's father. After a mile the road crests at a small cemetery with a sweeping view across Wallowa Lake to the snowpeaks of the Eagle Cap Wilderness. Winds shiver the silver leaves of quaking aspens and sweep across the lake's mirror like spirits of the sky. Here, among the sagebrush of the bank, a stone monument honors the remains of the last Wallowa Nez Perce chief to die on the band's homeland.

But now, a century after Chief Joseph died in exile and was buried in Colville, Washington, some of his descendants have begun to return to the Wallowa country. The Bonneville Power Administration, finally admitting that its dams have decimated the fish runs pledged to the Nez Perce, offered the tribe financial compensation in 1997. The tribe used the money to buy back 10,300 acres of Joseph Canyon, a valley west of Hells Canyon. A cave in this 2000-foot-deep canyon was the birthplace of Thunder Rolling in the Mountains—Chief Joseph. The tribe has dismantled the canyon's ranches and is managing the land as a wildlife refuge.

In another major step, the Wallowa Band of the Nez Perce formed a non-profit association that raised money to buy back a portion of the band's traditional summer campsite near the confluence of the Wallowa and Lostine rivers. Known as *Tamkaliks* ("from where you can see the mountains"), the site became a gathering point for the band's traditional summer powwow and friendship feast in 1998. Plans call for construction of a cultural center to tell the story of the Nez Perce.

Sometimes the greatest changes are reflected in small things. One such symbol is the gift exchanged on July 27, 1997, between two Northwest families: the descendants of Chief Joseph and the descendants of C.E.S. Wood. In 1877, Wood had been the Army lieutenant who wrote down Chief Joseph's surrender speech. The two men had impressed each other enough to become friends. In 1889, when Chief Joseph was living on the Colville Reservation, Wood asked if his young son Erskine might spend the summer with the tribe. Joseph agreed and let the thirteen-year-old boy share his teepee as a family member, taking him hunting and even sewing a feathered headdress for him. When it was time for Erskine to leave, the boy told Chief Joseph that his father had offered to do anything he wished in return.

"Joseph said he would like a good stallion to improve the breed of his pony herd," Erskine Wood wrote later at the age of ninety.

"I looked on Joseph as such a great man, a noble chief driven out of his ancestral home, I revered him so, that I thought his request for a stallion was too puny—was beneath him. I shook my head and said, 'No, that was not what my father meant.' Joseph accepted this calmly and we said no more. But I always regretted my utter stupidity. A fine stallion which would have upbred Joseph's herd of ponies would have been a wonderful thing for him. Just the kind of a thing in his Indian life that he needed, and of course well within the ability of my father to get for him. But just because I exalted him so high I deprived him of it, and it is something I shall always regret."

Years later, when a television documentary on the American West described the many unfulfilled promises of the white men to the Nez Perce, the Wood family felt spurred to a decision: they would begin making amends of their own. They traced Chief Joseph's closest living descendant on the Colville reservation—a man they identified as Soy Redthunder. Then they invited his family to a ceremony in the Wallowa Valley and presented them with a purebred Appaloosa stallion in trust for the words spoken a century earlier.

"I think Indian people are always skeptical at first," Redthunder admitted. "Treaties written down were never fulfilled. A word spoken ten years ago is likely forgotten. Yet this one family can turn around and fulfill spoken words between two people more than a hundred years old. To make those words good now is an extraordinary thing."

CHAPTER VIII

The Iron Horse

Whistling and clanking, snorting and rumbling, steam locomotives once rode steel rails through Oregon's rural valleys. As modern highways gradually stole the trains' thunder, the rails were torn up from most of the state's backwoods lines. But now some of the old grades have been reopened for hiking and bicycling. These routes are not only the flattest, straightest trails around, they're also quick tickets to an exploration of Oregon's past.

The Northwest's first locomotive started portaging travelers around the Cascade rapids on the Columbia River in 1862. But the short track there didn't connect with railroad lines anywhere else. Connections seemed the key to progress, especially after the much-publicized golden spike

Sumpter's restored "Stump Dodger."

completed a transcontinental railroad line from New York to Sacramento in 1867. By mid-1868, two competing railroad companies had already started building track south from Portland, both heading for Sacramento. The 700-mile route they surveyed traced the nightmarish Applegate Trail south to Ashland and then crossed the steep Siskiyou Mountains. Construction setbacks and rivalries delayed the two companies year after year. Oregonians began wondering if there wasn't an easier route to connect with the transcontinental railroad line.

The time was ripe for the entrance of Colonel T. Egenton Hogg, a flamboyant entrepreneur who would promise a shortcut—a transcontinental track east across the Cascade Range.

Santiam Pass

Drivers today still generally view Hogg Rock as the most frightening obstacle at Santiam Pass. The highway grade here clings to the cliffs of a rock mesa. Trucks belch black smoke and hug the guardrail, just inches away from a vast, forested canyon. The bald head of Hoodoo Butte glowers from a horizon full of peaks. Although drivers hardly have time to watch the scenery, passengers occasionally glance up the cliffs and marvel at the sight of carefully fitted stonework embankments a hundred yards almost straight up—the remnants of an unlikely railroad grade.

Over a thousand laborers helped chip the precarious rail route from the face of Hogg Rock in 1888. But who came up with the money for such a daredevil scheme? And why was the only train to run here an empty boxcar drawn by mules? For the answers, look to Colonel T. Egenton Hogg.

Hogg was not actually a colonel, but he did have a commission with the Confederate navy during the Civil War. His assignment was to serve as a pirate, attempting to disrupt Union shipping and whaling in the North Pacific. Before he could inflict much damage, however, he was captured and convicted. Like many Southern officers, he was sent to Alcatraz as a political prisoner. Although Indian prisoners (such as Tyee John from Oregon's Rogue River War) were also being held in federal facilities in San Francisco, Southerners were privileged with better access to the white man's world. The ambitious Colonel Hogg, for example, spent his days reading newspaper reports of the West's great entrepreneurs.

Hogg must have laughed out loud when he read that the millionaire stagecoach king Ben Holladay had sold his vast Western holdings to the Wells Fargo Company for a fortune in 1866, just three years before the transcontinental railroad would make many stagecoach lines obsolete. Two years later Hogg must have raised his eyebrows when he read that

Willamette Valley & Coast Railroad locomotives, circa 1877.

Holladay had decided to spend that fortune trying to build the difficult railroad line between Portland and Sacramento. Railroading was a high-stakes gambling game. Hogg was eager to be dealt a hand.

After Hogg was released from Alcatraz, he completed recovery from his war wounds in a hospital. Then he toured Oregon in 1871, laying plans for a railroad shortcut. He scoffed at Portland as a rail terminus, declaring that the treacherous Columbia River bar made that city unreliable as an ocean port. Instead he proposed converting the sleepy coastal village of Newport to a bustling seaport, with steamships docking in the deep water of Yaquina Bay. The new San Francisco he envisioned there would be connected by rail across the Coast Range to the Willamette Valley at Corvallis. Then the track would cross Santiam Pass and Eastern Oregon to a transcontinental link at Boise, Idaho. Hogg's rail line would provide a route to Chicago nearly three hundred miles shorter than Holladay's route south via Sacramento.

Corvallis citizens embraced Hogg as a genius. They raised seed money for Hogg to incorporate the Corvallis & Yaquina Bay Railroad Company in 1872. There wasn't enough money to actually build the railroad, but Hogg was able to reopen a defunct wagon road across the Coast Range and to assume its 60,000-acre federal land grant through the Siletz Indian Reservation to Newport. In 1874 Hogg reincorporated his dream as the bigger-sounding Willamette Valley & Coast Railroad. He still couldn't raise enough local money to start building track.

The colonel began looking elsewhere for the huge amounts of capital

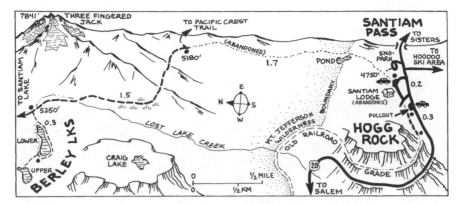

31. Santiam Pass

HIKE LOCATION

Easy (to Hogg Rock)
0.6 miles round-trip
No elevation gain

Explore an abandoned railroad grade at Santiam Pass.

Getting There: Drive Highway 20 to Santiam Pass. West of the Hoodoo Ski Area turnoff 0.2 mile, park at a big pullout on the north strewn with red cinders.

Hiking Tips: From the pullout, walk 50 feet into the forest, turn left on an abandoned service road for 0.1 mile, scramble down to the old rail grade, and continue 0.2 mile to an impassable rockslide. Turn back here.

If you'd like to see Santiam Lodge, return to the service road near the historical marker's pullout and continue straight 0.2 mile.

Season: The Santiam Pass railroad grade is usually snow-free May through November.

While You're in the Area: Three hikes to lookout sites are nearby: Sand Mountain (Hike #50), Black Butte (Hike #47), and Iron Mountain (Hike #48).

his vision demanded. The center of the financial universe was London. Why not start there?

Hogg charged into London in early 1877. He made an appointment with one of the most powerful financial lawyers in the world, Wallis Nash. A personal friend and neighbor of Charles Darwin, Nash knew how to raise money for big projects. One of his clients was Alexander Graham Bell; in fact, the first long-distance telephone call in England was from Queen Victoria's summer home to Nash's office in London.

Nash studied the tall, lean, blue-eyed Colonel Hogg and concluded that the drawling Southerner was "an interesting talker, evidently a man of foresight and imagination." Still, Nash decided that he himself would need to visit Oregon before offering bonds to investors. And so Nash and two colleagues returned to Oregon with Hogg that summer. The trip required twenty-one days of travel each way. They crossed the Atlantic by steamship, rode the train to California, and took the stagecoach north.

Nash liked Oregon so much that he wrote an effusive and entertaining book, *Oregon: There and Back in 1877*. Publicity from the book helped Nash raise $15 million in bonds for Hogg's project. Eventually Nash retired to Oregon. The hamlet of Nashville, on the train line between Corvallis and Toledo, was named in his honor.

Meanwhile, with $15 million in hand for his company—now renamed as the even grander-sounding Oregon Pacific Railroad—Hogg hired 1400 men to start construction. In the summer of 1881 they began building west from Corvallis toward Newport.

The project's scale alarmed Portland businessmen. They feared Newport really might upstage Portland as the state's primary harbor. "The tide and marsh lands around Yaquina Bay have absolutely no value," the *Oregonian* thundered editorially. "Portland, not Yaquina Bay, will become the focal point for shipments of wheat and other products grown in the state."

By the time Hogg got around to buying a right-of-way through Newport he discovered that Portland businessmen had already bought up key properties along the Yaquina bayfront. Hoping to squelch the rival town, the Portlanders demanded astronomical prices for a railroad right-of-way to Newport's harbor.

Furious, Hogg countered by announcing that Newport would not be the western terminus of his railroad after all. In 1885 he stopped laying track at the eastern edge of Yaquina Bay, three miles short of Newport. There he laid out Yaquina City, an entirely new town with its own harbor. He bought a steam-driven ocean liner, christened it the *SS Yaquina City*, and scheduled regular sailings between Yaquina Bay and San Francisco. With connecting rail service from Corvallis, the line became the quickest route from Oregon's heartland to California. And by offering ferry service across the bay to Newport, Hogg rendered the Portlanders' rights-of-way there worthless. The outmaneuvered Portland businessmen began quietly looking for other ways to defeat Hogg.

With the Coast Range crossing complete, Hogg turned to construction of the rail line from Corvallis east. His rail crews built through Albany in 1886 and raced to lay track up the North Santiam River into the Cascade Range. Hogg's franchise required that he complete the Cascade crossing before he

The 1888 railroad grade near Hogg Rock.

could claim a federal land grant across Eastern Oregon. The success of his plans hinged on getting free federal land. Meanwhile, time and money were both running short.

At first it seemed only a minor setback when Hogg's construction contractor quit in 1887. But then the replacement contractor also quit before the year was out. And then came a bigger blow: his steamship, the *SS Yaquina City*, ran aground at the mouth of Yaquina Bay on December 5, 1887. All hands were rescued, but the bar's surf pounded the ship to splinters.

What had caused the shipwreck? The captain reported that the rudder cable had mysteriously snapped as he was turning into the entrance of Yaquina Bay. The cable was only three years old. Sabotage seemed likely. Hogg suspected the rival Portland businessmen of trying once again to derail his plans, but he had no proof.

Hogg immediately ordered a new steamship built with the insurance money. Still, he knew his train to Yaquina City would lose riders in the meantime. Without that income, the Oregon Pacific Railroad no longer had enough money to build the final forty-three miles of track to the Cascade summit. And without a train at the Cascade summit, he'd lose his federal land grant. The company would be doomed.

Hogg decided to throw all his resources into one last, daring gamble. He abandoned the North Santiam track where it stood unfinished near present-day Detroit. Instead he hired a new contractor for a new task: to build an unconnected section of track atop Santiam Pass. Hogg would make a train run across the Cascade summit, even if it couldn't run anywhere else.

Hundreds of mule-drawn supply wagons rolled up the South Santiam

River canyon in the summer of 1888, following the old Santiam Wagon Road to a makeshift camp beside Santiam Pass at Big Lake. Over a thousand men — mostly Chinese — worked with picks, shovels, carts, and dynamite to build eleven miles of track across the summit and around Hogg Rock. Other workers in Albany disassembled a boxcar, packed the pieces into wagons, and hauled it up to the pass. There the car was reassembled on the deadend rail line and pulled back and forth along the track by mules.

At this point Hogg brazenly informed government officials that he had fulfilled the terms of his franchise: The Oregon Pacific Railroad was in fact running a train across the Cascade Range. Meanwhile he reassured his nervous bondholders that a replacement ocean liner, the 257-foot *SS Yaquina Bay*, was already on its way to Oregon from the San Francisco shipyards. Soon the company would be earning enough money to connect the train line at Santiam Pass and start building toward Idaho. It looked as though Hogg's bluff might pay off.

And then a wild card changed the game. On December 9, 1888, as a tug was helping maneuver Hogg's newly built steamship across the Newport bar, the towing cable suddenly snapped. The *SS Yaquina Bay* ended her maiden voyage by drifting to rest beside her derelict sister ship, where she too was smashed by the surf.

The tragedy mirrored the previous shipwreck so precisely that few observers believed it could be a coincidence. Still, Hogg had no proof that the cables had been sabotaged, or that the rival Portland entrepreneurs were responsible. And this time insurance did not cover the loss.

Within months, the Oregon Pacific Railroad defaulted on its interest payments to bondholders. In the next four years the bankrupt company was sold three times — for $1 million, $200,000, and finally $100,000. Each of the new owners defaulted. The bondholders lost every penny they had invested. Ruined and disgraced, Hogg left the state. Yaquina City became a ghost town, and Portland thrived.

What remains of the Oregon Pacific today? In fact, several sections of the track are still in use. Trainloads of wood chips cross the Coast Range to Corvallis from Toledo, where the tracks now end. Lumber trains still run up the North Santiam as far as Mill City. But the old grade at Santiam Pass never was connected, and never saw a real train.

After you drive east past Hogg Rock on the way to Santiam Pass, just before the highway crests at the turnoff for the Hoodoo ski area, look for a big highway pullout on the left, strewn with red cinders, on the north side of the road. To find the railroad grade, climb up the cinder bank beside the sign and walk fifty feet into the forest. You'll discover an ancient service roadbed, used by the railroad crews. Walk left, stepping over a few small logs. To the left you can see dirt embankments where a small railroad trestle once bridged a gully. After two hundred yards the old service road ends. Scramble down twenty feet to the railroad grade and continue along it to a viewpoint. The panorama here sweeps from Mt. Washington's spire past flat-topped Hayrick Butte and the bald hump of Hoodoo's ski area cinder cone to the cliffs of Hogg Rock. Rockslides have obliterated the grade beyond this point, making it too dangerous to continue. This is the end of Colonel T. Egenton Hogg's crumbled dream.

Part of Hogg's old railroad grade now serves as the boundary of the Mt. Jefferson Wilderness. A third of that wilderness was overswept by the B&B wildfire in 2003. The silver snags of dead lodgepole pines and mountain hemlocks stand as reminders of the fire along the old rail line. But as you walk here you'll also see evidence that fire is a natural part of healthy forests in the High Cascades. Triggered by the fire's heat, billions of pine and hemlock seeds have sprouted from the ashes. Wildflowers and huckleberry bushes have found fresh ground to thrive.

When the 2003 fire neared Santiam Pass, crews stepped in to save landmarks of human history. They unbolted and removed the wooden historical marker at the highway pullout. They wrapped nearby Santiam Lodge with fireproof fabric. Although the abandoned building is entirely built of wood, the fire swept over it without singeing a shake. As for Colonel Hogg's railroad grade, the fire has actually made it easier to find and follow. When a cold wind whistles through the snags of Santiam Pass, you can almost imagine it's the mournful wail of a distant, far distant train.

Deschutes River

The charms of a desert river are many: bright blue skies, the pungent smell of sage, birdsong across glassy water, and the cool grass of an oasis-like riverbank. These enticements would be reason enough to take a loop hike from the state park at the mouth of the Deschutes River. But the route has other attractions as well—whitewater rapids, canyon rimrock viewpoints, a fragment of the Oregon Trail, and two of Oregon's most interesting railroad routes.

Two railroad routes? The sinuous Deschutes River canyon is so crowded with lava cliffs that it seems an improbable place for a train at all. In fact, an 1855 U.S. Army railroad survey had dismissed the canyon route as impossible, observing that "nature seems to have guaranteed it forever to the wandering savage and the lonely seeker after the wild and sublime in natural scenery." A more detailed railroad survey in 1899 likewise

Bicyclists on the old railroad grade along the Deschutes River.

rejected the Deschutes River route as impractical. And yet in 1909, feuding railroad moguls launched a race to lay track upriver to Bend. By 1911, not one but two lines had been built through the desert river's seemingly impossible gorge.

The tycoons behind this battle were James J. Hill of the Great Northern Railroad (doing business here as the Oregon Trunk Railroad) and Edward H. Harriman of the Union Pacific (operating here as the DesChutes Railroad). Both men wanted first shot at Central Oregon's sixteen billion board feet of ponderosa pine timber. They also hoped to build through Bend to connect with their other rail lines in California and Idaho.

Hill's and Harriman's proposed routes up the narrow canyon conflicted at many points. Harriman wasn't about to wait for the courts to finish haggling about rights-of-way. In July, 1909, he hired twenty contractors with a thousand men to set up work camps along his route, planning to claim key crossings. Hill responded by quietly sending twenty-six carloads of workers into the canyon one evening, with orders to start work at midnight. Harriman's men awoke on the morning of July 27 to find parts of their survey line crawling with rival laborers.

In general, Hill's Oregon Trunk Railroad followed the river's west bank while Harriman's DesChutes Railroad followed the east, but contested areas became impromptu battlefields. Explosions echoed up the canyon as the men on both sides drilled and blasted their grades from the

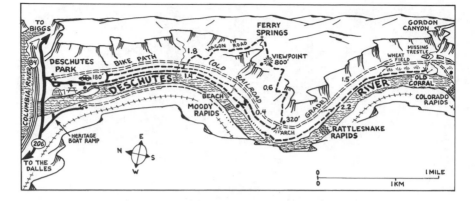

32. Deschutes River

HIKE LOCATION

Moderate
4.2 miles round trip
600 feet elevation gain

Hike a desert river canyon where steam trains once ran.

Getting There: From The Dalles, take Interstate 84 east past The Dalles Dam to the Deschutes Park exit (#97). Follow park signs 3 miles until you cross the river, and then turn right. Drive straight through the park to the far end of the last parking area. Dogs are allowed on leash only.

Hiking Tips: Walk upriver through a picnic area lawn 250 yards to a trail sign. Bicyclists must turn left here to the railroad grade/bike path, but hikers can keep right along the scenic riverbank. After 1.2 miles the river trail passes a small beach near Moody Rapids, a mild riffle. A few hundred yards later fork to the left on a small path that switchbacks uphill. Keep right at the next junction and continue 0.3 mile along a tableland to a viewpoint with a messageboard overlooking Rattlesnake Rapids. Here the trail joins the gravel bike path. If you're tired you could simply follow it to the left back to your car. But it's more interesting to go to the right 50 feet and head uphill past a "No Bikes" sign on a path that climbs 0.6 mile to Ferry Springs. Cross the creek, continue downhill 0.9 mile, and turn right on the gravel bike path to your car.

Season: Spring and fall are nicest. Skip August's heat and mid-winter's chill.

While You're in the Area: The eclectic Maryhill Museum features a full-size Stonehenge replica, 100 chess sets, Rodin sculptures, and Native American artifacts. To find the museum (open 10am-5pm from March 15 to November 15), drive east to Highway 97, cross the Columbia River, and turn left 2 miles on Highway 14.

cliffs. In the sweltering heat of late summer, the rival crews sometimes zinged rifle shots toward each other across the river. Miraculously, no one seems to have been hit. At night, squads crept through the sagebrush to locate and detonate their opponents' gunpowder caches. Shortages of black powder eventually slowed both sides.

After building seventy-five miles up the river's west bank to a cliff at the Warm Spring Indian Reservation, Hill's crews suddenly changed course, bridged the river, and built directly across Harriman's line. To avoid bloodshed, Congress swiftly passed the Canyon Act. The law required the two companies to share an eleven-mile stretch of track and observe a "cease-fire" for "a period of 999 years."

By early 1911, Hill appeared to be winning the race to Bend. His crews had already sprinted ahead to build the spidery Crooked River Bridge, a 350-foot steel span, arching from sheer cliffs 320 feet above the river. The historic bridge is still a tourist attraction, visitable from the Ogden Scenic Wayside on Highway 97, ten miles north of Redmond.

Using the Canyon Act as leverage, Harriman negotiated to share the use of Hill's final miles of track toward Bend. And so the two railroad titans ended their race with a tie. On October 5, 1911, when James J. Hill, the renowned "Empire Builder" of the Great Northern, drove a golden spike to complete the line at Bend, Harriman's Union Pacific agent was on hand to share the glory.

Hill had spent $16 million on the competition; Harriman had spent $9 million. The two lines were immediately recognized as redundant. Nonetheless, they competed for forty years before most of Harriman's east-side rails were finally removed. Hill's west-side track is still in use.

Today the twelve lower miles of the east-side grade have been reopened as a hiker/biker trail. If you're bicycling, simply follow the gravel grade up the canyon from the state park. If you're hiking, you can take a loop that more closely follows the river. Start by walking along the grassy riverbank from the state park's overflow camping area, listening for the melodious call of the western meadowlark, Oregon's state bird. This is also a good place to spot a long-tailed, black-and-white magpie — or even a bald eagle.

The riverbank is lined with sumac trees whose multi-leafletted boughs turn scarlet in autumn. The rest of the canyon is silvered with sagebrush, some of it ten feet tall and hundreds of years old. Also look for tumbling mustard. In spring this plant's shoulder-high stalks sprout tiny yellow flowers. In fall, when its dried skeleton rolls with the wind to spread seeds, the plant becomes a tumbleweed.

After about a mile and a half along the river, you'll pass a riffle called

Moody Rapids. For the loop hike, turn left on a trail that crosses the bike path—the old railroad grade. Continue uphill through a dry steppe of waving cheatgrass. The path climbs to a sweeping viewpoint, crosses a mossy creek beside Ferry Springs, and descends back toward the river. This downhill stretch is a remnant of a stagecoach road built in the 1860s to connect The Dalles with the John Day gold mines. When the path returns to the old railroad grade, turn right to complete the loop.

As you're walking back along the old grade to your car, don't be startled if you hear the whistle and rumble of a locomotive. The train you hear isn't a phantom. It's across the river, on the rival railroad line that survived from the heady days of the hard-fought race to Bend.

Row River

One of Oregon's prettiest railroads once followed the Row River from Cottage Grove past covered bridges and rustic farms to a reservoir hidden in the Cascades' wooded foothills. Today the trains are gone, but you can still ride this historic route. As part of the "Rails to Trails" movement, the abandoned track has been paved as a thirteen-mile path for hikers, bikers, and equestrians.

The United States once had the largest rail system in the world, boasting nearly 300,000 miles of track. Since that peak in the 1910s, more than half of the nation's rail lines have been abandoned. Two thousand additional miles of track are torn up each year. The Washington, D.C.-based Rails-to-Trails Conservancy began lobbying to save the old rail lines as public paths in 1985. The group has already preserved more than 8,000 miles of these linear parklands. The total acreage involved is usually quite small, because a mile-long right-of-way requires less than a single acre of land. The historic value of the routes, however, can be enormous. Near Boston, for example, the Minuteman Trail preserves a rail line along the route taken by British soldiers in 1776. In Pennsylvania, the Ghost Town Trail tours a string of deserted mining villages along an abandoned coal train track.

The railroad along the Row River is not as old as those eastern lines, but it has achieved fame as the setting for several classic movies. Buster Keaton filmed his five-star comedy blockbuster, *The General,* here in 1927. Keaton's silent film about a stolen Civil War train features slapstick stunts with steam locomotives. The Row River scenery resembles the Appalachians closely enough that it serves well as the backdrop for the movie's impressive Civil War battle reenactments. At the high point of the film, a locomotive crashes through a burning trestle into the river. The scene was not faked. Keaton steamed a genuine locomotive into the Row River.

While you're gearing up for the hike by watching *The General*, you might also pick up the four-and-a-half-star movie *Stand By Me*, filmed on the same tracks in 1986. A darker coming-of-age drama, the film stars River Phoenix as a boy searching for a missing schoolmate believed to have been hit by a train. Only late night TV now airs a third movie filmed here, *Emperor of the North*, in which Lee Marvin plays a seasoned hobo determined to ride the rails on every train in America — including an infamous run guarded by engineer Ernest Borgnine.

The railroad line itself dates to 1902, when Cottage Grove citizens raised the money to build tracks from their city upriver toward the Bohemia gold mining district. Trains hauled both ore and logs out of the backcountry. The railroad company's original name, Oregon & Southeastern (OSE), soon slipped in local parlance to "Old Slow & Easy." Perhaps to shake that nickname, the company later reincorporated as the Oregon Pacific & Eastern (OPE).

When the Army Corps of Engineers built Dorena Dam in the early 1940s, they moved the village of Dorena out of the reservoir's way and rerouted part of the railroad track along the new shore. By the 1970s, a steam excursion train called "The Goose" was sharing the line with Bohemia lumber company cars from the Culp Creek sawmill. After the mill burned in 1991, however, the track fell into disuse. The federal government acquired the line in lieu of $850,000 owed by Bohemia for forfeited timber sale

Mosby Creek's 1920 covered bridge.

contracts. The Bureau of Land Management converted the route to a gravel trail in 1994 and paved it in 1997.

The entire thirteen-mile trail is too long for most hikers, but you can sample the best of the route in the first few miles. The drive to the trailhead is also a pleasure, because you'll pass two of Lane County's most scenic covered bridges.

The Row River (or Currin) Bridge, along the road a mile before the trailhead, looks like a quaint, 105-foot garage straddling the stream. It dates to 1925, but replaced a covered bridge built on the same spot in

1883. Closer to the trailhead parking area, you'll drive through the Mosby Creek Bridge from 1920, the oldest of Lane County's eighteen remaining covered highway bridges. To sound like a local, pronounce "Mosby" like "Moe's bee," and make sure "Row River" rhymes with "cow liver."

In 1920 it cost just $4,125 to build the Mosby Creek Bridge, a 90-foot Howe truss span, sided in the classic board-and-batten style. In those days bridge-building crews set out with little more than tools, hardware, and camping equipment. They felled trees on the spot, cut their own lumber, split their own roof shakes, and fished for their dinners.

Why did Oregon's early bridges have roofs? Of course the covered spans were a welcome shelter for horse-and-buggy travelers in downpours. But the roofs made economic sense too. When the Row River railroad was first built in 1902, the owners tried to save money by leaving the trestles uncovered. By 1909, one bridge was already so badly rotted that the timbers gave way, plunging a passenger train car thirty-five feet into the Row River. No one was killed, but the mishap launched an investigation. The report revealed that the rainy climate had caused the uncovered bridge to rot in just seven years, while a covered span could easily have lasted forty. With that news, covered bridges became the standard.

From the trailhead beside the Mosby bridge, the path promptly crosses a red steel bridge over the lazy creek and sets off arrow-straight across flat valley bottomland. Expect giant cottonwood trees, mossy oaks, blackberries, teasels, queen anne's lace, views of grassy oak hills, and a few cows looking up from farm fields along the way. The trail itself consists of an eight-foot-wide asphalt strip with a two-foot gravel shoulder designed for horse use.

After a mile and half you'll cross the hundred-foot-wide Row River on an impressive steel railroad bridge. This is where the uncovered bridge

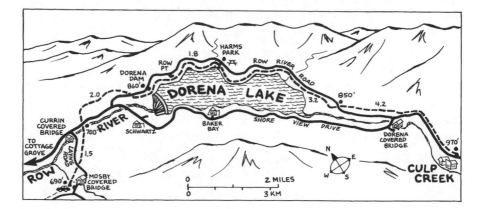

collapsed in 1909. It's also near the spot where Buster Keaton's stunt locomotive took its dive in 1927. Just beyond the Row River, you'll cross a paved road and climb for two miles through second-growth Douglas fir woods to Dorena Dam. Then the trail traces the edge of Dorena Reservoir, with views to forested hills beyond. After almost two miles along the reservoir you'll cross a footbridge to Harms Park, where the Lane County Parks Department has a gravel boat ramp. This makes a good turnaround point for hikers.

If you're bicycling, you might want to pedal another three miles past Harms Park to where the path recrosses the Row River Road. The path continues four miles beyond that point, mostly behind farms or near the road, to its end at the community of Culp Creek. On a bicycle, the trip back is an easy downhill cruise. With the rural scenery slipping past, you could even imagine you're riding the Old Slow & Easy on the railroad track that was such an attraction for Hollywood.

33. Row River

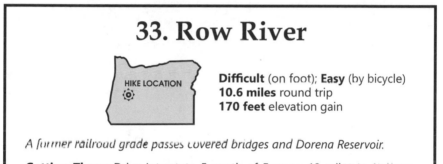

HIKE LOCATION

Difficult (on foot); **Easy** (by bicycle)
10.6 miles round trip
170 feet elevation gain

A former railroad grade passes covered bridges and Dorena Reservoir.

Getting There: Drive Interstate 5 south of Eugene 18 miles to Cottage Grove exit 174 and follow "Dorena Lake" signs east on Row River Road for 3.2 miles. Immediately after passing the Currin covered bridge, turn right on Layng Road for 1.2 miles, cross the Mosby Creek covered bridge, and park in a well-marked gravel parking lot on the right.

Hiking Tips: The trail crosses fields for 1.5 miles to a Row River footbridge. Then the path climbs through woods 2 miles to Dorena Dam and traces the reservoir's shore 1.8 miles to Harms Park, the recommended turnaround point for hikers. Foresighted hikers will have left a shuttle car here, allowing them to hike the trail only one way. Bicyclists who continue will find the path follows the reservoir's shore only another mile before following the highway and crossing more farm fields en route to trail's end at Culp Creek.

Season: Open all year.

While You're in the Area: Visit the Cottage Grove Museum at Birch and H Streets, open 1-4pm on weekends (Wednesday-Sunday in summer).

CHAPTER IX

Beacons to Sea

If you're hunting for the haunted, look no further than the lighthouses of Oregon's perilous coast. Shipwrecks, salty storms, and the lonely vigils of lighthouse keepers have left the state's coastal beacons loaded with tales. Some of the spookiest stories are true.

Plan on combining a tour of Oregon's haunted lighthouses with several short hikes. Of the seven century-old towers open to visitors, three can be accessed only by trail. The paths lead past some of the Pacific shore's most precarious panoramas—smashing surf, forested bluffs, and craggy islands where screeching seagulls soar.

After an initial Pacific Coast survey in the early 1850s, Congress originally authorized fourteen lighthouses for the new state of California, while the entire Oregon Territory was granted only two—a beacon at Cape Disappointment to warn of the treacherous Columbia River bar, and a light by Fort Umpqua to mark the Umpqua River mouth. An earlier chapter (Hike #10) describes how the ship bringing a "lighthouse kit" to Cape Disappointment sank on the Columbia River bar in 1853, taking its cargo of bricks and lantern equipment to the bottom. A second ship in 1855 had better luck, and the resulting lighthouse remains to this day, perched atop the Washington side of the river a short walk from the Lewis and Clark Interpretive Center.

The Umpqua River lighthouse location also proved troublesome. The ship carrying a lighthouse kit there landed successfully, but engineers built the tower on the river's sandy spit, so floods soon began crumbling the nearby bank. After just four years, in the apocalyptic 1861 flood that realigned many Oregon rivers, the Umpqua tower toppled into the river without leaving a trace. Thirty-three years passed before a replacement lighthouse was built, this time on a bluff nearly a mile inland.

After Oregon won statehood, Congress authorized construction of nine additional lighthouses, hoping to light the state's rugged coastline and mark its tricky ports. Not all of these beacons, built between 1868 and 1896, functioned as planned either. If you tour the Oregon coast from north to south in search of the old lights, you'll start with two of the most spectacular failures.

The lighthouse at Point Adams, built in 1875 just south of the Columbia River entrance, was set so low among the dunes that most ships failed to notice it at all. Its nearly useless light was extinguished in 1899. The building was demolished thirteen years later.

The coast's most dramatic failure, however, is twenty miles farther south: the derelict Tillamook Rock lighthouse, on an island beside Tillamook Head (see Hike #11). The beaconless tower there resembles a haunted ship forever moored at sea. And in fact this unmaintainable lighthouse remains the setting for the strangest of the coast's true ghost stories. Cursed by its former keepers as "Terrible Tilly," the tower briefly emerged in its afterlife as a kind of mausoleum—a privately-operated, desolate repository for the ash-filled urns of souls who wish to spend eternity in a lighthouse when they pass on.

Newport's Lighthouses

"The somber stillness of the darkening day was rent by a shriek so wild and weird that they who heard it felt the blood freeze suddenly in their veins."

So wrote Oregon author Lischen Miller in 1899 about the mysterious disappearance of a strange young girl in Newport's abandoned Yaquina Bay lighthouse. Although Miller's short story was fiction, it launched one of the most hair-raising legends about Oregon's coastal beacons.

Mystery and fright would surround Newport's two lighthouses even without the invention of a local ghost. The genuine mystery is why this town has two lighthouses at all. The true horror story tells how one of the lighthouses' scenic capes nearly vanished altogether. To track down the tales, plan on visiting the lights and exploring their scenic settings on foot.

Begin at Yaquina (*yuh-KWIN-uh*) Bay, where a lighthouse guided ships into Newport's harbor for the surprisingly short period of three years, from 1871 to 1874. This white clapboard lighthouse is not only Newport's oldest building, it's also the only Oregon lighthouse without a tower. To simplify construction, the architect designed a turret-shaped lantern room that mounted onto the roof of a Cape Cod-style house. The building also briefly served as the lighthouse keeper's home.

Park in the Yaquina Bay State Park picnic area and walk up the stairs for a free tour of the building, now open as a museum every day from 11

The Yaquina Bay lighthouse.

am to 4 pm (in winter, noon to 4 pm from Wednesday through Sunday). You'll find the restored kitchen outfitted with a cast-iron woodstove, a pantry, and antique cooking gear. A spooky, narrow staircase climbs past the bedrooms to a locked lantern room. The walls are crooked and the floorboards squeak. Author Lischen Miller was right to choose this as the setting for a ghost story.

In Miller's 1899 tale, a bedraggled sloop sails into Newport. The captain comes ashore with his genteel young daughter Muriel and says the sea voyage is proving difficult for the girl. He asks to lodge her at a boarding house for two weeks while the ship sails to Coos Bay and back.

The captain and the sloop are never seen again. At first Muriel doesn't seem to care. She joins a group of young people on outings about the town. In the abandoned lighthouse, they discover a hidden closet with a secret shaft descending to the sea. After they leave the lighthouse, however, Muriel insists on going back alone to retrieve a handkerchief she dropped.

Then comes the scream. The friends rush back to see what has happened, but they find the closet is now sealed shut. The only trace of Muriel is a pool of blood and a handkerchief.

"Of an afternoon when the fog comes drifting in from the sea and completely envelopes the lighthouse, it is the loneliest place in the world," Miller writes at the conclusion of her story. "At such times those who chance to be in the vicinity hear a moaning sound like the cry of one in pain, and sometimes a frenzied call for help pierces the death-like stillness of the waning day."

Miller's tale struck a chord because many locals already suspected this long-deserted building was cursed. But it wasn't a ghost that shut down the Yaquina Bay lighthouse in 1874. It was a government mistake.

Congress had originally authorized two beacons for the central Oregon Coast: the Yaquina Bay lighthouse and a supporting light ten miles north atop Cape Foulweather. Before the ship sailed with the parts for the second lighthouse, however, a local Army colonel changed its destination. He felt the cliffs at Cape Foulweather would make construction too difficult, so he ordered the materials off-loaded at Yaquina Head instead. Certainly the tower went up more quickly on that easily accessible headland. Wagons could drive there from Newport in just over an hour. The problem was that the new lighthouse was simply too close—less than four miles from the old light. After both had operated for thirteen months, bewildering mariners with their competing beacons, authorities decided simply to abandon the one at Yaquina Bay.

The derelict Yaquina Bay lighthouse deteriorated for a century before history buffs helped raise money to restore the building in 1974. In 1996 they convinced the Coast Guard to install a smaller, less confusing beacon in the old lantern room, allowing the long-neglected lighthouse to shine purposefully once more. Today volunteers staff the museum and run a gift shop in the basement. They also show videos dramatizing Lischen Miller's ghost story—almost as strange a tale as the true story of the lighthouse's untimely retirement in 1874.

After you've explored the lighthouse at Yaquina Bay, drive north through Newport to investigate the horror story—and the happy ending—behind Yaquina Head, site of Newport's second lighthouse. Park at a turnaround at the end of Yaquina Head's road and hike the short, paved path to the 93-foot lighthouse tower.

This is Oregon's tallest lighthouse, so you can be forgiven for feeling a little dizzy as you climb the 114 steps of the cast-iron spiral stairs to the lantern room. At the top, a two-ton lens dominates the glass-walled chamber like a gigantic chandelier in a greenhouse. In contrast to Newport's older lighthouse, this one has been in continuous use since it was first lit in 1873. Although the lens no longer rotates to flash a beam of light across the sea, a thousand-watt electric bulb installed inside the lens achieves much the same effect by blinking every few seconds.

The lens itself consists of an eight-foot-diameter array of glass prisms capable of focusing the light from a single light bulb into a beam visible twenty miles out to sea. August Jean Fresnel, a French physicist who had studied refraction in the early 1800s, designed the lenses used here and at many other lighthouses around the world. Fresnel lenses (pronounced

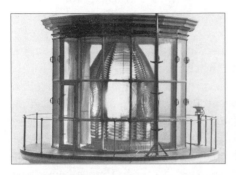

A Fresnel lighthouse lens.

fray-NELL) contain as many as a thousand curved triangular prisms, mounted in tiers around a thick central bullseye lens like stadium seats around a baseball field. The round bullseye lens in the middle resembles a three-inch-thick, glass dinner platter. Because of the prisms' precise shape and positioning, they catch light coming from the lamp in almost any direction and refract it toward the horizon.

Ground by hand in Paris , the massive lens array was shipped around Cape Horn and hoisted up from the beach with pulleys and mules. Surprisingly, the lens assembly originally rotated by hand power, using a larger version of the mechanism in a wind-up cuckoo clock. Every four hours the lighthouse keeper or his assistant would crank a weight up to the top of the tower. As the weight slowly descended, it powered gears that rotated the lens. To minimize friction, the heavy lens assemblies of Oregon lighthouses were designed either to ride on polished ball bearings or to float in a circular trough of liquid mercury.

After inspecting the lens, head back down the tower to a large railed deck. Here you'll have a close-up view of rocky islands where cormorants, murres, and seagulls nest. Bring binoculars to watch for the spouts of gray whales from December to June. Up to 20,000 whales migrate each year from Alaska to Mexico. Sometimes as many as thirty per hour round this prominent cape.

This is also a good place to imagine the alarm of the lighthouse keeper who once looked out from this viewpoint to see a flaming ship steaming past at full speed. The date was May 19, 1910, and the assistant engineer of the 600-ton *J. Marhoffer* had just made the mistake of overpumping a gasoline blow torch. The torch had exploded and set the entire engine room on fire. As the ship plowed onward, the captain desperately tried to flood the room. By then, however, the water valves were already red hot. Finally, ten miles north of Yaquina Head, the captain turned the ship's wheel straight toward the rocky shore and gave the order to abandon ship. He sent his first mate and his protesting wife off in the first lifeboat. Then he narrowly escaped with the remainder of the crew in a second lifeboat.

Still at full speed, the *Marhoffer* crashed into the rocks and broke up. Meanwhile, the two lifeboats bobbed onward to the north. The boat with the captain's wife and first mate landed safely on a small beach at Whale Cove. The captain's lifeboat capsized at Fogarty Beach, but most of the hands swam ashore. Only the injured cook drowned. Today the *Marhoffer's* rusty, barnacle-covered boiler can still be seen on the rocks at low tide from Highway 101 in a cove now known as Boiler Bay.

After taking in the view from the lighthouse deck, walk back to the parking turnaround. This exposed, wind-swept site seems an unlikely place for one of the Oregon Coast's earliest known settlements, but excavations show a tribal village stood here from 4100 to 2000 years ago. Archeologists have unearthed scrapers, arrowheads, shells, fishbones, and campfire remains. Tree pollen in the strata suggests that a large forest covered the headland then, providing shelter from the wind. Yaquina Head was probably larger then, too. Wave erosion has been whittling back the cliffs here for fourteen million years, ever since basalt lava flows from Hells Canyon poured across Oregon to the sea, leaving black rock headlands like this one all along the northern Oregon Coast.

To see one unusual side effect of the cliff's gradual erosion, take a staircase down to a beach of round black cobbles. As each wave froths onto the beach, the rocks roll up and back with a clattering roar, slowly grinding away at each other and at the headland itself. Collecting the naturally polished rocks on this rare cobble beach

The Yaquina Head Lighthouse stairway.

is forbidden, but feel free to take home samples of the beach's rounded driftwood. At low tide you can explore tidepools along the beach's edge, too. Be sure to look for the dozens of harbor seals that like to lounge in the sun on nearby Seal Island. The seals are so lazy and gray that they are often mistaken for driftwood logs.

The erosion of Yaquina Head has not always been natural, and therein lies the cape's most frightening tale. Using the archaic Mining Law of 1872—a piece of gold-rush-era legislation that lets almost anyone claim valuable minerals on federal land—a Newport gravel company staked a claim to Yaquina Head in the 1950s. Arguing that the cape's basalt was a "valuable mineral" because it could be converted to gravel, the company forced the U.S. government to sell. For less than three dollars an acre, the company snapped up nearly all of Yaquina Head's priceless oceanfront property.

Incredibly, once the gravel company owned the cape, they did not divide it up for condo sites. Instead they started quarrying the landmark to fill their gravel trucks. The excavators announced they would leave the lighthouse on an island where the cape's tip used to be.

The horror of this prospect did not escape Senator Mark Hatfield, whose only Oregon residence at the time was a Newport home with a view of the headland. He convinced Congress to pass a multi-million-dollar buyback that transferred Yaquina Head to the Bureau of Land Management in 1980.

For several years the BLM debated what to do with the half-demolished headland. The quarry had changed the cape's silhouette forever, leaving a gigantic crater on the south side. In fact, part of the excavation was already below sea level, kept dry by a dike.

Finally BLM planners came up with an unusual proposal, and if you walk back along the road from the headland's tip, you'll see the result. The plan involved three steps: First, build concrete paths through the pit. Second, blow up the dike and let the sea rush in. Third, announce the opening

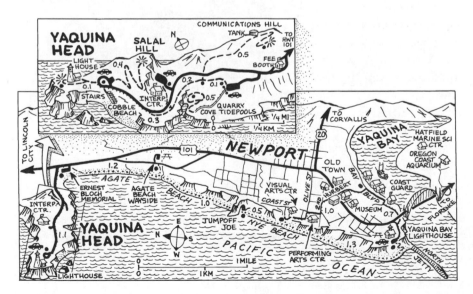

of Oregon's only wheelchair-accessible tidepools.

At first the plan appeared to be working without a hitch. Visitors who toured the Quarry Cove Tidepools Trail shortly after its grand opening in

34. Newport's Lighthouses

Easy
3 miles round trip
300 feet elevation gain

HIKE LOCATION

Visit two lighthouses—and see tidepools, birds, and seals along the way.

Getting There: In Newport, drive Highway 101 to the north end of the Yaquina Bay Bridge. Then follow state park signs to a picnic area below the Yaquina Bay lighthouse. To continue to the second lighthouse, drive Highway 101 north 3 miles and turn left at a sign for Yaquina Head. Stop at the headland's entrance booth to pay the $7-per-car fee, and then drive on half a mile to the large Interpretive Center parking lot on the right. After touring the displays here, walk or drive another 0.3 mile to a small parking area and turnaround at road's end, near the headland's tip.

Hiking Tips: Yaquina Bay State Park lacks hiking trails, but Yaquina Head offers 5 short paths. From the turnaround at the end of Yaquina Head's road, take a short, paved path to the Yaquina Head lighthouse, open daily 10am-4pm (9am-5pm in summer). Next return to the parking turnaround and take a staircase down to a beach of black cobbles. Then return to the parking turnaround to find a trail behind the restrooms that switchbacks 0.4 mile up through wildflowers to Salal Hill and a bird's-eye view of the cape. Before leaving Yaquina Head, drive down to the Quarry Cove trailhead for a 1-mile hike on concrete paths through an old gravel quarry, converted to wheelchair-accessible tidepools.

Season: Open all year.

While You're in the Area: Don't miss 2 spectacular aquariums at the south end of Newport's Yaquina Bay Bridge: the Oregon Coast Aquarium (with live otters, seals, and sea birds) and the Hatfield Marine Science Center (with an octopus and interactive indoor exhibits). The Oregon Coast Aquarium is open 9am-6pm daily in summer (otherwise 10am-5pm) for an admission of $19.95 for adults and $12.95 for kids age 3-12. The Hatfield Marince Science Center is open 10am-5pm daily in summer (otherwise 10am-4pm Thursday through Sunday), with admission by donation. For a walking tour of Newport's Old Town (see map), take the stone stairs down from the Yaquina Bay lighthouse picnic area, turn right along the beach 1.3 miles, head inland through the historic Nye Beach district, cross through Old Town, and return along the bayfront, completing a 3-mile loop.

1994 saw how the former gravel pit was being colonized by acorn barnacles, turban snails, and scores of other intertidal species. Today, however, you'll find the trail mostly blocked by sand.

What the government planners overlooked was that genuine tidepools rely on vigorous surf action to keep them clear of sand. The calm waters of Quarry Cove are rapidly turning the tidepools into a beach.

Government officials, weary of arguing with the headstrong headland, are letting the sand stay. After decades of abuse, Yaquina Head has obviously decided to heal its scars in its own way.

Heceta Head

A different tale is set at the next old lighthouse to the south, on picturesque Heceta Head. One year, if you called for reservations at Heceta House (an adjacent building that now serves as a bed-and-breakfast inn) the answering machine would cackle spookily, "Leave a message — or the ghost of Rue will haunt you forever."

Mike and Carol Korgan decided to manage scenic Heceta House partly out of a fondness for ghosts. For twenty years, while the two certified executive chefs owned and operated Portland's Strudel House restaurant, they lived in a million-dollar Victorian mansion with a ghost named John.

According to the Korgans, John is on record as the avid builder who had nearly finished work on that house when the bank threatened to foreclose on a $3000 debt. Rather than be forced to leave, John went upstairs and hanged himself. They claim John's spirit has been hanging around the place ever since. When the Korgans were ready to retire from Portland, they regretted leaving John behind. They jumped at the chance to move into a lighthouse complex with a resident ghost of its own.

Even Rue's staunchest believers admit she does not haunt the lighthouse itself, but only Heceta House, the white clapboard, 1893 Queen-Anne-style building next door. This duplex once housed the two assistant lighthouse keepers and their families.

As Mike Korgan tells the story, a little girl who once lived at Heceta House fell off a cliff and was never found. He suspects the local ghost might be either the lost girl or the anguished mother looking for her child.

"Rue has a lot of love for the house," Korgan says. "The only people she has scared are workers doing things to the house she didn't like."

Rue's appearances date to the early 1970s when Lane Community College was leasing the building from the Forest Service. Workers' tools began vanishing, only to reappear later in the same spot. Padlocks mysteriously opened by themselves. In November, 1975, Florence's *Siuslaw News*

Heceta House and the Cape Creek bridge.

reported that a container of rat poison in the attic had apparently been exchanged for a single silk stocking. Later, a workman claimed to have seen a gray-haired woman in the attic wearing an 1890s-style gown.

"When they started converting one of the best view bedrooms into a pair of dormitory-style toilets, the horror stories began," Korgan says. "Workmen left their jobs and wouldn't come back."

Rue's name presented itself in a Ouija-board seance, shortly after a Coast Guard lighthouse keeper noticed that an attic window kept opening on its own. When the keeper later visited the Korgans to reminisce, he explained that he could track Rue's wanderings because of a weird, special creak that issues from the seventh step of the empty stairway.

If you choose to stay at Heceta House—otherwise an excellent base for walking tours of the area—think twice before renting the west bedroom. That room not only contains the stairs to Rue's attic, but it also faces the lighthouse. As a result, a glaring beam bursts in through the window every ten seconds. One visitor wrote in the room's guestbook, "I dreamt I was at a Hollywood premiere all night, dressed in nothing but my nightgown."

If you'd rather visit Heceta Head on a day trip, the easiest place to start is at a beachside picnic area. Locals still call this delightful picnic spot Devils Elbow State Park. The name refers to the park's L-shaped ocean cove, where tricky currents bedeviled mariners in the late 1800s. Bureaucrats in the 1990s, determined to purge satanic references from state park names, rechristened the park Heceta Head Lighthouse Viewpoint. But the new, sanitized name is having trouble catching on—in part because the park does not actually have a very good view of the lighthouse. To see it properly, you'll want to hike up a half-mile path from the picnic area.

From the Devils Elbow, the lighthouse trail climbs gradually amid sa-lal meadows and Sitka spruce groves. Along the way you'll pass Heceta House, with its dramatic view of the graceful arch of Highway 101's Cape Creek Bridge. The trail ends beside the 56-foot tower of the 1890 light-house, at a railed lawn methodically trimmed by rabbits.

Bring binoculars to get a good look at the other wildlife here. From April through August, seven thousand Brandt's cormorants roost on the rocks below the lighthouse, often standing in comic poses as they dry their wings. Heceta Head has the nation's largest mainland nesting colony of these black, long-necked birds. Tufted puffins once roosted here in profu-sion, too. Parrot Rock, the large island just offshore, was named not for parrots, but rather for its brightly plumed puffins. Because early light-house keepers and their families gathered eggs from the island, however, the colorful birds have become rare visitors here.

The name "Parrot Island" may be inappropriate, and "Devils Elbow" may be controversial, but none of the place names here is as hotly debated as "Heceta" itself. Most people pronounce the word *huh-SEE-tuh*. A vehe-ment minority, however, contend it should really be spoken *HECK-uh-tuh*. A few sticklers point out that the cape's discoverer, Bruno de Heceta, was captaining a Spanish ship, and that in Castilian Spanish his name would be pronounced *ay-THAY-tuh*. Considering that Bruno de Heceta was actu-ally Portuguese, and thus probably referred to himself as *ay-SAY-tuh,* the argument is unlikely to be settled anytime soon.

The Spanish had sent Captain Heceta north toward Oregon on a secret mission. On March 16, 1775, he sailed from San Blas, Mexico in the *Santiago* with forty-five men and one year's provisions. His secret orders were to "land often, take possession, erect a cross, and plant a bottle containing a record of the act of possession" along the Pacific Coast as far north as Alaska. By the time Heceta named this Oregon headland, however, scurvy had ravaged his crew so badly that he was forced to turn back.

The lighthouse here was the last of Oregon's dozen major lighthouses to be built. A boat delivered the two-ton Fresnel lens, with its 640 deli-cate, hand-ground prisms, through the Devils Elbow's tricky currents to the beach below the lighthouse site in October, 1892. Bricks for the tower were shipped from San Francisco to Florence, carted down the beach,

35. Heceta Head

HIKE LOCATION

Easy (from Devils Elbow)
1 mile round trip
200 feet elevation gain

Moderate (from Highway 101)
2.6 miles round trip
600 feet elevation gain

Walk to Oregon's most photographed lighthouse—and a haunted house.

Getting There: Drive Highway 101 north of Florence 12 miles. Just beyond a tunnel, turn downhill to Heceta Head Lighthouse Viewpoint (alias Devils Elbow State Park). Expect a $5-per-car fee in summer.

Hiking Tips: The trail starts at the far end of the parking lot and climbs 0.3 mile to a service road. First walk to the right to Heceta House, where an interpretive center is open from noon to 5pm Thursday through Monday in summer. For bed & breakfast reservations call 866-547-3696 or check *www.hecetalighthouse.com*. Then walk left on the road 0.2 mile to the lighthouse, open for tours 11am to 5pm daily from March through October.

A slightly longer trail to the lighthouse avoids crowds and parking fees. To find this path, drive 1 mile north of the tunnel on Highway 101 to a paved pullout on the right signed "Overnight Camping Prohibited." Walk 100 feet north and cross the highway to find a Beach Trail post. When the path forks after 50 feet, keep left. After 1.3 miles the path switchbacks down to the lighthouse.

Season: Open all year.

While You're in the Area: Drive a mile south of Heceta Head to the Sea Lion Caves, one of the few really worthwhile commercial attractions on the Oregon Coast. The 100-foot-tall sea grotto still has dozens of wild sea lions, although 200,000 tourists ride an elevator down to see them each year.

The Heceta Head lighthouse.

and hauled over the hills on wagons. Workers completed construction of the tower and adjacent buildings by August, 1893, but the light still did not become operational for seven months, until the lamp and the Head Keeper himself finally arrived. The tower first opened for public tours a hundred years later, in 1994. If a volunteer is on hand, you can climb up to see the giant, rotating lens. On clear days the lens is shielded from the sun by a curtain to prevent the prisms from melting the metal lamp fittings or igniting forest fires on the wooded slope nearby.

As you walk back from the lighthouse, imagine the lighthouse keepers who trudged this trail in all kinds of weather, every day for years, on their way to work. Military efficiency structured their lives. Three employees took shifts around the clock to tend the light—carrying kerosene, trimming the wick, winding the lens mechanism, and polishing the glass. The Head Keeper earned $800 a month. He lived nearest the lighthouse in an elaborate house (now demolished) that was decorated with a six-armed chandelier. The two assistant lighthouse keepers had quarters next door in Heceta House. The first assistant earned $600 a month and lived in the side of this duplex with a five-armed chandelier. The second assistant had to live on the side farthest from the lighthouse. He earned only $500 and had to be satisfied with a four-armed chandelier. The Heceta House chandeliers remain as testimony of the strict hierarchy.

The staff's families formed an active little community, gardening and fishing for their food. They sometimes complained, however, that the wagon road to Florence was so rough and muddy that the trip took five to seven hours each way. Things changed dramatically in 1931-32, when ninety workers camped nearby to finish construction of the Roosevelt Highway — known today as Highway 101. Named for President Theodore Roosevelt, the highway had begun as a military project in World War I to provide for troop movement along the West Coast. By 1931, the route's only remaining gaps were a few unbridged rivers and the rugged shoreline near Heceta Head. Workers arduously blasted a tunnel through the cliffs above the churning Devils Elbow. Then they built a high, connecting bridge that leapt 220 feet across Cape Creek's chasm to Heceta Head. Conde McCullough, an inspired Oregon highway engineer famed for his graceful bridge designs, modeled the $150,000 bridge after Roman aqueducts he had seen in Europe.

When electric powerlines arrived along the new highway in 1934, the Coast Guard replaced the lighthouse's kerosene lamp with a 500-watt bulb. The staff shrank to two men, and then just one. The last lighthouse keeper left when the light was completely automated in 1963.

After years of neglect, many of the lighthouse complex's original buildings were torn down. But a handful of concerned citizens succeeded in preserving Heceta House as a historic landmark in 1978. Were they perhaps aided by the mysterious Rue? To this day, the ghost seems determined to defend the old house against change.

"Not long ago the Forest Service decided to insulate Rue's attic," says bed-and-breakfast host Mike Korgan. "The unopened bags of insulation are still sitting up there, right next to the staple guns the workmen abandoned." He laughs. Then he adds, "What self-respecting spook would want to live in an insulated attic?"

Cape Blanco

The story of the Patrick Hughes family keeps cropping up in the history of the picturesque 1870 lighthouse in Cape Blanco State Park, on the Southern Oregon coast near Port Orford. In fact, the story lines cross so often that it's fair to start the tale — and your Cape Blanco hike — two miles away from the lighthouse, on the doorstep of the Hughes' restored Victorian mansion.

Hang onto your hat as you walk up to the ornate porch, because a bracing breeze nearly always blows across the grassy slope surrounding the 1898 house. Cape Blanco is Oregon's westernmost point, jutting so far out to sea that the North Pacific winds seem genuinely surprised to find this solidly build Victorian house in their way. Most visitors, too, wonder why such a lavish old home should be standing alone on an isolated part of the Southern Oregon coast.

When you step inside you'll see a rose-colored chandelier lighting a

The Cape Blanco lighthouse.

tall-ceilinged foyer. Doorways lead to two formal parlors and a dining room. A mahogany banister curves upstairs to a Roman Catholic chapel. Throughout the house, the walls have been built not merely with two-by-fours, but rather with two-by-eight beams of rare, straight-grained Port Orford cedar. Altogether the cross-shaped Victorian house cost Patrick Hughes $3800—a very large sum in 1898.

And yet Patrick Hughes grew up a pauper in one of the world's poorest nations. Born in 1830 in County Tyrone of Ireland, Patrick survived the Potato Famine that claimed the lives of one million Irish in the 1840s. Another million of Patrick's eight-and-a-half million countrymen emigrated to the United States. In 1850, he joined that hopeful migration, fired by word that gold had been discovered in California. Many of the emigrants would die on board the ship to America, and most of the survivors ended up in Boston's Irish ghetto, barred from well-paid jobs. Patrick worked five years in Boston before he could afford the fare to California. During that time he met and married Jane O'Neil, an Irish girl from his home county.

The heyday of California's gold rush had long since passed when Patrick finally reached San Francisco in 1855. Tantalizing reports of gold in the black sands of Southern Oregon's beaches, however, lured Patrick and Jane north. In Oregon, too, Patrick found the best mining land already claimed. Without the cash to buy in, he took the only work he could get, as a farm laborer. In 1860, when his employer couldn't pay his wages, Patrick shrewdly offered to accept land instead: eighty acres of pasture on the Sixes River beside Cape Blanco. He and Jane started a dairy and soon were shipping high-quality butter to San Francisco. They prospered, gradually expanding their holdings until they owned the entire 1800 acres now preserved as Cape Blanco State Park. In 1868 Patrick even managed to realize his gold rush dream by buying a small beach mine from William O'Sullivan, a fellow Irishman who had been the first to stake a claim nearby.

Meanwhile, Patrick and Jane raised a family of five boys and two girls. The first son became a bachelor schoolteacher. The second served for twenty years as Head Keeper of the nearby lighthouse. The third son, bowing to the devout Patrick's wishes, became a Roman Catholic priest. The two daughters married and moved away to Port Orford and Eugene. The last two Hughes sons stayed on their parents' farm. The youngest son's bride, Annie, outlived the rest of the family to become the last resident of the Hughes mansion.

After touring the Hughes House, drive or walk a quarter mile down to a trailhead beside the Sixes River. The river's name recalls a Tututni village that once stood near the ocean here. The villagers called themselves *Sik-ses-tene,* "people by the far north country," because they had settled so close to the border with the Coquille tribe to the north. By the time Patrick Hughes arrived, however, the village was empty. The Tututnis had already lost battles against the whites at Port Orford (see Hike #13) and in the Rogue River canyon (Hike #29), and had been transported by the U.S. Army to a distant reservation in the northern Oregon Coast Range.

The 1898 Hughes House museum.

From the picnic area, follow a mowed path across the Hughes' long-abandoned dairy pasture to the beach. Walk left along the sand a mile, with the lighthouse ahead winking at you every thirty seconds. From here Cape Blanco's flat-topped headland looks like a beached aircraft carrier. It's hard to imagine why Sebastian Vizcaino, a Spanish explorer sailing north from Mexico in 1602, named this dark ochre headland *Cabo Blanco,* "white cape." Even the Tututnis' poetic name for the protruding cape, *Penyekwet,* "fingernail upon," lends itself to more plausible interpretations.

A stone's throw before the beach runs out of sand, take a trail up a slope to the neck of the cape. Then walk along a service road to the lighthouse plateau, nearly two hundred feet above the sea. A substantial spruce forest once grew on this windy plateau, perhaps a remnant of a time when the cape was larger. When the U.S. Lighthouse Board bought the headland's tip in 1867, they ordered the forest cleared to improve the view and to "prevent to some extent the fogs that so frequently hang over the cape." They contracted to have 200,000 bricks made at a makeshift kiln on Patrick Hughes' land, but found them worthless and ordered new ones made. The rest of the lighthouse materials arrived from San Francisco by ship. The ship had time to unload only part of its cargo here, however, before a storm drove it offshore and wrecked it. The lens arrived safely with a separate ship in 1870.

The oldest continuously operated lighthouse in Oregon, the beacon burned lard oil for its first seventeen years, then switched to mineral oil and finally to electricity. Before Patrick Hughes' son took over as Head Keeper, the lighthouse had its share of personnel problems. In 1887, for example, Second Assistant Keeper John Goodman hit First Assistant Keeper August Miller over the head with a stick, sending him to Port Orford for a doctor. Goodman resigned the next day, but was hired back the next year as a laborer.

After visiting the lighthouse, return to the Hughes House museum on a different route, following a path through the blufftop fields. But before

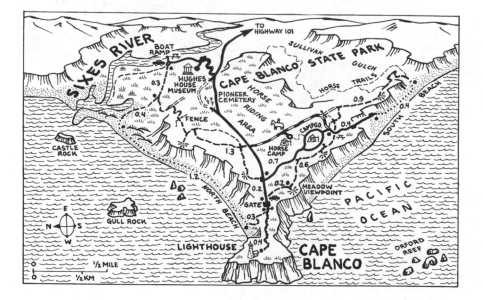

driving away from Cape Blanco State Park, stop along the lighthouse road to visit the crooked marble tombstones of a small pioneer cemetery. Here, five years before Patrick and Jane Hughes started work on their mansion, they built a small Catholic church, Mary Star of the Sea. And here their third son, John, dedicated to the priesthood by his devout parents, laid to earth the family's members one by one. That devotion, perhaps, may help explain why there are no ghost stories at Cape Blanco.

36. Cape Blanco

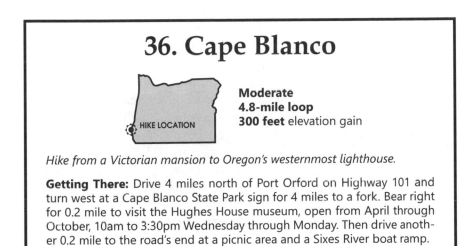

Moderate
4.8-mile loop
300 feet elevation gain

Hike from a Victorian mansion to Oregon's westernmost lighthouse.

Getting There: Drive 4 miles north of Port Orford on Highway 101 and turn west at a Cape Blanco State Park sign for 4 miles to a fork. Bear right for 0.2 mile to visit the Hughes House museum, open from April through October, 10am to 3:30pm Wednesday through Monday. Then drive another 0.2 mile to the road's end at a picnic area and a Sixes River boat ramp.

Hiking Tips: Two mowed paths cross a pasture from the trailhead gate at the Sixes River boat ramp. Take the left-hand trail for 0.3 mile, and then fork to the right for 0.4 mile to the beach. Walk left along the beach 1.2 miles toward the lighthouse. Just before the beach runs out of sand, look for a trail up a meadowed slope to the left. Climb this path 0.3 mile to the cape's crest and follow a service road 0.4 mile to the lighthouse. It's open for a $2 fee from April through October, 10am-3:30pm Wednesday-Monday.

To return on a loop, hike back on the road 0.6 mile to a trail post on the left, opposite the campground entrance. Go left on a mowed path across a meadow. Then keep left at junctions for 1.3 miles, passing cliff-edge viewpoints and brushy fields before descending to the pasture by your car.

Season: Open all year.

While You're in the Area: Cape Blanco State Park's 58-site campground is open year round and does not accept reservations, but usually fills only on summer weekends. If you're driving south on Highway 101, stop by Port Orford to see Battle Rock and Humbug Mountain (Hike #13). If you're heading north, pull into Bandon (Hike #6) to see its Old Town and beach.

CHAPTER X

Boom Years

A wave of prosperity and optimism flooded through Oregon at the beginning of the 1900s, launching grandiose development schemes from Portland to the backwoods of Josephine County. Although the arrival of the Great Depression in 1929 dried up many of those dreams, hikers today can still find parks, beaches, and streets that echo with memories from the heady days when money made all things seem possible.

Start with a street ramble through Portland's Old Town, the financial heart of Oregon's economic booms. Next hike to the sites of a vanished amusement park, a vanished coastal resort, and the vanished country mansion of a family dynasty. Then plan to visit two famous parks where the gleam of Oregon's gilded age has been restored to its brightest polish.

Old Town Portland

When MAX, Portland's modern light-rail train, slides into downtown weekday mornings, crowds of commuters step off at Pioneer Courthouse Square, raise their umbrellas against the drizzle, and hurry into the urban canyonlands. One of the umbrellaed businessmen on the paved plaza is forever frozen in mid-stride, a bronze statue capturing the modern spirit of the city's center. But other sculptures nearby — depicting life-sized deer, bear, otters, and ducks — recall that this was not always the center of a metropolis. In fact, Portland arose from the forest by fits and starts, with setbacks and scandals interrupting the boom years.

For a walking tour of Portland's checkered past, head downhill across Courthouse Square to Yamhill Street, and set your sights toward the river. The riverbank is where Portland's written history began, but these days you'll have to squint pretty hard to picture the original Willamette view. Imagine peering through the woods to a small riverbank clearing, an abandoned campsite of the Multnomah tribe. Now imagine a business-man named Asa Lovejoy bumping into a rollicking drifter by the name

Bronze statue of a commuter at Portland's Pioneer Courthouse Square.

of William Overton in that clearing. During that 1843 encounter, Overton mused that he'd like to stake a 640-acre homestead claim on the spot if only he had twenty-five cents for the filing fee. The cagey Lovejoy replied that he would gladly provide two bits in exchange for half the land. And thus Portland's financial heart began to beat.

Within a year Overton had drifted on to other adventures, merrily trading the remaining half of his claim to a speculator named Francis Pettygrove for fifty dollars' worth of traveling supplies. This left Pettygrove and Lovejoy to plat the streets for the new town. When they went to file the plat at the Oregon City recording office, however, they couldn't agree on the new town's name. Each wanted to honor his home port. Lovejoy hailed from Boston while Pettygrove came from Portland, Maine. They tossed an 1835 copper penny three times to decide. Pettygrove won the toss and kept the penny—a coin you'll be able to see later on your street ramble through Old Town.

In 1844 Lovejoy and Pettygrove built Portland's first house, a log cabin that served as a store and tavern at First and Washington, hoping that trade would come their way. They knew several other cities already were vying to become the supply point for farms in the rich Willamette and Tualatin Valleys. The upstart settlement at Portland leaped to prominence in 1846 when the influential Captain John Couch of Massachusetts chose it as his headquarters, declaring, "To this very point I can bring any ship that can get into the mouth of the Columbia River. And not, sir, a rod further."

With the completion of the Canyon Road—a muddy track through the West Hills—Tualatin Valley farmers had a way to drive their wheat and cattle down to the town's riverbank. The road's promoter, Daniel Lownsdale, bought up land near the road in 1848 and opened a tannery on the site of what became Multnomah Stadium (now Providence Park). Sawmills opened in 1849 and 1850, supplying the lucrative San Francisco gold rush trade by clearing nearby forests. Soon the townsite had so many stumps they were painted white to keep people from tripping over them in the dark. Envious boosters of rival towns derided the white-dotted village as "Stumptown-on-the-Willamette." But by then Portland was unstoppable.

As you start your urban ramble down Yamhill Street, you'll walk alongside the Pioneer Courthouse. When Portland's city fathers sold the U.S. government this block for a post office in 1869, locals ridiculed the sale as a scam. The site, they declared, was so far from Portland's riverfront center that postal officials would need a pony express to deliver mail. Other critics complained about the building's design, noting that the roof's octagonal wooden cupola was antique even for 1869. When a new federal courthouse made the building obsolete in 1933, it was almost razed. But by then Portlanders had grown fond of the landmark, and a public outcry saved it from the wrecking ball. Renovated in 1971 for use by the Ninth U.S. Circuit Court, the courthouse is now one of Portland's treasures—and the West's oldest public building still in use.

Looming behind the Pioneer Courthouse is the elegant twelve-story terra cotta face of the Meier & Frank Building. Completed in 1932 under the motto "Portland's Own Store," the building remains a landmark to the city's most powerful merchant dynasty. Aaron Meier had originally set up a small general store on Front Street in 1857. Fifteen years later he hired a young German music student, Sigmund Frank, as a clerk. Frank proved so ambitious that he became a partner in 1874, married Meier's daughter Fanny in 1885, and took over the business after Meier's death in 1889. The family gained influence as the store grew. In 1931 company vice president Julius Meier was elected Oregon governor. The family finally sold the building in 1967 to Macy's, which still runs a department store there.

Just the opposite kind of emporium, a ragtag public market, thrived on the other side of the Pioneer Courthouse from 1914 to 1933. As you walk down Yamhill Street, picture the curbs lined with colorful stalls from Fifth to Third Avenue. For nearly twenty years, crowds jammed this street bazaar to buy fresh fruit, vegetables, and flowers direct from local growers.

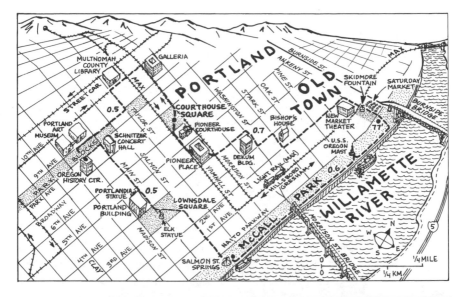

37. Old Town Portland

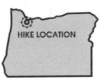

HIKE LOCATION

Easy
2.3-mile loop
100 feet elevation gain

Take a street ramble through Old Town to Portland's riverfront.

Getting There: Instead of driving to downtown Portland, take MAX or a bus. Get off at Pioneer Courthouse Square at 6th and Yamhill.

Hiking Tips: Use the map to find your way along Old Town's city streets to the riverfront and back. When you reach the park blocks, note that the Oregon History Center is open Tuesday-Saturday 10am-5pm and Sunday noon-5pm. Admission is $11 for adults, $9 for students and seniors, and $5 for children age 6-18.

Season: Open all year.

While You're in the Area: Oregon's largest bookstore, Powell's City of Books, occupies an entire block at 10th and Burnside. The store's 1-million-plus titles include a good history collection. On the riverfront, the Oregon Maritime Museum is housed aboard the 1947 steam-powered sternwheeler *Portland*. Docked at the foot of Pine Street, the ship is open Wednesday, Friday, and Saturday 11am-4pm. Admission runs $7 per adult, $4 for kids age 13-18, and $3 for ages 6-12.

The Yamhill Public Market was not only popular with shoppers, but it also launched the careers of scrappy young merchants—most notably the German-born, Brooklyn-raised Fred Grubmeyer. At the age of nineteen, Grubmeyer had ridden the rails out West, hoping to strike it rich in the Klondike gold rush. But gold fever had already passed when he arrived in 1905. Innocently, the young man let a slick-talking Seattle salesman sell him a Portland store, sight unseen. The store proved to be a ruin in a rundown neighborhood near the train station. Sobered by this deception, the determined Grubmeyer loaded the store's goods into a wagon and peddled them to local logging camps. He used the profits to open coffee and tea stalls downtown at the new public market on Yamhill Street. By 1917, bowing to anti-German sentiment in World War I, he shortened his name to Fred Meyer.

The Bishop's House.

Despite the Yamhill Public Market's immense popularity, City Council businessmen grumbled that vendors were using city property rent-free and were leaving rotten vegetables in the gutters. The politicians voted to force the free-spirited market into a building on the waterfront in 1933, where the market died. But Fred Meyer, with increasingly savvy business sense, was already a step ahead of them. He opened a store at Fifth and Morrison, pioneering the use of coupons, case lot discounts, and products priced with stickers so customers could choose purchases by themselves. By the time the modest, bow-tie-wearing Fred Meyer died in 1978, his business had grown to the nation's forty-fifth largest retailing chain, with more than a hundred self-service superstores.

Today the ragtag market stalls along Yamhill Street have been replaced by Saks Fifth Avenue and Pioneer Place. Veer left into Pioneer Place, cutting diagonally through this upscale, four-story atrium to take a look at its seventy shops and central fountain. Then zigzag another two blocks toward the river to the Dekum Building, an ornate 1892 office tower. The original builder, Frank Dekum, was a Bavarian pastry chef who founded Portland's German Songbird Society. Dekum insisted that his entire building be constructed solely from materials native to Oregon. Note the decorative sandstone griffins and the red brick of the upper five stories—nicely restored in the 1980s by Portland businessman Bill Naito.

Walk onward another block to Stark Street and you'll pass another nineteenth-century relic, the Bishop's House. With its Gothic windows and seventeen-foot high ceilings, this was once the elegant domain of Archbishop Blanchet. The Roman Catholic Church built Blanchet's house in 1879 to accompany a cathedral next door. After the cathedral moved in the 1890s, however, the Bishop's House fell on hard times. For years it served as the incense-clouded headquarters of a tong, a Chinese society. Later it reeked with cigarette smoke as a Prohibition-era speakeasy. Restored in 1965, it now houses a restaurant and a private apartment.

When you turn the corner onto Old Town's Second Avenue, you'll start seeing more taverns. This was especially true in the 1870s, when Portland had one saloon for every forty inhabitants. In fact, alcohol took such a toll on the early city's family life that Portland women formed the Women's Temperance Prayer League on March 18, 1874, vowing to "pray down saloons." The ladies of the league launched their crusade by singing hymns outside the notorious Webfoot Saloon at First and Morrison. For a while the owner, Walter Mofett, tried to compete by shouting Bible passages at them. Then he tried banging a Chinese gong. When the women simply kept on singing, Mofett's frustrated bartender doused them with a fire hose. Drenched but defiant, the stalwart women still sang. Gradually a crowd of a thousand gathered to watch the standoff. Eventually, a rock thrown from somewhere in the mob of bystanders sailed through saloon's front window with a crash. Other vandals pushed their way inside and began smashing glassware. Meanwhile, the ladies outside did nothing but sing hymns.

Finally Mofett called in the police. They arrested twenty-one of the hymn-singing women and hauled them before a judge for inciting a riot. The judge sentenced them to five dollars apiece or twenty-four hours in jail, fully expecting that the ladies would never sully themselves by doing time in Portland's crowded, dirty lockup. To his surprise, the women refused the fine, declaring that this was a matter of principle. Heads high, they marched to prison. That evening Portland's jailhouse rocked with a festive atmosphere. Visitors brought food and tea and helped the ladies belt out hymns. Finally the jailors threw up their hands and released the women — ahead of schedule.

Temperance protests did not prevent August Erickson, a Portland immigrant from the Swedish-speaking portion of Finland, from opening the world's longest bar ten years later. The colossal tavern is no more, but when you reach the bend of Second Avenue, stop for a moment to imagine it on the corner ahead. Filling most of a city block on Burnside between Second and Third Avenues, Erickson's establishment boasted a counter that snaked around a gigantic main floor for a record-breaking total of 684 linear feet. Perhaps to discourage protests, females were not allowed on the floor. The tavern's walls, however, were decorated with huge, "classical" oil paintings of female nudes. A concert stage featured a "$5000 Grand Pipe Organ." Visitors lured by Erickson's advertisements for a "Dainty Free Lunch" discovered that this gratis Scandinavian feast consisted of a roast quarter steer cut into one-and-a-half-inch-thick slabs, pails of pickled herring, platters of cheese and sausage, and quart jars of homemade mustard. Pint schooners of beer were for sale to wash it all down, of course, but even they cost only a nickel. Shots of whiskey were available at the reasonable price of three for a quarter.

The fame of Erickson's bar spread so far, and its clientele became so devoted, that even the flood of 1894 could not staunch the flow of spirits. The accommodating Finn simply moored a houseboat in the middle of Burnside Street and shifted operations there. Customers who managed to pole logs or paddle boats to this haven often stayed aboard for days—high, if not entirely dry.

By this point on your walk you probably will have noticed the four-armed drinking fountains that dot Old Town's sidewalks. These bronze fixtures represent a later salvo in the temperance wars against Portland's saloons. Simon Benson, developer of the Benson Hotel, donated twenty of the fountains in 1912 after he discovered he couldn't order a glass of water in downtown Portland without ordering a beer. Benson's water fountains are said to have cut saloon business twenty-five percent. Prohibition arrived eight years later, dealing the town's barkeeps a body blow. Erickson's closed for good, and his long-time supplier, the Blitz-Weinhard brewery a few blocks up Burnside, only survived by bottling fruit drinks during the dry years. Even today, who can say if the temperance wars are over? Microbreweries have sprouted throughout Old Town. But on the other hand, the number of Benson-style, saloon-battling water fountains on the streets has gradually climbed to fifty.

Old Town Portland has had trouble keeping dry in other ways as well. When the Willamette River jumped its banks in 1876, businessmen piled bricks on the wooden sidewalks to keep them from floating away. Rickety bridges spanned streets to shops, but pedestrians often fell in anyway. One hotel installed a temporary false floor several feet above the original. During the flood of 1894, when Erickson's bar moved to a barge, 1500 boats crowded Old Town's canal-like streets. Chinese locals staged a gala boat race from the New Market Theater up Second Street to Stark and

Morrison Street in the flood of 1894.

back on First. Winning time for the eight-block course was five minutes flat, a record that is likely to stand for some time.

Look for the floods' high-water marks on the stone building at 133 Second Avenue. The lines show that water stood five feet deep here in 1894, and two feet deep in 1948. The '48 flood has gone down in history as the deluge that washed away the 18,500-population city of Vanport a few miles downriver, but it also dunked Portland pretty thoroughly. At the flood's height, one quick-thinking angler managed to catch a fifteen-pound steelhead *inside* the Union Station train depot.

When you reach Ankeny Street, turn right at the corner of the New Market Theater. Actually this "new" theater is one of the city's oldest buildings, a posh establishment built by Alexander Ankeny for the phenomenal sum of $100,000 in 1875. Ankeny modeled it after London's chic Covent Garden, with a public market on the ground floor, a theater on the second, and a cafe on the third. An immediate success, the theater became the place to see and be seen in the Northwest. Ankeny swapped the lucrative theater and an entire surrounding city block in 1879 in exchange for the Sterling gold mine in Southern Oregon. The new owner was David Thompson, a former Idaho Territory governor and future Portland mayor. Thompson had no trouble packing the hall year after year — notably for an 1884 boxing exhibition by world champion John L. Sullivan.

From the New Market Theater, cross First Street to the soothing water sounds of the Skidmore Fountain. When prominent druggist Stephen Skidmore died in 1883, he left $5000 for a fountain to quench the thirst of "horses, men, and dogs." For its unveiling in 1888, Henry Weinhard offered to run a hose from his brewery so the fountain could spout beer on opening day. City fathers refused the heady donation. The following year, however, when people at the fountain looked up to see a professor dangling from a hot-air balloon, they might well have wondered what they had been drinking.

The hot-air balloon exhibition was one of three staged by Philadelphia professor P. H. Redmond along Portland's riverbank on successive Sundays in September, 1889. On the first Sunday thousands watched as the professor ascended from the east bank of the Willamette, hanging from a trapeze. The balloon dipped, however, dragging him ignominiously through the river. The following Sunday winds tore the balloon loose before Professor Redmond could climb onto his trapeze. Meanwhile, however, an overeager twelve-year-old boy had become tangled in the balloon's lines. The lad zoomed up a thousand feet in the air, dangling perilously for seven minutes. He landed, frightened but unharmed, in Southeast Portland and was promptly put on display in the New World's Museum on First and Madison, where hundreds of people paid ten cents apiece to view him. On Professor Redmond's third and final Sunday show, a crowd of 3500 turned out to watch the bungling scholar attempt his trapeze stunt one last time. To their satisfaction, he soared 3000 feet into the sky, leapt free of his trapeze according to plan, successfully inflated a parachute, and then sailed to a painful landing on a picket fence.

Since the 1970s the block between the Skidmore Fountain and the Naito Parkway has been home to Saturday Market, a tie-dyed reincarnation of Portland's freewheeling old Yamhill Public Market. Rain or shine, every Saturday and Sunday from March through December the place sprouts colorful booths where local craftsmen and artists sell their wares.

Cross the Naito Parkway to the lawns of Governor Tom McCall Waterfront Park and turn right on a promenade along the riverbank's concrete seawall. Certainly no part of Portland's Old Town has changed so much over the years as the riverfront. For most of the city's first century, unusual two-story docks lined the river, so that even during the high water of spring floods, goods could be unloaded onto the wharves' upper level. During the rest of the year, however, the shadowy, lower level became notorious as a harbor for rats, drunks, shanghai men, and pimps. Pipes

Tom McCall Waterfront Park.

poured the entire city's sewage into the river here with a dizzying stench. Finally in 1929 the city tore down the old docks, laid a sewer main, and filled in the waterfront to a new seawall, adding a wide strip of reclaimed land to downtown.

This new riverfront land became the final resting place for the Yamhill Public Market. In the depths of the Great Depression, the city built a massive, three-block-long concrete barn to replace the market's popular street stalls. Eighteen thousand customers and 246 farmers petitioned the city, objecting that the new building would be too far away and too expensive. The petitions fell on deaf ears. When the echoing hall opened in 1933, blocking the riverfront from Morrison to Salmon Street, two hundred of the vendors boycotted it. Those who came had to raise their prices, demanding five cents a pound for sugar, twenty-two cents a pound for coffee, and sixteen cents a pound for deer meat. After just three years, the cavernous building had to be put up for bankruptcy sale. In 1943, the Harbor Drive freeway completed the destruction of the old riverfront. Another generation passed before Portlanders began clamoring for a return to the river, the old town's heart. Finally the city demolished the monstrous building in 1968 and tore up the freeway in 1974, making room for the popular lawns and promenades of Governor Tom McCall Waterfront Park.

Like an empty fireplace mantle, the riverside park keeps collecting knickknacks. First you'll pass the salvaged mast of the *USS Oregon*, the

1893 "Bulldog of the Navy" that fought proudly in the Spanish-American War, ran humble coastal patrols in World War I, and finally was downgraded to an ammo barge in World War II before being intentionally scuttled in a Guam lagoon. Next you'll see a bronze plaque commemorating James B. Stephens, the Virginia pioneer who opened the mule-powered Stark Street Ferry here in 1853. Portland's first bridge opened next door at Morrison Street in 1887, but because it was privately owned, the toll was set relatively high, at a nickel per person. As a result, the Stark Street Ferry kept running until 1895, when the city bought the bridge for $150,000 and dropped the toll. Nine years later the original Morrison Street Bridge had to be replaced with the current structure.

A few blocks beyond the bridge, head inland to Salmon Street Springs, a gigantic fountain with 185 jets controlled by a computer panel hidden underground. Dedicated in 1988, the fountain's display changes at different times of the day, spouting up to 4924 gallons of recycled water a minute. That kind of water power might have saved Portland in 1873, when a devastating fire wiped out twenty-two city blocks in this area—essentially every building between the river and Second Avenue from Morrison to Clay streets.

Cross the Naito Parkway and head inland on Salmon Street beneath the glass skybridge of Portland's World Trade Center. After a couple of blocks, angle across Lownsdale Square, a park block donated in 1852, at a time when an elk was still said to graze here. The current elk statue in the middle of Main Street dates to 1900, when Portland mayor David Thompson (owner of the New Market Theater) paid sculptor Roland Perry $20,000 for the work. He invited the Exalted Order of Elks to attend the unveiling. They refused, criticizing the statue as a "monstrosity" with a neck that would be "the envy of a giraffe." Since then, others have tried to dislodge the elk as a traffic hazard, or to have it painted, deriding it as a "gargoyle quadruped" and a "fossilized stag." But it remains, watching over Lownsdale Square and the adjacent park block, Chapman Square. Surveillance was particularly needed here in 1924, when city officials conceded that the two blocks were plagued by an "infestation of mashers." To restore decency, the city segregated the two parks for decades, reserving one for men and the other exclusively for women.

As you continue up Main Street from the elk you'll pass the Portland Building, a postmodern office tower that raised eyebrows in 1983 for its daring angles and its teal-rust-cream color scheme. Critics have since relented, perhaps swayed by *Portlandia,* an arresting, two-story-tall copper woman crouched triumphantly above the front door. The hammered copper sculpture is the world's second largest, after the Statue of Liberty.

A couple more blocks up Main Street brings you to the Portland Center for the Performing Arts. To your right, a palatial old movie theater has been revamped to create the Arlene Schnitzer Concert Hall (popularly, "the Schnitz"). In the process, the movie house's gaudily lit, seven-story "Paramount" signboard was subtly relettered to read "Portland."

Beyond the concert hall, turn left along Park Avenue to the Oregon History Center. Here you'll find four stories of exhibits—including Pettygrove's famous 1835 penny. The museum's site was once the start of Canyon Road, the muddy track that allowed Tualatin Valley farmers to bring their produce to Portland's docks. Daniel Lownsdale championed this road from the first, and was on hand here in 1851 when a gold coin was placed under the first board in a plank pavement that eventually covered the route's notorious mud. The next year, the civic-minded Lownsdale convinced Benjamin Stark and two other major landowners to help him set aside a string of twenty-five blocks along Park Avenue for public use.

As you walk north through the park blocks to complete your street ramble, you'll notice that the original series of twenty-five blocks is broken in the middle. Benjamin Stark's heirs reneged on the agreement with Lownsdale and sold seven central park blocks to private buyers. That loss has long been a sore point for Portlanders. Finally, when one of the developed blocks was scheduled to become a parking garage in 1998, developer Thomas Moyer donated $5 million to put the garage underground and create another park block for the city after all.

At Taylor Street, at the corner of the newly opened park block, detour left to visit the stately Multnomah County Central Library. Built in 1913 and renovated in 1997, the library retains the elegance of Portland's boom years. It also houses more than seventeen miles of bookshelves. A block later, turn right at the corner of the Galleria. This building opened in 1910 as Olds, Wortman, and King, the first department store west of the Mississippi. Now it houses a Target department store.

Walk back beside the MAX rail lines to conclude your loop hike at Courthouse Square. This plaza was the site of Portland's first genuine schoolhouse in 1858. Later it was home to the opulent Portland Hotel. Then it languished as a parking lot. In the 1970s, more than 64,000 citizens helped fund its conversion to an urban park by buying pavement bricks inscribed with donors' names. In many ways, Courthouse Square's past mirrors the entire city's history, careening through boom years, depression, and renewal. Caught as bronze statues, the plaza's otters and the umbrella-carrying commuter remain to serve as bookends for that multi-volume tale.

Council Crest

At the peak of Portland's early 1900s boom, dashing gents in bowler hats and elegant ladies with parasols would ride an electric trolley to the city's highest point, Council Crest, where a roller coaster circled an amusement park. Today the trolley and the amusement park are gone, but the wide-angle view still beckons, sweeping across Portland to five Cascade peaks. Of course it's now possible to drive to Council Crest, but it's more fun to hike there on the Marquam Trail. Then you can return on a 4.4-mile loop that includes a free ride on Portland's aerial tram.

Start at the Oregon Zoo, walk an overpass across Canyon Road, and hike the Marquam Trail up through a forest of maples and Douglas firs. In spring, watch for white woodland wildflowers: three-petaled trillium, star-flowered solomonseal, and bell-shaped fringecup. In summer, the delicate fronds of maidenhair ferns wave on black stalks above the trail. In autumn, vine maple's pinwheel-shaped leaves paint the woods scarlet.

In the late 1800s, developers lamented that hiking trails like this were the only way to reach the panoramic real estate atop Council Crest and Portland Heights. This otherwise valuable land lay only a mile from downtown, but nearly a thousand feet higher. During Portland's early boom years, the demand for construction of a streetcar line up these imposing hills was so great that two companies went bankrupt trying.

Portland's love affair with light rail began rather slowly in 1872, when Ben Holladay, czar of the Oregon & California Railroad, opened a simple horse-drawn trolley along First Avenue from Union Station to downtown. The little streetcar must have seemed insignificant compared to Portland's fleet of thirty steam-driven riverboats and the heavy railroad trains that rumbled off each day toward Eugene and Hillsboro. Ten years passed before a second urban trolley was added, this time along Third Street. But once the Steel Bridge opened in 1889, enabling tracks to cross the river, steam-powered streetcars were suddenly everywhere. A dozen competing trolley companies sprang up. At the height of the craze in the early 1900s, a thousand streetcars a day rattled across the river's bridges.

One of the trolley system's most daring efforts began in 1887, when the Portland Cable Railway Company bought the rights to try San Francisco's cable car system in Portland. The company also purchased most of Portland Heights, the hill halfway to Council Crest. Then engineers built a 1,040-foot trestle at a terrifying twenty-degree grade from 18th and Mill straight up to the new property, and the company began selling view lots.

The Council Crest streetcar line and amusement park, circa 1906.

Cable car experts from San Francisco briefly trained the new line's employees, but conductors still had trouble getting the hang of it. The hardest part was smoothly engaging the car's grip to the moving cable beneath the track. More than once, conductors accidentally jerked themselves through the glass of the cars' front windows. On one occasion, a car sped out of control and tipped on a corner. Although no one was seriously injured, the mishaps made view property hard to sell. The line lost money and sold at auction after just five years.

The Marquam Trail briefly follows a street on Portland Heights and then climbs through a wooded park to Council Crest's park lawn. Cross the lawn to the observation patio on the summit, where plaques identify sights from Mt. Rainier to Mt. Jefferson. Even in less-than-perfect weather, views still extend from Beaverton to the Fremont Bridge.

A widely circulated tale claims Council Crest won its name because Multnomah tribespeople met on the hilltop, built powwow fires, and overlooked their domain. But there is no evidence of native use here, and until developers cut the forests, the hilltop had no view. In fact, this was known as Talbot Mountain until 1898, when six carriage-loads of delegates to a Congregational Church Council drove up here for a picnic and rechristened the crest to commemorate their outing.

Eight years later, in 1906, the hilltop was converted to an amusement park, complete with roller coaster, observation tower, gigantic carousel, and landlocked riverboat. Pennants flew gaily about a carnival midway.

At about the same time, a competing amusement park opened at the end of a different streetcar line at Oaks Park, south of Portland. Council Crest's carnival is gone, but the one at Oaks Park survives, recalling the glitter and devil-may-care optimism of Portland's turn-of-the-century boom.

Portland's sudden infatuation with amusement parks was a spinoff of the grandest carnival of all, the 1905 Lewis and Clark Exposition and Ori-

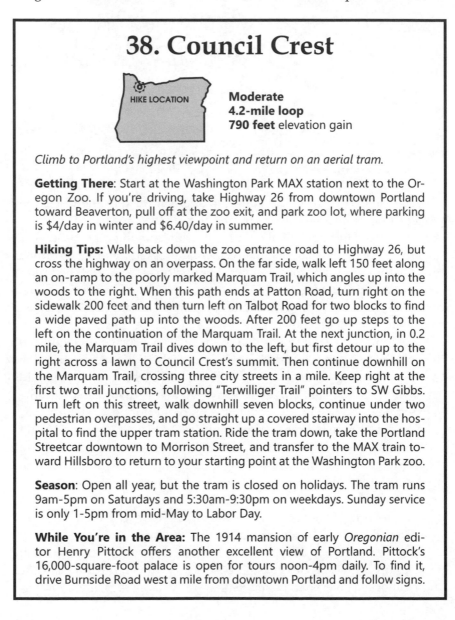

38. Council Crest

HIKE LOCATION

Moderate
4.2-mile loop
790 feet elevation gain

Climb to Portland's highest viewpoint and return on an aerial tram.

Getting There: Start at the Washington Park MAX station next to the Oregon Zoo. If you're driving, take Highway 26 from downtown Portland toward Beaverton, pull off at the zoo exit, and park zoo lot, where parking is $4/day in winter and $6.40/day in summer.

Hiking Tips: Walk back down the zoo entrance road to Highway 26, but cross the highway on an overpass. On the far side, walk left 150 feet along an on-ramp to the poorly marked Marquam Trail, which angles up into the woods to the right. When this path ends at Patton Road, turn right on the sidewalk 200 feet and then turn left on Talbot Road for two blocks to find a wide paved path up into the woods. After 200 feet go up steps to the left on the continuation of the Marquam Trail. At the next junction, in 0.2 mile, the Marquam Trail dives down to the left, but first detour up to the right across a lawn to Council Crest's summit. Then continue downhill on the Marquam Trail, crossing three city streets in a mile. Keep right at the first two trail junctions, following "Terwilliger Trail" pointers to SW Gibbs. Turn left on this street, walk downhill seven blocks, continue under two pedestrian overpasses, and go straight up a covered stairway into the hospital to find the upper tram station. Ride the tram down, take the Portland Streetcar downtown to Morrison Street, and transfer to the MAX train toward Hillsboro to return to your starting point at the Washington Park zoo.

Season: Open all year, but the tram is closed on holidays. The tram runs 9am-5pm on Saturdays and 5:30am-9:30pm on weekdays. Sunday service is only 1-5pm from mid-May to Labor Day.

While You're in the Area: The 1914 mansion of early *Oregonian* editor Henry Pittock offers another excellent view of Portland. Pittock's 16,000-square-foot palace is open for tours noon-4pm daily. To find it, drive Burnside Road west a mile from downtown Portland and follow signs.

ental Fair. This world-class festival, honoring the centennial of Lewis and Clark's visit, cost the U.S. Congress $1,775,000 and the Oregon Congress $450,000. The fairgrounds covered 406 acres overlooking Guilds Lake near Montgomery Park in Northwest Portland. The marshy slough had been dredged and then pumped full of water from the nearby Willamette River. A "Bridge of Pleasure" crossed to a peninsula with a race track, Wild West show, and livestock display. The midway, known as "The Trail," featured a contingent of Fiji Island "headhunters," camel rides in the "Streets of Cairo," a life-sized cow sculpture made entirely from butter, a Temple of Mirth, an Egyptian mummy, the shocking "Fatima" belly dancer, and the daring Floradora girls, who danced the Hootchy Kootchy with bare knees. Also on display was the Willamette Meteorite, a fifteen-ton rock resembling a six-foot peach pit. The alien stone had been discovered in the West Linn woods three years earlier when a farmer happened to hit it with an ax and it rang like a bell.

On June 5, 1905, President Theodore Roosevelt pressed a telegraph key in Washington, D.C to open the Lewis and Clark Exposition. The connection failed, but the fair opened nonetheless, drawing 39,577 visitors the first day. New-fangled electric lights allowed the carnival to continue long into the night, astonishing fairgoers with a "witchery of light." Two and a half million people visited in the fair's 137-day run. To transport the crowds, 125 specially built, open-sided electric streetcars ran a shuttle downtown, leaving every twenty seconds.

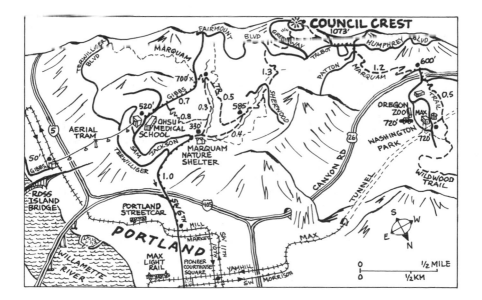

Portland's various competing trolley companies had merged in 1904 to form the Portland Consolidated Railway Company. With the success of the Lewis and Clark Exposition, the new company dared to reconsider construction of the problematic line to Council Crest. This time the planners nixed cable cars and massive trestles. Instead an ordinary streetcar track would run up Burnside Street to 23rd, turn left on Vista, wind through Portland Heights, and climb to a loop around Council Crest's new amusement park. The line opened successfully on September 20, 1906.

The Council Crest amusement park survived three decades, until the Great Depression finally squeezed the gaiety out of carnivals. The park's owners traded the land to the city in 1937 in exchange for an abandoned firehouse. Five years later the city built a huge water tank here. By then buses had replaced trolley lines on most streets. The Council Crest streetcar made its final trip in 1950, the last Portland trolley for half a century.

After you've taken in the view from Council Crest, return to the Marquam Trail, turn right, follow the path downhill through Marquam Nature Park. This quiet, forested canyon was originally saved from development because of the unstable geology that makes Portland's west hills such a tricky place to build. Although Ice Age glaciers never reached Portland, their outwash plains repeatedly filled the flatlands with dusty silt. During arid interglacial periods, huge dust storms blew this silt onto the hills, leaving a layer of slippery topsoil up to thirty feet thick. Prolonged rains can launch landslides, especially where this layer is disturbed by houses or roads. Despite the danger, a trio of dentists proposed building two hundred apartments in this canyon in 1968. Instead of merely protesting, a scrappy group of volunteers raised over $1 million in a citywide campaign and bought the land for the public.

When you reach the Marquam Nature Shelter, hike the Connor Trail up to the Oregon Health Sciences University (OHSU) medical center, where you can catch a ride on Portland's aerial tram.

The OHSU area, familiarly known as "Pill Hill," was originally part of the federal land grant awarded to the Oregon & California Railroad for building its line through the Willamette Valley. The railroad's German investors sent Henry Villard to Oregon to keep an eye on the company's solvency. Villard straightened the books, but he also snapped up this scenic hilltop for himself. He never built here, perhaps because of the poor access. A later owner donated the land for the medical school.

An early attempt to build a tram line up this hillside ended in failure. In the early 1900s, promoter Frank Prantl built a cable car line with an innovative "gripwheel" technology. With this system, a motorized pulley inside the car was supposed to spool its way up the hill along a fixed cable. The machinery never did work, however, and Prantl ended up going insane.

The current aerial tram finally connected OHSU's hill to the riverfront area in 2006. Originally budgeted at $15 million, the tram's cost soared to more than $45 million because of the site's engineering challenges. Now the tram's two 78-passenger, Swiss-made gondolas depart every five minutes and complete the three-minute trip at 22 miles per hour, jiggling stomachs as they pass the central support tower. Views en route extend from the skyscrapers of downtown to Mt. Hood. Although a $4 ticket is required for the uphill trip, you can ride the tram downhill for free.

From the tram's lower station, take the Portland Streetcar downtown to Morrison Street. This modern streetcar line opened in 2001. The sleek cars shuttle across downtown every 13 minutes. Then transfer to the MAX light-rail train and ride back to your starting point at the Washington Park zoo. The loop you have toured is known as the 4Ts because it involves a trail, a tram, a trolley, and a train.

As you glide back on the rails, you can close your eyes and reel back a century to the days when streetcars once climbed to an amusement park on Council Crest, the city's highest point.

Bayocean

Oregon's economic boom in the early 1900s financed more than just amusement parks. People had the time and money to visit vacation resorts too. Although inadequate roads and harbors hindered travel to the Oregon Coast, the broad, sandy beaches proved an irresistible lure. And so the stage was set for the rise and fall of a peculiar resort city, Bayocean.

Built on the narrow sand peninsula between Tillamook Bay and the Pacific Ocean, Bayocean grew to become one of the largest cities on the Oregon Coast. But because the area's development subtly changed the ocean currents, the town eventually crumbled into the sea. Today if you stroll the beaches of the four-mile-long peninsula you'll find no trace of the once glamorous city. But you are almost certain to see pelicans, herons, and seals. Wildlife and hikers now share this remote and hauntingly beautiful shore with the ghosts of Oregon's boom years.

Start your visit to the mysterious lost city by parking at a gate beside Tillamook Bay. Then set off amid the bayshore's yellow-blooming Scotch broom, strolling along a sandy old road for a mile toward the original townsite. Bring binoculars to watch ducks and long-necked loons paddle on the bay. Great blue herons stand like sticks in the mudflats. Curlews

Bayocean's natatorium featured an indoor pool with a wave machine.

stride along the shore, probing the sand with long, thin bills.

Perhaps if Bayocean's early developers had paid more attention to local tribal legends, this sand spit might never have become a townsite at all. With an earthiness that shocked Victorian-era pioneers, the Tillamook tribe insisted that the entire peninsula was actually a demigod's dismembered penis.

According to the Tillamook myth, the Bayocean spit originally belonged to *As-ai-yahal,* the powerful trickster spirit of the south wind. Each spring As-ai-yahal traveled north to break winter's spell by warming the Tillamook area — and the Tillamook maidens. One year for a prank he turned his penis into a clam digging stick. As-ai-yahal laughed at the tribe's women who unwittingly used it in their work, thrusting it rhythmically into the mud. But then one of the older women figured out his game and rammed the stick in so hard that even As-ai-yahal couldn't pull it loose. He was so angry that he stomped on Tillamook Bay's salmon, flattening them to flounders. To this day the bay still has more flounders than salmon. And of course the South Wind's abandoned digging stick has proven a fickle piece of real estate.

After walking a mile along the sandy track you'll reach another gate at the base of a forested hill. At this point you are standing near what once was the center of Bayocean's downtown. The two-story Mitchell general store and the bayside docks were to your right. To your left, twin concrete boulevards and the tiny tracks of a miniature steam locomotive led three blocks to the resort itself, where a massive hotel, an indoor swimming pool, and a dance hall faced the ocean. Today a small sandy path to the left of the gate ducks through salal brush and shore pine for a quarter mile to an apparently pristine beachfront. As you follow this trail to the lonely beach, it's hard not to wonder what on earth happened to the town.

The city's story begins in 1906, when a Kansas City real estate promoter named T. B. Potter visited Oregon on a hunting trip. He fell in love with the four-mile-long peninsula and platted Bayocean Park, billing it as the "Atlantic City of the West." Within eight years he had sold 1600 lots for a total of $600,000. For his part, Potter built the three-story concrete hotel, the dance hall, and the natatorium—a gigantic building with a fifty-by-sixty-foot indoor swimming pool. Said to be the largest on the West Coast, the natatorium's saltwater pool featured an artificial surf machine powered by an electric generator.

Utilities were always a problem at Bayocean. Potter built a pipeline to bring fresh water from springs on Cape Meares, but pressure was so low that water would not reach many of the lots. He built a local telephone system, too, but he never managed to connect it to the outside world. Similarly, Potter's much-touted concrete streets didn't connect with the mainland's road system for two decades, so cars were rare.

The difficulties of building a city on such an isolated sand spit must have weighed heavily on Mr. Potter's mind. One night Mrs. Potter reported that her husband had gone violently insane. He ran out of their Bayocean home and was never seen again.

Mr. Potter's dramatic exit did not improve the sandy city's troubles. Transportation, for example, remained a headache. In the early years, most visitors arrived on Potter's white steamship, the *SS Bayocean*, which sailed weekly from Portland to the town's bayside dock. The cruise took three days, frightening passengers with a rough crossing of the bay's undeveloped bar. From the first, Potter and other Bayocean boosters had clamored for a better channel into the bay. Tillamook fishermen and merchants added their voices, calling for construction of a jetty and a dredged channel for large ships.

The U.S. Army Corps of Engineers studied the bay mouth and announced in 1910 that the most reliable solution would be to build two jetties at a cost of $2.2 million. At least half of the money, the Army said, would have to be raised locally. Bayocean residents blanched at that astronomical amount. They suggested meekly that if the Army built a single jetty for the more modest sum of $814,000, locals might be able to pay half. And so, despite warnings about the unreliability of a single jetty, contractors

39. Bayocean

HIKE LOCATION

Moderate (to sandy draw)
3.9-mile loop
100 feet elevation gain

Difficult (to jetty)
8.1-mile loop
No elevation gain

Stroll quiet beaches to a ghost town that's now home to birds.

Getting There: From Highway 101 in downtown Tillamook, follow "Three Capes Scenic Route" signs west of town. After 2 miles you'll turn right on Bayocean Road. After another 5 miles look for a large signboard on the right describing the Bayocean Spit. Turn right on a gravel road along a dike for 0.9 mile to a big parking area.

Hiking Tips: The trail starts as an old gated road along the bayshore. If you bring a bicycle you can ride this flat road out the spit to the jetty, but hikers see more birds and can take the loop along the beach. After a mile on the road you'll reach a gate. Turn left here on a sandy path 0.2 mile to the beach. Head right along the beach 0.6 mile to a big sandy gap in the forested bluff on the right.

If you're ready to head back on a short loop, turn inland through the grassy dunes in this draw. After 0.3 mile the sandy opening narrows to a trail that descends into the forest. The path dives through dense salal before emerging at the bayshore road. Your car is 1.6 miles to the right.

If you'd prefer the long loop, continue along the ocean beach 1.9 miles to the jetty. Turn right for a few hundred yards to find the start of the bayshore road. While you're following it 4.4 miles back to your car, scan across the bay to spot Garibaldi's docks to the left and the distant roof of the huge Tillamook blimp hangar to the right.

Season: Open all year.

While You're in the Area: Visit the lighthouse 3 miles south at Cape Meares State Park. In Tillamook, stop by the restored 1905 county courthouse to see the Pioneer Museum's blacksmith shop and steam donkey engine. At 2106 2nd Street, it's open Tuesday through Sunday 10am to 4pm for a $4 admission fee. Then drive 5 miles south on Highway 101 and turn left to a gigantic World War II blimp hangar that now houses one of the nation's largest collections of flying World War II aircraft, open 9am to 5pm daily; adults are $9.

went to work on a single, 5400-foot North Jetty. But as the rock breakwater lengthened, the swirling ocean currents at the mouth of the bay subtly began to shift.

TO PORTLAND

TILLAMOOK

101

TILLAMOOK

BAYOCEAN

BAY

N

E

S

W

SPIT

CRAB HARBOR

2.8

BARVIEW

0.5

LOCKED GATE

DIKE

BAYOCEAN RD.

THREE CAPES LOOP

GATE

0.6

1.0

0.4

CAPE MEARES LAKE

1.9

0.2

1.1

SOUTH JETTY

PACIFIC

0.6

0

1 MILE

SANDY DRAW

BAYOCEAN TOWNSITE

OCEAN

CAPE MEARES

0   1KM

Ironically, by the time work on the risky jetty began in 1917, steamship service was already obsolete. After 1911, when the Pacific Railway & Navigation Company opened its line from Portland to Tillamook, most visitors preferred to pay $5.57 for the seven-hour train trip to the bay. From there they could take a ferry across to Bayocean without crossing the bar at all. The journey was relatively expensive and slow, but safer.

Bayocean's business district, near the bayfront ferry landing, held its grand opening party on June 22, 1912. In addition to a general store, the town boasted a trap shoot, a bowling alley, a machine shop, a bakery, and several cafes. A tent park and forty rental bungalows were nearby.

Although Potter had been the first to promote the Bayocean development, he was not its most determined booster. That honor goes to Francis Mitchell, a man described by a 1931 visitor as an exuberant, apple-cheeked gnome who bounced with enthusiasm when he talked. Mitchell had bought Bayocean's very first lot in 1907 and had built a two-story general store across from the wharf. He married in 1923 and enlisted his wife to help run the business.

Between 1920 and 1925, Bayocean's broad beach mysteriously began to narrow. By then the town's residents had forgotten the U.S. Army Corps of Engineers' warning that a single jetty might have unpredictable effects. At first residents gave the advancing surf little heed, worrying instead that the nation's economic downturn might scare away visitors and lower property values. Since the stock market crash of 1929, tins of caviar on the shelves of the Mitchells' general store had begun gathering dust. But the danger of the narrowing beach struck home in 1932, when winter waves devoured the colossal natatorium. Over the next six years the concrete hotel slowly crumbled, wall by wall, from the lip of its oceanfront bluff. Each winter the breakers advanced farther into town, swallowing street after street until fifty-nine houses were gone.

Meanwhile, the ever optimistic Mr. Mitchell painted the words "Watch Bayocean Grow" on his storefront window. A wry newspaper photographer took a picture of a man holding his hands over two of the sign's letters, turning the last word to "Go."

Beginning in 1939, storm waves began occasionally sweeping entirely across the peninsula's neck to Tillamook Bay. After one midwinter wave left a foot of sand in Mitchell's store, the old man was seen working alone on the mudflats with his shovel and wheelbarrow, quixotically trying to open the road to the mainland. Finally in November, 1952, the ocean ripped through the peninsula for keeps, creating a mile-wide breach deep enough for fishing trawlers. Bayocean became an embattled island. Sand poured into Tillamook Bay through the huge gap, destroying a thousand acres of valuable oyster beds. The bay's salinity surged, raising fears that the estuary's fishery would collapse.

Brown pelican at Bayocean's jetty.

into Tillamook Bay through the huge gap, destroying a thousand acres of valuable oyster beds. The bay's salinity surged, raising fears that the estuary's fishery would collapse.

Telephones, power, and fresh water were gone, but the Mitchells refused to leave their battered home. A friend ferried groceries and mail from the mainland to the shrinking island of Bayocean. And then, one dark day, Mrs. Mitchell suffered a stroke. By the time Mr. Mitchell could signal the Coast Guard to bring help she was so ill that medics could not save her. Wracked by the loss and no longer able to care for himself, Mr. Mitchell allowed himself to be committed to Salem's Oregon State Hospital. There he spent his final days a broken and disillusioned man.

Meanwhile, although the destruction of Bayocean had not spurred the government to action, the impending loss of Tillamook Bay's estuary did. In 1956, a $1.75 million breakwater dike reconnected Bayocean with the mainland, plugging the new gap. In 1973, contractors finally built a second jetty at the mouth of Tillamook Bay, calming the angry ocean currents. Gradually Bayocean's broad beach returned. Today the peninsula's sandy plain once again sweeps from the site of the vanished town to the base of Cape Meares, where a lighthouse warily watches the waves.

When you emerge from the trail onto the beach, walk north (to the right) for two and a half miles to South Jetty, the rock barrier that finally reversed the peninsula's erosion. Loons, tufted puffins, and brown pelicans often fish in the bay mouth here. Even if you're not an avid birdwatcher, the pelicans are hard to miss. With six-foot wingspans, they cruise above the water like formations of B-52 bombers. When one of the pelicans sees a school of fish below, it tucks its wings and nosedives into the water, scooping up gallons of seawater, fish and all. Seagulls often lurk nearby, hoping to pick up wounded fish that slip from the pelicans' bills.

From the jetty, turn right for a few hundred yards to find the start of an old road that leads back along the quiet bayshore. When you return to your car you'll have hiked more than eight miles, looping around the lonely peninsula's perimeter. Quite probably you'll have seen a thousand times more birds than people. You'll have passed no hotels, no streets, and no billboards. Emptying the sand from your shoes after such a hike, it's easy to think that Bayocean's erstwhile boomtown, tidied by the tricky South Wind, may have become the pleasantest hideaway on the Oregon Coast after all.

Shore Acres

Breakers crash against the tilted sandstone cliffs of Cape Arago on the rugged Southern Oregon coast near Coos Bay. Sea lions bark from off-shore rock reefs. Wavelets lap the beaches of hidden coves. If this seems an unlikely backdrop for a formal English garden, welcome to the sur-prises of Shore Acres State Park.

North Bend timber baron Louis Simpson bought this dramatic seaside estate as a 1906 Christmas surprise for his wife. Today Simpson's man-sion is gone, but a state park preserves the elaborate gardens and a lovely hiking trail along the grand old estate's shore. Start your exploration by walking across the park lawns to a glass-walled observation building overlooking the ocean cliffs.

So far you will have walked only a few hundred feet, but it's almost precisely the same route explored by Louis J. Simpson in 1905 on his first visit. Simpson was overseeing one of his many timber cruising crews when, following an ancient path, the group stumbled upon the cabin of Jake Evans, a wizened hermit whose Indian wife had died years before. Simpson saw a glint of ocean through the trees and decided to take a clos-er look.

"It was a perfect day and the sun was shining gloriously," Simpson later recalled. "I determined to work my way down to the headland to see what the view might be like. I did have to crawl on my hands and knees through . . . the densest undergrowth you ever saw outside of the tropics.

The Simpsons' Shore Acres estate in 1943, shortly after its purchase by the state.

Finally, hot and breathless, I emerged on a little open space. Immediately I saw what a place for a country home! I went back to the cabin and I said, 'Jake, did you ever think of selling.' 'This property isn't worth anything to anybody, it's uncleared and out of the world,' he answered. 'But,' I urged, 'think how it would be if you should die out here alone; you wouldn't be found perhaps for months.' At last the old man put a price of $400 on his 320 acres, and I took him up at once."

The view today is still inspiring. Giant waves below the observation building's bluff pound onto outcroppings of yellow sandstone. The surf is slowly leveling the tilted sandstone strata, creating weirdly stepped reefs in the process. The plateau you're standing on was similarly leveled by waves thousands of years ago, before the coastline here rose.

Louis Simpson built a summer mansion on this bluff—right where the little observation building now stands—and presented it to his wife in 1906. Styled after homes he had seen in Massachusetts, the shake-covered building featured bay windows and an enormous pillared porch that faced the ocean. The entry hall was richly paneled with Oregon myrtle-wood and lit with specially ordered Tiffany lamps. Navaho rugs and a massive stone fireplace lent the living room a casual, cozy atmosphere. Guest bedrooms, each with its own bath, filled the second floor, while the third floor housed a vast ballroom.

Louis Simpson could never have afforded such a posh retreat if it had not been for his father Asa, the man who amassed the Simpson fortune. Born a humble farmer's son in Maine, Asa Simpson learned the shipbuilding trade and sailed to California with his two brothers in time for the Gold Rush. He opened a lumberyard and sent his two brothers to scout sawmill sites along the Pacific Coast. Both brothers died during those voyages. One brother's ship capsized with a load of timber on the Columbia River bar. The second brother's

The original mansion at Shore Acres.

ship wrecked while bringing sawmill machinery across Coos Bay's bar.

With grim determination, Asa salvaged the equipment from the Coos Bay wreck in 1856 and opened a mill nearby at what is now North Bend. To reduce the risk of shipwrecks like the ones that killed his brothers, Asa bought a steam tugboat that could tow sailing ships across the treacherous bar in relative safety. Then he built a Coos Bay shipyard that began turning out a two-masted freighter every nine months. The finest of his ships, the three-masted schooner *Western Shore*, broke all records in 1875 by sailing from Astoria around Cape Horn to Ireland with a full load of 1800 tons of Oregon wheat in just 101 days.

Asa's son Louis grew up amid luxury. The family owned palatial homes in both Stockton and Oakland, and often traveled to the East Coast and Europe, collecting fine art. Louis studied briefly at the University of California in Berkeley. Still, he had almost no business training when he was given charge of the family's Coos Bay operations in 1899 at the age of twenty-one.

When Louis arrived at North Bend, the white buildings of the Simpson Company lined the bay, but he noticed that the woods behind were undeveloped. Because his father still dictated every detail of work at the shipyard and sawmill, Louis decided to save up his salary to undertake a different kind of enterprise. In 1902 he borrowed $25,000, bought up the nearby land, platted a townsite, established a post office, and incorporated the city of North Bend. He was promptly elected mayor—hardly surprising, given that he owned all but two of the town's lots. Then he wrote his father that he was raising the rent on land the company had been using. Furious, Asa took the next ship to North Bend to browbeat his upstart son. But Louis didn't budge.

Within a year Louis had built a city he could call his own. He sold lots to company workers and to ambitious entrepreneurs from the entire Pacific Coast. He raised capital to open an iron works, ice factory, hotel, gas works, milk condensing plant, door factory, and woolen mill. He donated land for a public dock and for Mercy Hospital. Later he helped organize the Bank of Oregon.

While riding the crest of these business successes, Louis married Cassie Hendricks and presented her with the Shore Acres mansion as a Christmas gift. The Simpsons' country home became the scene of parties and gay summer gatherings for the social elite of both California and Oregon. Guests often arrived on Simpson ships to stay for weeks.

Gradually Louis made the summer estate grander and grander. In 1914 he added an enormous wing to the mansion with a 52-foot, heated indoor swimming pool in the style of a Roman bath. A Palm Room connected the addition to the main house. Upstairs were still more bedrooms and a new, 76-by-36-foot ballroom. A Chinese cook and three servants kept the estate in order. North of the house stood a two-story carriage house and a path to two concrete tennis courts. South of the house, beyond the private beach at Simpson Cove, Louis added a fifteen-cow dairy farm that also supplied the estate with vegetables, chickens, and eggs. He cleared the forest near the house and hired crews to build four acres of formal gardens, including a Japanese garden pool lined with boulders hoisted up with horse teams from Simpson Cove.

To tour the estate's grounds, turn left along the cliff edge from the

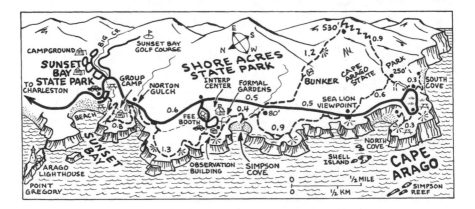

observation building. Then veer left into the fabulous formal gardens. Simpson's ship captains brought exotic plants from around the world to fill the beds. Replanted in the 1970s, the gardens now feature more native species, including twenty-two varieties of rhododendrons and azaleas. Walk through the boxwood hedges' geometric designs, circle the Japanese garden's pool, and return to the paved oceanfront trail. Then turn left for a

40. Shore Acres

Easy (to Simpson Cove)
0.6 miles round trip
100 feet elevation gain

HIKE LOCATION

Moderate (to Cape Arago)
4.6 miles round trip
500 feet elevation gain

Stroll along a scenic seashore bluff to an estate's formal gardens.

Getting There: From Highway 101 in Coos Bay, follow "Shore Acres" signs 9 miles to Charleston, and then continue straight 4 miles. A mile past Sunset Bay State Park, turn right into the Shore Acres entrance, stop at a booth to pay the $5-per-car fee, and park by the oceanfront lawns at the far end of the parking area. Dogs are not allowed in the park.

Hiking Tips: Walk to a little observation building and turn left on a paved oceanfront path. Detour left to tour the formal gardens. Then continue along the paved path to the beach at Simpson Cove. For a longer hike, hop the cove's inlet creek, take an unpaved path up a gully 300 yards, and keep right at all junctions for the next 0.9 mile to the Simpson Reef Overlook. Then cross the road to a trail that traverses through a coastal rainforest 0.6 mile to a T-shaped junction. Turn left, climbing steeply at times for 0.9 mile, and turn left on a downhill trail. After 0.6 mile look sharp for a path back to your left to find a roofless 4-room concrete bunker. Then continue 0.6 mile down to the paved road, jog left 50 feet on the road to a path on the other side, and keep right for 0.4 mile top return to your car.

Season: Open all year, the park features rhododendron blooms from March through June and a 250,000-light holiday display from Thanksgiving through New Year's weekend.

While You're in the Area: Perhaps the state's best ocean swimming beach is sheltered within Sunset Bay's scenic, cliff-rimmed cove, a mile north of Shore Acres. Low tide exposes tidepools on sandstone reefs at the base of cliffs on either side of the cove. Across the road is a popular, 130-site, year-round state park campground with rentable yurts. On the drive home, stop at the north end of the downtown Coos Bay waterfront to see the Coos County Historical & Maritime Museum, which opened here in 2015.

quarter mile down to the beach at Simpson Cove, a broad triangle of sand embraced by sheer ochre cliffs. This makes a good turnaround point for an easy walk. For a longer hike, you can continue on a loop trail that tours a coastal bluff to a sea lion viewpoint and returns over a hill with the ruin of a World War II observation bunker.

The turnaround point for Louis Simpson's fortunes came after a spectacular peak in World War I. The war had revived the sagging demand for the Simpson Company's wooden ships and lumber. When Asa Simpson died in Oakland in 1915, Louis became sole ruler of the company's empire. He brought a shipload of the family's European art treasures to Shore Acres, including marble statues and copies of oils by Italian masters. In 1916 he moved his family from North Bend to Shore Acres, making the mansion

Formal English garden at Shore Acres.

their year-round home. To cap off his success, Louis entered the race for governor, inviting the newspaper editors of Oregon to help kick off his bid with a luncheon bash at Shore Acres. How could he lose? The debonair six-term mayor of North Bend, known throughout the state as the "handsome stranger," was active in the state's YMCA and Elks club. He ran on a populist Democratic platform to develop Oregon and to extend the state's new women's suffrage law nationwide.

But Simpson did lose the governor's race, and within days World War I ended, canceling demand for wooden ships. In 1920, his wife died of kidney failure at Shore Acres. Suddenly his world was crumbling.

As you hike back on the blufftop trail from Cape Arago you'll be following in the hurried footsteps of Louis Simpson on the night his dream home went up in flames. No one knows why Louis was out walking near the dairy farm at 2 am on the morning of the Fourth of July, 1921. But when he noticed a glow on the horizon to the north he raced down the dark trail to Simpson Cove and sprinted through the formal garden paths. The mansion was already engulfed by the fire. By dawn, it was gone. No one had been hurt, but all of the house's artworks and all of his company's records were lost.

Insurance paid only half of the fire's loss. Louis moved temporarily into the caretakers' cottage that still remains beside the formal gardens. Later that year he married a second wife, Lela. Two years later, when one of his company's schooners wrecked on Simpson Reef, dumping three million board feet of lumber onto the shore here, he tried to make the best of tragedy by salvaging the wood for construction of a new mansion on the ashes of the old. Plain but huge, the great shingled barracks that began to rise in 1927 was 224 feet long, with seventeen rooms in its two stories. Work stopped on the new mansion, however, when the stock market crash of 1929 staggered Simpson's fortunes yet again. He moved into the shell of the uncompleted house, hastily finishing a few of the rooms. In 1932 he donated 134 acres south of the estate for Cape Arago State Park. In September, 1936, the wildfires that destroyed the town of Bandon also swept toward Shore Acres. The Simpsons fled to North Bend. Although the mansion survived the fire, most of the outbuildings were lost. On December 10, 1942, he sold the remaining 637 acres of the Shore Acres estate, including the rambling second mansion, to the state of Oregon for a mere $29,000. The Army converted the house to a barracks for troops guarding the Southern Oregon coast. Then it fell into disuse.

Meanwhile, Louis Simpson's long-time business competitor from Coos Bay, Ben Chandler, had become chairman of the State Highway Commission that oversaw state parks. Sensing an opportunity to score a symbolic victory over his rival, Chandler ordered Simpson's run-down mansion destroyed in December, 1948. Louis J. Simpson died three weeks later in a small Barview cottage near North Bend.

Today, with 400,000 visitors a year touring the old Shore Acres estate, parks officials have begun to regret Chandler's vindictive decision. Together with the 250-member Friends of Shore Acres, the Department of Parks and Recreation has been considering ways to rebuild the original 1906 Simpson mansion. Complete with bay windows and pillared porch, the replica would house an interpretive center and restaurant in the manner of other great park lodges where the glory days of Oregon's boom years still shine.

Oregon Caves

The same era of prosperity that launched the Bayocean resort and the Shore Acres mansion also spurred Congress to create Oregon's most famous parks, Oregon Caves National Monument and Crater Lake National Park. Most Oregonians claim to have visited these places — but chances are the trip was actually a dimly remembered camping vacation at the age

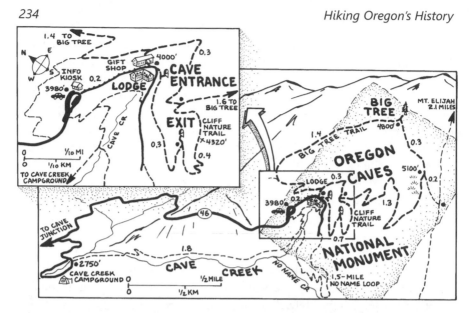

of twelve or a whirlwind car tour with Aunt Martha from North Dakota. In either case a re-visit is in order, especially now that the parks' recent restoration projects are complete. And this time, don't miss the best part of the parks—the scenic hiking trails near the historic lodges.

As you drive up the narrow, winding mountain road to the Oregon Caves, deep in the Siskiyou range, you might well wonder how the remote cave's modest entrance was discovered at all. Apparently, local tribes never stumbled across it. In 1874, however, a hunter named Elijah Davidson was chasing after a bear with his dog Bruno when both animals suddenly disappeared into a mountainside. Davidson cautiously lit matches to follow. He found narrow passageways and hidden rooms of dripstone formations. When his last match died he was deep inside the cave. He managed to find his way out of the darkness only by crawling along a cave-floor stream until it led outside.

At first, word of Davidson's find spread slowly. Visitors had to endure a multi-day horse ride on a crude pack trail. Then the renowned poet Joaquin Miller made the cave famous overnight by lauding it in one of his popular books as the "Great Marble Halls of Oregon." Miller's praise helped the caves win national monument status in 1909.

Before long, early entrepreneurs had damaged the cave extensively. From the first, guides had encouraged visitors to break off stalactites as samples and to hug the white dripstone columns, darkening the rock. Once a road arrived in 1922, a new, more theatrical cave operator took over. He hoked up his tours with ghost stories, colored lights, and hidden growling men in lion skins—the origin of Grants Pass' mascot, the caveman.

In the 1930s, "improvements" by the Civilian Conservation Corps resulted in still more damage. The crews destroyed natural cave formations while trying to widen passages and build rock staircases. Heavy doors at the entrance blocked bats and other animals that had made the cave their home. Asphalt pavement leached tar into the cave's stream. Then the tour route was wired with fluorescent lighting, and the resulting growth of algae and moss turned much of the white rock green.

In an attempt to reverse a century of damage, the National Park Service launched a fourteen-year, $1.2-million restoration project in 1985. Today when you take the half-mile guided cave tour, you'll see the results of that work. A thousand tons of rubble from earlier construction projects have

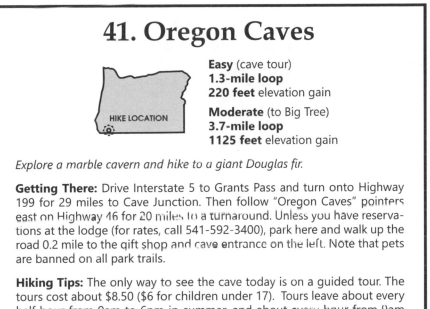

41. Oregon Caves

HIKE LOCATION

Easy (cave tour)
1.3-mile loop
220 feet elevation gain

Moderate (to Big Tree)
3.7-mile loop
1125 feet elevation gain

Explore a marble cavern and hike to a giant Douglas fir.

Getting There: Drive Interstate 5 to Grants Pass and turn onto Highway 199 for 29 miles to Cave Junction. Then follow "Oregon Caves" pointers east on Highway 46 for 20 miles to a turnaround. Unless you have reservations at the lodge (for rates, call 541-592-3400), park here and walk up the road 0.2 mile to the gift shop and cave entrance on the left. Note that pets are banned on all park trails.

Hiking Tips: The only way to see the cave today is on a guided tour. The tours cost about $8.50 ($6 for children under 17). Tours leave about every half hour from 9am to 6pm in summer, and about every hour from 9am to 4pm in spring and fall. There are no tours between early November to the end of April. You don't need a flashlight, but because it averages 44 degrees Fahrenheit in the cave year-round, you'll want warm clothes. The tour lasts 90 minutes and climbs 0.6 mile through the cave to an upper exit. From there the quickest return route is a 0.3-mile trail to the right.

To hike to Big Tree, walk through the gift shop's breezeway arch and then fork to the left for 1.4 miles. To complete the loop, keep right at all junctions for another 1.9 miles.

Season: Snow covers the trail to Big Tree from December until late April. Lodge reservations, however, are available year-round.

been removed. Bats have been allowed to return. Some of the broken stalactites have been painstakingly repaired with epoxy and powdered marble. A subtler incandescent lighting system lessens algae growth. The new tour recaptures the thrill and wonder of exploring a natural cave.

The tours now also showcase Ice Age animal bones discovered during the restoration project. The bear that Davidson's dog chased into the cave was not the first to discover this hibernation hideout. Grizzly bear bones in the cave have been dated to be more than 50,000 years old. Other bones have been found that belonged to black bears, a bobcat, bats, small rodents, and two jaguars—a mammal that has been extinct in Oregon for millennia.

One collection of historic graffiti along the tour route has not been

The Chateau, the Oregon Caves' lodge.

removed. In the late 1800s, when only the lower part of the cave had been discovered, tour groups were often allowed to sign their names in pencil on the dripstone of what was then the cave's innermost chamber. The Park Service tried to erase those names in 1917 but failed because the cave's drips had already covered the pencil marks with a thin layer of transparent calcite. Today the rock covering is even thicker, but you can still read the names of early visitors—including an entire class of University of Oregon geology students from the late 1800s. Thomas Condon's signature reveals that the class was led by the pathbreaking Oregon professor who discovered Ice Age bones at Fort Rock's Fossil Lake (see Hike #2).

If you've hiked through other caves in Oregon, chances are you've been in lava tubes, volcanic tunnels in lava flows. But the Oregon Caves have a much older, metamorphic origin. The rock here began as a tropical coral reef in the Pacific Ocean. Recent research has pushed the presumed date of this reef's formation from 200 million years ago to as much as a billion. The coral and seashells eventually compacted to form limestone. Then, when the advancing North American continent scraped up this seafloor debris to create the Siskiyou Mountains, the resulting pressure cooked the limestone to rough marble.

At first the land here was so wet that percolating ground water dissolved parts of the marble, forming pockets. Then the land rose and the caves drained. After that, dripping water gradually deposited calcite inside—much as a dripping faucet can stain a sink.

Drips inside the marble cave start out by forming "soda straws," thin tubes hanging from the ceiling. Once the tubes get plugged, water runs down the outsides and forms thicker stalactites. If the drip is fast, it carries dissolved calcite to the cave floor to form a stalagmite.

When you emerge from the guided, 90-minute cave tour, you'll probably have to blink in the bright sunlight to get your bearings. Then walk down to the Chateau, the park's rustic, six-story lodge. Completed in 1934, the gabled building is entirely faced with slabs of shaggy incense cedar bark. If you can't stay for dinner in the lodge's restaurant, at least drop by the basement soda fountain for lunch. This Art Deco malt shop retains its original 1930s charm.

After lunch, burn off those calories with a four-mile, aboveground loop hike to Big Tree, one of Oregon's largest Douglas firs. To find this trail, walk through

The Oregon Caves in the 1920s

the gift shop's breezeway arch and then fork to the left. The path climbs a slope of marble outcroppings and manzanita bushes before entering old-growth woods. Expect lots of golden-mantled ground squirrels, chipmunks, and dark blue Stellars jays with pointy black topknots. At Big Tree (a fir that's thirteen feet in diameter) the loop trail switchbacks up to the right. Keeping right at junctions you'll pass high meadows of aromatic mint and cow parsnip. Then the path descends through a grove of Port Orford cedars to return to the gift shop by the cave entrance.

Crater Lake Lodge

The prettiest trail in Crater Lake National Park follows the lake's craggy rim from the lodge to the wildflowers and views of Garfield Peak.

The path starts from the back porch of the grand old Crater Lake Lodge. Truth be told, the lodge here wasn't always grand. Built from 1909-1915 for the relatively modest price of $50,000, the building originally opened with tarpaper on its outside walls and flimsy beaverboard between rooms. Years of makeshift maintenance and harsh winters left the building slated for demolition in the 1980s. But a public outcry pushed the Park Service to renovate it instead. The $35 million makeover proved to be the most expensive hotel construction project in the history of Oregon. Workers had to disassemble the entire lodge, numbering each of the rocks in its walls. Then they built what is essentially a brand new hotel and replaced the facade. The lodge reopened in 1995 with elegant woodwork in the Great Hall and a modern bath for each guestroom.

Surprisingly, the lodge's rustic ambiance seems to have survived intact. If you settle into the rocking chairs on the spectacular stone terrace behind the lodge, for example, it's easy to imagine yourself transported back to the early 1920s. As you gaze across the blue lake, liveried waiters decorously offer to bring you drinks. But don't take them up on the offer until after your hike.

Start by following the paved promenade to the right along Crater Lake's rim. Pavement soon yields to a trail through meadows of pale blue lupine, bright orange paintbrush, yellow groundsel, purple fleabane, and white pearly everlasting. Views improve with each switchback. The trail climbs past cliffs of *breccia*—welded volcanic rubble from Mt. Mazama's early mountain-building eruptions. The breccia here was long buried with

Garfield Peak rises behind the restored Crater Lake Lodge.

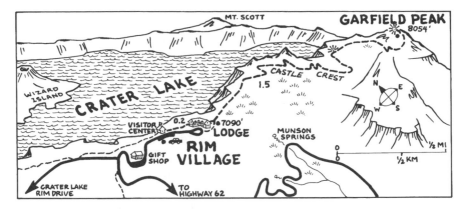

42. Crater Lake Lodge

HIKE LOCATION

Moderate
3 miles round trip
970 feet elevation gain

Climb from Crater Lake's lodge to a viewpoint on Garfield Peak.

Getting There: From Medford or Klamath Falls, follow "Crater Lake" signs on Highway 62 to the park turnoff and turn north to the national park's entrance booth. Expect to pay a fee here of about $10 per car for a week-long pass or $20 for an annual pass. Then continue seven miles to Rim Village, and turn right through this beehive of tourists for 0.3 mile to a turnaround at the Crater Lake Lodge.

Hiking Tips: From the lodge's back porch, follow a path to the right up 1.5 miles to its end atop Garfield Peak. As on all park trails, pets and flower-picking are banned.

Season: The trail is open from mid-July through October. The lodge is open late May to mid-October. For reservations call 888-774-2728.

While You're in the Area: Hike to a lookout atop the Watchman (Hike #49) or take a boat tour to Wizard Island (Hike #4).

lava flows, but these were stripped away by glaciers. The glaciers, in turn, vanished in Mt. Mazama's cataclysmic blast 7700 years ago.

Near the top, snow patches linger across the trail until August. The only trees that can survive at this elevation are five-needled whitebark pines. The gnarled limbs of these short trees are so limber that they literally can be tied in knots. Flexibility gives whitebark pines an edge during winter windstorms. When gales snap other trees, these pines merely bend.

The long-term health of the whitebark pine population, however, relies on the Clark's nutcracker, a bird first identified by explorer William Clark. You probably have noticed these raucous, crow-sized, black-white-and-gray birds along the trail. Because whitebark pines only grow in isolated patches atop mountain peaks, they need help to spread their seeds. By occasionally carrying pine nuts from one summit to the next, the friendly nutcrackers improve the pines' gene pool. And this is why you should never share your lunch with nutcrackers, no matter how boldly they beg. If the birds fill up on peanuts, they won't go after pine nuts, and the age-old partnership between nutcrackers and whitebark pines may collapse.

When you reach Garfield Peak's summit, the glowing blue of Crater Lake gapes below like a four-cubic-mile pool from a high-dive tower. If you're quiet you might see foot-long marmots and guinea-pig-sized pikas watching from cliff-edge rocks a few feet north of the summit. To the east, Mt. Scott looms above Phantom Ship's small craggy island. To the south stretch the distant flats of Klamath Lake, with the tip of Mt. Shasta and the cone of Mt. McLoughlin to the right.

Garfield Peak's name honors President Garfield's son, who became a politician in his own right and visited the lake as Interior Secretary in 1907. The man who deserves the most credit for winning national park designation here, however, was not a politician at all. It was William Gladstone Steel, the pioneer who damaged the lake's ecosystem by introducing fish (see Hike #4). Steel also came up with the idea of building Crater Lake Lodge. As you hike back down to the comforts of the lodge's rocking chairs you might weigh Steel's contributions to the park.

Born in Ohio in 1854, Steel read about the discovery of Oregon's "Deep Blue Lake" as a boy. He was captivated by the romantic tale. By the time the Steel family came to Oregon in 1872, however, William couldn't find anyone who had heard of the magic lake. In 1880 he started his own paper, the Albany *Herald.* The following year he switched to what seemed like steadier work in the Portland post office. But Steel was a Republican, and when the Democrats elected Grover Cleveland President in 1885, Republicans like Steel were fired.

Suddenly at loose ends, Steel went looking for adventure. He climbed Mt. Hood and traveled to Crater Lake. Then he published *The Mountains of Oregon,* a book calling for creation of a national reserve for the "lake in an extinct crater." Steel took his book in person to Washington D.C., where he managed to secure an audience with the President who had fired him

Crater Lake from Garfield Peak.

the previous year. More surprising still, the headstrong young lobbyist succeeded in convincing the President to set aside 360 square miles to protect the lake until it could be surveyed properly. The next summer the U.S. Geological Survey asked Steel to help outfit a scientific expedition to examine the lake. When the new survey reported that the lake was an astonishing 1996 feet deep (a figure since corrcted by sonar to 1943 feet), Congress introduced a bill to preserve the eerie lake as a national park. Timber and grazing interests stalled the legislation for seventeen years, but Steel lobbied tirelessly, traveling often to Washington D.C. at his own expense. In the meantime, he organized the founding of the Mazamas outdoor club at a meeting on the summit of Mt. Hood in 1894.

Once Steel won national park designation for Crater Lake in 1902, he shifted his focus to development. He pressed for construction of a lodge, a commercial village, and a road around the rim. Those projects have all been realized. But Steel also proposed building an aerial tramway from the rim to the Wizard Island summit.

Today, park planners are grateful that the most intrusive of Steel's schemes remained unbuilt, just as Tillamook Bay's peninsula is prettier without Bayocean's concrete buildings and the Oregon Caves are more authentic without early developers' "improvements." Nonetheless, after hiking down from Garfield Peak to the lodge's terrace, it's tempting to raise a silent glass to the giddy optimism that filled Oregon's boom years with dreams.

CHAPTER XI

The Horseless Carriage

Of the many luxuries introduced during Oregon's economic boom in the early twentieth century, few seemed as frivolous as the private automobile. The first roads built for cars were designed for pleasure, not speed. Bypassed today by more businesslike thoroughfares, the scenic old byways remain as goals for short hiking trips—particularly in the Columbia Gorge and along the Oregon Coast.

Portland's first horseless carriage, a Locomobile, arrived in 1898. By 1905 the city still only had forty cars, but their owners had already banded together to form the Portland Automobile Club. Within a year they had successfully lobbied the city council to raise the town's speed limit from eight miles per hour to the breakneck speed of ten.

By 1909, the number of autos in Portland had shot up to 552. Outside the city, however, travel on the countryside's rutted old wagon roads was rough indeed. After a group of owners drove to Mt. Rainier—a muddy, major expedition—they resolved to try to raise $10,000 for an all-weather excursion road, perhaps to Mt. Hood.

The donor who stepped forward with $10,000 for an automobile road was Simon Benson, the man who later financed Portland's bronze drinking fountains, the Benson Hotel, and the Benson Polytechnic School. Born in Norway, Benson had come west in 1878 to try his hand at the timber business. During his first thirty years in Oregon he bought 45,000 acres of Coast Range forest, built donkey engines to haul out the logs, and invented a system of towing huge, 835-foot log rafts by sea to San Diego for the California home building market. In 1910 the self-made timber baron suddenly left the woods forever. He sold his forest land and dedicated his fortune instead to hotels and public works.

When Benson made his donation to the good roads movement he directed that the first project be a scenic drive through the Columbia Gorge. Because the state had no highway department and no roadbuilding crews at that time, the money paid for convicts from the state prisons to start digging out a roadbed at Shellrock Mountain in the middle of the gorge. Soon it became obvious that more money was needed. Much more money.

A wealthy but eccentric railroad lawyer by the name of Sam Hill came to the project's rescue. For some time already, Hill had been toying with improved road designs at his Maryhill estate across the Columbia River from The Dalles. In February, 1913, he invited the entire Oregon state legislature to ride his private excursion train through the Columbia Gorge to see his estate. Hill wined and dined the lawmakers, and then launched into his "good roads" sermon. Impressed, they returned to Salem, created a state highway department, and funded the Columbia River Highway. Hill himself moved on to other projects, assembling memorabilia of the Queen of Romania, collecting chess sets, and building a life-size replica of Stonehenge in concrete—all of which are preserved at his Maryhill estate, now a fascinating museum.

With government money on tap, the Columbia River Highway project moved quickly. By August of 1913, engineer Samuel Lancaster had started a survey of the new road. He based his design on tourist roads he had seen in the Swiss Alps, built by Italian engineers. Lancaster dictated that the roadbed be twenty-four feet wide throughout, that curves arc gracefully with a minimum 100-foot radius, and that the steepness not exceed a

Vista House on Crown Point in the Columbia River Gorge, circa 1917.

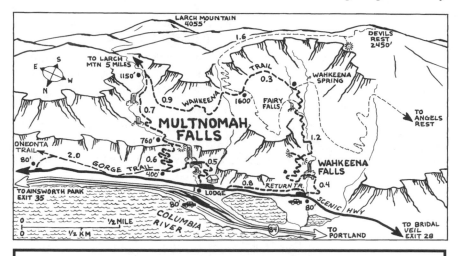

43. Multnomah Falls

HIKE LOCATION

Moderate
2.2 miles round trip
680 feet elevation gain

Walk from a historic lodge to a 542-foot falls on Oregon's most popular trail.

Getting There: For the quick route to the falls, drive Interstate 84 east of Portland to Multnomah Falls exit 31, park, and walk under the overpass. If you'd prefer the scenic route, drive 18 miles east of Portland on Interstate 84 to Lewis and Clark State Park exit 18 and follow signs through Corbett on the old Columbia River Highway to Multnomah Falls Lodge.

Hiking Tips: Walk past the lodge on a paved path to a stone bridge between the falls' two tiers. Then continue a total of 1.1 mile, keeping right at junctions, to a viewpoint at the top of the falls. From here you can simply return the way you came. Or, if you continue keeping right at all junctions, you'll return on a more difficult but quieter 5-mile loop via Fairy Falls and Wahkeena Falls. This longer route follows the Wahkeena Trail and Return Trail to your car.

Season: Open all year.

While You're in the Area: Other fragments of the Columbia River Highway are at Starvation Creek Falls (Hike #44) and McCall Preserve (Hike #45). In addition, two carefully restored segments of the old highway reopened in 2000 for hikers, bicyclists, and equestrians. The first extends 3.5 miles from the Tooth Rock Trailhead (at Bonneville Dam exit 40 of I-84) to Cascade Locks (at exit 44). The other section, with a pair of restored tunnels, extends 4.7 miles from Hood River (follow signs from exit 64) to Mosier (exit 69).

moderate five percent grade. Though unusually generous for 1913, these specifications now make the road seem narrow and twisty. Lancaster intentionally detoured the highway to cliff-edge viewpoints and hidden waterfalls. His route looped up hillsides and leapt across chasms. Ornate concrete bridges and decorative stonework railings completed the plan.

After just two months of survey work, Lancaster opened a construction camp near Multnomah Falls. He hired an army of workers, including many immigrant Italian stonemasons. Less than two years later, the entire western half of the highway was done. On July 6, 1915, dignitaries officially opened the road by driving from Portland to Hood River. At that time, Oregon still only had 23,000 automobiles. Portland wouldn't have a stoplight for another twenty-two years. But the culture of the car was already here to stay.

Multnomah Falls

Multnomah Falls is not only Oregon's tallest waterfall, it's also one of the most visited tourist sites in the state. Each day thousands of visitors pull off the Interstate 84 freeway to snap photos of the 620-foot, two-tiered cascade.

For a quieter, more scenic route to the falls, however, take the old Columbia River Highway. To find this route, turn off the freeway at Lewis and Clark State Park (exit #18) and follow signs through Corbett to Crown Point. Atop this dramatic bluff the old highway loops around Vista House, an elaborate 1917 Art Nouveau rest stop, viewpoint, and memorial to Oregon Trail pioneers. The building suffered so many cost overruns during its construction that critics dubbed it the $100,000 outhouse.

Beyond Crown Point, the old highway passes Latourell Falls, Bridal Veil Falls, and Wahkeena Falls (each with its own picnic area, paths, and views) before reaching the old stone lodge at the base of Multnomah Falls. A simpler roadside inn stood here from the highway's opening in 1915 until 1925, when the entire loop road around Mt. Hood was completed. For that grand opening, Multnomah County authorized renowned Portland architect A. E. Doyle to build a lodge of stone, in the style of National Park lodges.

Park at the lodge and walk straight toward the falls to find a paved trail that switchbacks up to a stone bridge between the two segments of Multnomah Falls' long cascade. Although this is the most popular trail in the state, it may be the most dangerous. In 1991 a forest fire swept across the trail, stopping just short of the lodge. In 1996 a bus-sized chunk of the waterfall's cliff broke loose, landed in the splash pool, and sprayed rock splinters as far as the stone bridge. The incident permanently altered the shape of the waterfall and caused the Forest Service to close the splash pool area to adventurers. In 1998, torrential rainstorms launched a gigantic landslide of rocks, mud, and trees that wiped out the trail altogether just beyond this bridge.

The path beyond the stone bridge has been reopened, so if your courage holds, continue climbing for a mile to an overlook on Multnomah Falls' lip. From there, a dizzying view aims down the cataract to the antlike crowds and toy-sized lodge far below.

The cliff at Multnomah Falls exposes six layers of basalt lava flows, stacked like chapters in a stone history text. The Columbia River has been migrating northward for the past 25 million years, shoved around by lava flows like these. Originally the river flowed past what is now Mt. Jefferson, reaching the ocean near Salem. As the Coast Range rose, the river stretched farther west to the Newport area. Then came the basalt lava floods, pouring west from Hells Canyon. The eruptions repeatedly filled the old river channel. Because the river itself was flowing south from headwaters in Canada, it kept carving new channels on the northern edge of the lava flows. Today the Columbia Gorge is riddled with cross-sections of the river's old routes, cast in stone.

Multnomah Falls' lodge opened in 1925.

The Columbia Gorge's waterfalls owe their elegance to more recent cataclysms. During the Ice Age, a glacier from Canada repeatedly dammed the Clarks Fork of the Columbia River, backing up a huge lake into what is now Montana. When the lake got deep enough to break its ice dam, the water suddenly burst west across Washington. At least 120 of these Missoula Floods surged through the Columbia Gorge before the Canadian glacier finally retired some 12,000 years ago. The floods filled the gorge 600 feet deep, undercutting the cliffs on either hand so thoroughly that side creeks have been left plummeting into thin air.

Starvation Creek Falls

After visiting Multnomah Falls, continue driving east along the old Columbia River Highway. After two miles, pause at a bridge where Oneonta Creek emerges from a dramatic, slot-like gorge. The original highway bridge, to the right of the modern version, leads into a tunnel through the gorge's mossy rock wall. Like most of Sam Lancaster's tunnels along the old route, it was later filled with rubble and sealed off. But this one was reopened for pedestrians in 2012.

Drive another two miles beyond Oneonta Creek and then take Interstate 84 east to hunt down other remnants of the original highway. One restored section opened in 2000 as a 3.5-mile hiker/biker trail between the Tooth Rock Trailhead (near Bonneville Dam) and Cascade Locks. Another old highway section traverses the Starvation Creek Rest Area, a hungry-sounding picnic ground ten miles east of Cascade Locks.

From the rest area, follow a paved path a hundred yards up to the base of 186-foot Starvation Creek Falls. This waterfall earned its name during an 1884 blizzard, when thirty-foot snowdrifts marooned two trains nearby. At first the stranded passengers burned

Train in the Columbia Gorge, circa 1885.

the locomotives' coal to keep warm. Then they burned chairs and woodwork to keep from freezing. Meanwhile the railroad company dispatched skiers from Hood River to bring emergency food. Able-bodied passengers were offered three dollars a day to help dig out the track. Finally, after two weeks in the grip of the storm, the trains steamed loose of the wintry trap.

The abandoned Columbia River Highway has been reopened as a hiking trail in both directions from the Starvation Creek Rest Area. The prettiest trip is a loop to the west past several other waterfalls. To start, walk back toward the freeway and follow its noisy shoulder briefly west. The

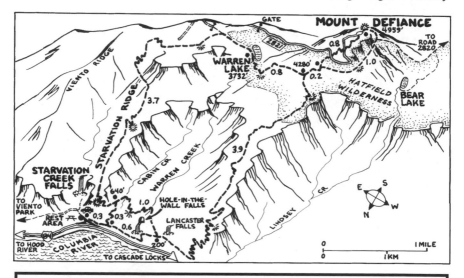

44. Starvation Creek Falls

HIKE LOCATION

Difficult
2.5-mile loop
600 feet elevation gain

Trace a historic roadbed past three Columbia Gorge waterfalls.

Getting There: Take Interstate 84 east of Cascade Locks 10 miles to the Starvation Creek Rest Area exit near milepost 54. This exit is only accessible from the west, so travelers from Hood River will have to turn around at Wyeth exit 51 and return 3 miles.

Hiking Tips: After looking at Starvation Creek Falls, walk back toward the freeway and follow its shoulder briefly west to find the trail to the abandoned highway. After 0.9 mile turn left on the Starvation Creek Trail for a mile. Then turn left on the steep, slippery Starvation Cutoff Trail 0.3 mile to complete your loop. For a much tougher option—in fact, one of the most physically demanding day hikes in Oregon—extend this walk to an 11.8-mile loop to Mount Defiance, Warren Lake, and Starvation Ridge. The loop gains nearly 5000 feet of elevation on its way to the highest point in the Columbia Gorge.

Season: Open all year.

While You're in the Area: Walk the other direction from Starvation Creek Falls (east) to follow the old Columbia River Highway 1.1 mile to a freeway interchange beside Viento State Park. To explore other fragments of the old road, visit Multnomah Falls (Hike #43) and Tom McCall Preserve (Hike #45).

trail soon veers into the woods and passes mostly-hidden Cabin Creek Falls. After almost a mile the path crosses a footbridge below Hole-in-the-Wall Falls, which plummets 100 feet from a tunnel. The Oregon Highway Department created this oddity in 1938. Upset that spray from Warren Creek Falls occasionally wetted the Columbia River Highway's pavement, engineers diverted the creek sideways through a cliff.

Just beyond Hole-in-the-Wall Falls, turn left on the loop's return path. This trail switchbacks up over a grassy ridge to a clifftop viewpoint. From there you can see the entire sweep of the Columbia Gorge—and your car in the parking lot below, at the end of the loop.

Tom McCall Preserve

Wildflowers blaze for a few months each spring on the tablelands at the dry, eastern end of the Columbia Gorge. Then the heat of summer again bakes the desert brown. To catch the vernal fireworks, plan an April drive along the loops of the old Columbia River Highway between the forgotten hamlets of Mosier and Rowena. Then hike across a nature preserve perched on the rimrock cliffs.

Although Sam Lancaster designed the Columbia River Highway between Troutdale and Hood River, the eastern segment to The Dalles is mostly the work of Conde McCullough, a brilliant young engineer who joined the state's highway department in 1919. McCullough went on to

The Rowena plateau from McCall Point.

design many of the Oregon Coast's spectacular bridges, including the Cape Creek Bridge at Heceta Head (Hike #35) and the Conde McCullough Bridge spanning Coos Bay.

Park at a viewpoint pullout at the top of the Rowena Loops, where the old highway begins its serpentine descent from the rimrock. Two trails begin at this viewpoint. Both explore a nature preserve belonging to the Nature Conservancy, a non-profit organization that quietly purchases ecologically sensitive land. The easier path visits several ponds on a plateau overlooking the Columbia River, while a steeper path climbs to the breathtaking mountain viewpoint atop McCall Point.

Start with the easy plateau path. From March through May the grasslands here bloom with sunflower-like balsamroot, purple vetch, blue bachelor buttons, and white yarrow. Ground squirrels zip about the fields gathering seeds and shoots from February to June. The squirrels hibernate the other seven months of the year when this plateau is either too hot, too cold, or too barren to support their active lifestyle.

Where the path crosses a narrow neck onto the plateau you'll notice an old stone wall that once fenced sheep. Just beyond, fork to the right around a pond full of lilypads and cattails. Listen for the melodious warble of redwing blackbirds. Then continue out the plateau's main trail past a smaller, poison-oak-fringed pond. The path ends at a cliff with a view across the Columbia River to the town of Lyle at the mouth of the Klickitat River. Note the eight layers of basalt in the opposite cliffs, evidence of the many lava flows that filled the Columbia Basin and created this plateau ten to fifteen million years ago.

The Missoula floodwaters that repeatedly surged through the Columbia Gorge during the Ice Age could not wash away the basalt, but the floods did cover this plateau two hundred feet deep, scouring it to bedrock. Since

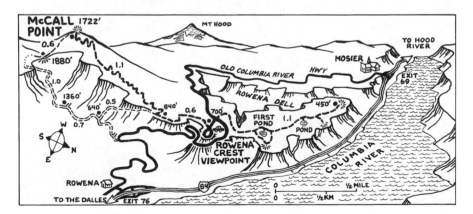

then, eruptions of Mt. St. Helens have dumped a total of three feet of ash here. Of course this volcanic soil must have been evenly distributed at first, but now, especially in the evening light, you'll notice the powdery dirt is heaped into low, circular, fifty-foot-wide humps. What created these mysterious "biscuit mounds?" Early geologists attributed the phenomenon to everything from glaciers to ground squirrels. Today the most widely accepted theory is that earthquakes shook the powdery soil together, in the

45. Tom McCall Preserve

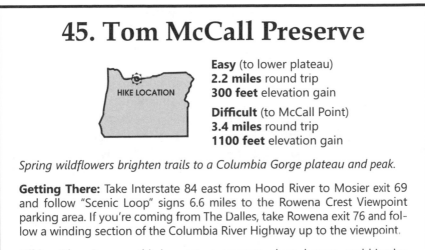

HIKE LOCATION

Easy (to lower plateau)
2.2 miles round trip
300 feet elevation gain

Difficult (to McCall Point)
3.4 miles round trip
1100 feet elevation gain

Spring wildflowers brighten trails to a Columbia Gorge plateau and peak.

Getting There: Take Interstate 84 east from Hood River to Mosier exit 69 and follow "Scenic Loop" signs 6.6 miles to the Rowena Crest Viewpoint parking area. If you're coming from The Dalles, take Rowena exit 76 and follow a winding section of the Columbia River Highway up to the viewpoint.

Hiking Tips: Because this is a nature preserve, dogs, horses, and bicycles are not allowed. Camping and flower picking are also banned, and hikers are asked to stay on designated trails. Remember to wear long pants if you're taking the upper trail, as it passes poison oak. The easy path to the lower plateau starts at a fence stile on the opposite side of the highway from the viewpoint's entrance road. To find the steeper path up McCall Point, look for a trail sign on the right at the start of the parking loop. This path joins an ancient road and turns left along the rim edge. When the trail forks at a large signboard, switchback up to the right on a steep path that climbs to the grassy summit.

Season: Spring is the best time to visit this dry eastern end of the Columbia Gorge, when flowers dot the slopes. Avoid the heat of July and August.

While You're in the Area: A 4.7-mile section of the old Columbia River Highway, complete with 2 spectacular tunnels, is now a hiker/biker/equestrian trail between Mosier and Hood River. From the village of Mosier, take Rock Creek Road a mile to the trailhead. Then it's an 0.8-mile walk to the tunnels, and another 3.5 miles to the far trailhead near Hood River. Afterwards, you might drive 10 miles east to visit the Columbia Gorge Discovery Center, a first-rate museum at The Dalles exit 84 of Interstate 84. It's open daily 9am-5pm, except holidays, for $9 (adults), $7 (seniors), and $5 (age 6-16).

same way that vibrating a cookie sheet makes an even layer of flour collect in rhythmic piles.

To try the more challenging trail, return to the parking area and hike up a ridge to the view atop Tom McCall Point. Along the way you'll climb through higher-elevation wildflower fields of red paintbrush and blue lupine. At the top, the view encompasses Mt. Hood, Mt. Adams, and the graceful loops of the Columbia River Highway across the plateaus.

This summit's name honors the maverick Oregon governor who, when

Mt. Hood from McCall Point.

given a chance to promote tourism on the CBS Evening News in 1971, bewildered a nationwide audience by telling them to "Come visit us again and again. This is a state of excitement. But, for heaven's sake, don't come here to live."

The lanky, unpredictable McCall had already created a Willamette Greenway to clean up the Willamette River, organized a rock festival at McIver State Park, and launched the nation's first Bottle Bill to outlaw no-deposit beverage containers. Now the straight-talking governor had dared to stand up against pro-development business interests and announce that the Oregon Trail was closed. Quality of life, rather than quantity, would become the state's new goal.

Oregonians reelected McCall by a landslide. Fans founded the James G. Blaine Society, a mysterious group named for an early Maine governor whose chief accomplishment was that he had never, ever, visited Oregon. When McCall passed away, proposals were floated to rename Mt. Washington, Mt. Jefferson, or even Mt. Hood in his honor. Finally the heroic politician's handle landed on this humbler, more strategically located peak instead. Tom McCall Point forever watches over the highways and trails of the Columbia Gorge, the traditional gateway for Oregon newcomers.

Hug Point

Early road builders threw up their hands at the frustratingly rugged terrain of the Oregon Coast. As late as the 1930s, coastal settlers were forced to drive on the beaches instead. For horseless carriages, this sandy alternative was no easy street. At Cannon Beach, for example, drivers trying to reach bungalows at the beach's remote southern end had to conquer soft sand, creek fords, incoming tides, and protruding headlands. Today cars zip past such obstacles on Highway 101. But you can relive the scenic drama of the old route by strolling the beach to a sea-level roadbed chipped out of Hug Point's cliffs.

Start at the Hug Point Wayside, a picnic area among the shore pines at the southern end of Cannon Beach. As you walk a railed path down to the beach you'll see the dark capes of Os West State Park looming into the sea at your left. Travelers on Highway 101 sometimes ask locals if there isn't a matching Os *East* State Park somewhere inland.

In fact, Oswald West was the name of the clever Oregon governor who decreed in 1913 that the state's beaches were official public highways. To be sure, drivers sometimes did use beaches as roads in those days, but West's underlying motive was subtler. By claiming the sand as public property, he prevented the private developments and "No Trespassing" signs that plague beaches in most other coastal states. Os West's ruling gave control of Oregon's beaches to the newly formed highway department. Since then the land has been transferred to the state's park department, and cars have gradually been banned from most beaches in favor of hikers, beachcombers, and wildlife.

When you reach the sand and turn right along Cannon Beach, you'll be very near the spot where the cannons were discovered that give this beach its name. The U.S. Navy schooner *Shark* foundered in 1846 while trying to cross the Columbia River bar. The crew survived, but the ship broke up, strewing fragments down the coast. The first cannon to show up was found here in 1898. It's displayed in Cannon Beach's history museum. Two more cannons were discovered here by beachcombers in March 2008. The ship carried a total of twelve guns, so keep your eyes peeled.

After a few hundred yards along the beach you'll pass a waterfall that spills from a bluff to a beach pool. If you like, you can explore two short, sandy caves beside the falls. Then continue along the beach to the rock headland of Hug Point, where the beach appears to end. Surf laps against the cliffs most of the day.

Early beach travelers named this headland Hug Point because they had to wait for low tide and "hug" the shore to get past. Now you'll notice that an eight-foot-wide ledge allows hikers to stroll around the base of the cape at all but the highest tides. The convenient ledge dates to about 1920, when a driver was trying to take a Maxwell car south along Cannon Beach to his home at Arch Cape. A wave caught his car at the tip of Hug Point and stalled the engine. The frightened driver fled on foot to higher ground. After the tide had ebbed, he drained the sea water from his prized car and managed to get it started, but the experience left him so angry that he raised subscriptions from other Arch Cape residents, bought dynamite, and built this bypass route.

The walk to Hug Point only takes half an hour. For a longer stroll, continue along the beach to a little island by Humbug Point, the next headland. This smaller cape won its name when Cannon Beach drivers mistook it for the notorious Hug Point and rounded it easily, only to see the real Hug Point ahead.

If you're still going strong, set your sights on the cafes and ice cream shops of downtown Cannon Beach, another three miles along the sand. Cannon Beach was the farthest point reached by the Lewis and Clark expedition in 1806 (see Hike #11), when Sacajawea joined Clark and several others to trek across Tillamook Head in search of a stranded gray whale. The group found the whale by a creek in front of a village of five huts. When Clark learned that the natives' word for whale was Ecola, he used the word to name the creek that ran beside the village.

What Clark did not learn from the natives, however, was that their village had been wiped out by a tsunami 106 years before. Likewise, the

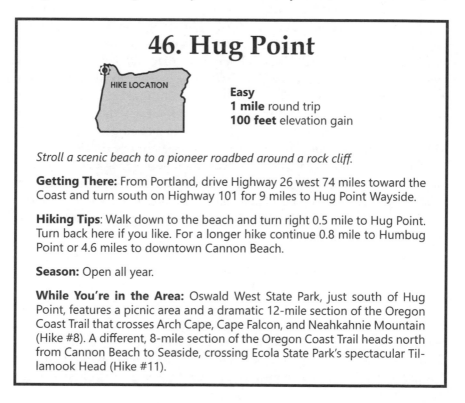

46. Hug Point

HIKE LOCATION

Easy
1 mile round trip
100 feet elevation gain

Stroll a scenic beach to a pioneer roadbed around a rock cliff.

Getting There: From Portland, drive Highway 26 west 74 miles toward the Coast and turn south on Highway 101 for 9 miles to Hug Point Wayside.

Hiking Tips: Walk down to the beach and turn right 0.5 mile to Hug Point. Turn back here if you like. For a longer hike continue 0.8 mile to Humbug Point or 4.6 miles to downtown Cannon Beach.

Season: Open all year.

While You're in the Area: Oswald West State Park, just south of Hug Point, features a picnic area and a dramatic 12-mile section of the Oregon Coast Trail that crosses Arch Cape, Cape Falcon, and Neahkahnie Mountain (Hike #8). A different, 8-mile section of the Oregon Coast Trail heads north from Cannon Beach to Seaside, crossing Ecola State Park's spectacular Tillamook Head (Hike #11).

settlers who followed Clark, eventually packing this exposed beachfront with boutiques and motels, had no idea that seismic sea waves ravage Cannon Beach every few centuries.

Native tales of giant earthquakes and sea floods were considered mythology until 1984, when CalTech geologists noted that the Northwest's coast is flanked by a "subduction zone." Along this 1100-mile-long fault, about 60 miles off the coast of Oregon and Washington, the North American continent is overriding (subducting) the Pacific Ocean seafloor plate at the rate of about an inch a year. But the contact zone is sticky. Instead of sliding smoothly, the edge of the continent is arching like a giant bow, building up pressure. Every 300 to 600 years it suddenly jerks westward about 30 feet.

Subduction earthquakes are the largest quakes on the planet. They create enormous tsunamis that can circle the globe. Japan has a subduction zone very similar to Oregon's. In 2011 a subduction earthquake there launched a tsunami that killed 23,000 people.

After the 1984 CalTech report, researchers examined estuaries along the Pacific Northwest coast. Their excavations revealed tsunami debris — sand, mud, and driftwood — as much as five miles inland. The researchers also found an ominous explanation for the puzzling "ghost forests" of ancient stumps that emerge on Oregon and Washington beaches each winter. When storms wash away much of the beaches' sand, the gnarled roots of long-dead cedar forests lie exposed at Neskowin, Lincoln Beach, and many other Northwest beaches. Obviously the trees could not have grown in salt water. By counting the trees' rings, the scientists determined that the trees died in 1700 AD, when our most recent subduction earthquake lowered the coastline here as much as ten feet.

The researchers verified that date by turning to Japan, an island nation

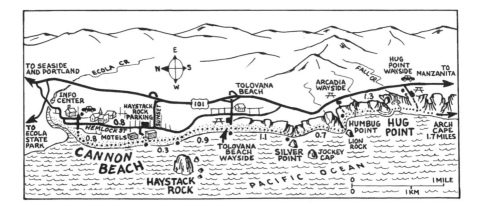

so plagued by tsunamis that records have been kept for a millennium. Japanese historians reported that a devastating wave had rolled in off the Pacific without warning on the morning of January 27, 1700. Knowing that such waves travel at 440 miles an hour across the Pacific, the researchers were able to pinpoint the time when the Northwest Coast shook. The quake that lowered the shore and launched the tsunami struck Oregon at 9 pm on January 26, 1700.

As you walk toward the coastal city of Cannon Beach, picture the effect such an earthquake would have today. Measuring about nine on the Richter scale, the initial shock would be roughly thirty times more powerful than the earthquake that destroyed San Francisco in 1906. Here in Cannon Beach, the ground would jolt so violently for three minutes that you would not be able to stand up. Brick buildings would collapse, highway bridges would fall, and streets would buckle. After the ground stopped shaking, you would have about ten minutes to walk to safety. Driving a car on the damaged roads would probably not be possible.

Surprisingly, the ocean might not surge forward at once. In fact, the water might even retreat for ten or twenty minutes, exposing first the tidepools at Haystack Rock, and then the mudflats beyond. By that time sirens would already be wailing, warning people to walk to high ground or to seek refuge in the upper stories of well-built concrete or steel buildings.

Cannon Beach is one of many towns on the Pacific shore that practice tsunami evacuation drills. Unfortunately, the tests show that a majority of people who hear the sirens do not evacuate to a safe location. Some people actually head toward the beach, hoping to see a tidal wave first hand.

The waves visible at the front of a tsunami are often unimpressive breakers, but each one builds on the last, creating a surge that pours inland like a sudden high tide. The tsunami itself consists of waves that may be a hundred miles wide. For perhaps ten minutes, the water level at the shore continues to rise. Cars and wooden buildings float or are smashed. Then the surge retreats, sucking everything a mile or more out to sea. Because the earthquake generates a series of waves — like gigantic ripples in a pond — similar surges inundate the coast at intervals of five to forty minutes for many hours.

More than three hundred years have passed since Oregon's last subduction earthquake, so the odds of another are rising. Already, the risk posed by living in a low-elevation wooden beachfront home is comparable to the risk of death posed by smoking cigarettes. Of course, many generations might yet pass without calamity. On any given day, the risk of walking along the beach is probably less than the risk of commuting to

Cannon Beach and Haystack Rock.

work by car. Still, whenever you spend much time at the beach, it's a good idea to keep an eye on potential escape routes. Could you walk within ten minutes to ground that is at least fifty feet above sea level? And if not, could you climb to the upper story of a concrete or steel building that's solid enough to withstand the tsunami?

When you reach Cannon Beach you'll have a hard time overlooking the Surf Sand Resort, a solid-looking motel that crowds audaciously close to both surf and sand. This was the site of a legal standoff in 1967, when the motel's former owner sparked public outrage by fencing off the beach for his guests. Oregonians rose up in protest, sending 30,000 letters to the state legislature. Governor Tom McCall took up the battle, thundering that Oregon's beaches have belonged to the public since the days of Governor Oswald West. When the legislators still wavered, objecting that West's decree had not identified specific boundaries, McCall staged a helicopter landing in Cannon Beach to publicize his side of the case. Victory came on July 6, 1967, when McCall signed into law the landmark Oregon Beach Bill. The law decreed that all land within sixteen vertical feet of the average low tide mark belongs to the people of Oregon.

And so private development stopped at a line drawn in the sand of Cannon Beach. Today, laughing children build sand castles and fly kites on the popular public beach. Governor West's stratagem to save the beaches by declaring them public highways has succeeded. But as you stroll here it's hard not to think of a different threat to the Oregon Coast, and to wonder when the ground will shake, launching the next giant tsunami.

CHAPTER XII

The Fire Line

Oregon's forests were once dotted with 805 fire lookout towers, staffed each summer by isolation-tolerant souls willing to trade civilization's comforts for a glass-walled viewpoint in the wilderness. Now that most fire-spotting work is done by airplane, fewer than a hundred of the old lookout buildings remain. The trails to these cabins may be steep, but their panoramic views—and their nostalgic stories—make them among the state's most popular hiking destinations.

Alarmed that the nation's forests were rapidly disappearing, conservationists such as John Muir convinced President Benjamin Harrison to set aside the Cascade Range Forest Reserve in 1893. For the next ten years, however, the new reserve's only on-the-ground protection consisted of a few rangers on horseback. Each man was assigned to roam hundreds of miles of wilderness woods, single-handedly trying to put out wildfires, guard against timber thieves, and keep out the illegal shepherds who often set fires to clear land for grazing.

After the Forest Reserve was divided into smaller National Forests in 1908, foresters began working on a more scientific way to locate fires: triangulation. If people in three different locations could report the precise direction of a smoke plume, fire crews could theoretically pinpoint the blaze by plotting the sight lines on a map. The problem was getting accurate measurements while working out in the woods.

William Osborne, a young graduate from the Yale School of Forestry, invented a way to make triangulation practical in the field. While assigned to the Forest Service office in Portland in 1914, Osborne built a firefinder table. The device consisted of a circular table covered with a map that was centered on the lookout's location. To determine the direction to a fire, a staffer sighted through a swiveling scope (in later versions of the device, a swiveling slot with a cross hair). When a smoke plume came into the sights, the staffer merely had to read the bearing on the table's rim. Osborne's fire-finders remain standard equipment in lookout towers to this day.

Osborne first tried out his firefinder on a platform bolted between two trees atop the Columbia Gorge's Larch Mountain in 1914. He decided he needed a higher viewpoint. Osborne knew that California foresters had built a lookout atop Mt. Lassen the year before, and that it had just blown up in that volcano's cataclysmic eruption. He decided to climb Mt. Hood, looking for more stable peaks. When he came down, he recommended that the Forest Service build lookout stations with his firefinder device atop Mt. Hood, Mt. St. Helens, Mt. Adams, Mt. Jefferson, and Mt. McLoughlin.

Of these five lofty candidates, the Forest Service rejected only Mt. Jefferson as inaccessible. Within a few seasons, bold little buildings rose on the other four summits. Although all of these early lookout cabins were later demolished by storms and eruptions, the stories of their heroic staffers succeeded in glamorizing forest fire protection to a nationwide audience. Lookouts like the one atop Mt. Hood, for example, set the stage for a second, more successful round of Oregon lookout tower construction in the 1920s and 30s—including the surviving buildings on Black Butte, The Watchman, and Sand Mountain.

Mount Hood

The first lookout cabin in Oregon was also the highest, atop 11,240-foot Mt. Hood. Even today, scaling this peak is a genuine mountain climb, and not a hike. However, if you hike the trail to the Silcox Hut above Timberline Lodge (a route described in Hike #53), you'll get a close enough look at Mt. Hood's summit to understand the trials faced by early lookout staffers.

As you trudge up the sandy mountainside past timberline, you'll be following the route of a 1915 mule train overseen by thirty-three-year-old Elijah ("Lige") Coalman, a mountaineer who had been climbing Mt. Hood since the age of fifteen. This time, however, he was determined to stay. The mules carried the equipment for Mt. Hood's first lookout station: a circular twelve-foot tent, an Osborne firefinder table, and four miles of insulated copper telephone wire. When the lookout project had been announced, critics had scoffed that no man could set up a permanent camp on the top of Mt. Hood. The supervisor for the Oregon National Forest, T.H. Sherrard, had interviewed candidates for the seemingly impossible job. If anyone could build a base on Mt. Hood's icy summit, he decided, it was Coalman.

Beyond what is now Timberline Lodge, the route steepens across snowfields to the Palmer Glacier. When the mules reached the entrance to Mt. Hood's crater, they could climb no farther. Ahead loomed cliffs of hoarfrost, sulfurous fumaroles, and gaping crevasses. Coalman chiseled steps out of the ice and packed the gear the rest of the way to the top on his back. After carrying the last of dozens of loads, he raised a wind-tattered American flag above his summit tent on July 21, 1915. Then he picked up his field telephone and called Sherrard in Portland. The Mt. Hood station, he reported, was officially in service.

Lige Coalman's achievement made him a national celebrity. Hundreds of admirers and curiosity-seekers climbed the mountain to meet the man who had set up camp on the summit. An entire wedding party, complete with silk gown, orange blossoms, and crampons, came to exchange vows before his wind-whipped tent.

As the summer of 1915 wore on, Coalman began planning to replace his tent with a more permanent cabin built of wood. On September 1 he sent a crude sketch of a proposed lookout building to Sherrard. His design, known later as the D-6 model, featured a twelve-foot-square wooden cabin with a cupola — a quarter-size second story where lookouts could peer out windows on all sides. Sherrard wasted no time in granting the celebrity's wish. Four days later, another mule train was already on its way, carrying two tons of building materials to the base of the summit. Sherrard had hired nine former loggers to pack the boards up the rest of the way to Coalman's camp. The laborers had agreed to be paid at the rate of two cents a pound. But when the loggers saw the thousand toe-holds that Coalman had chipped up the glacier to the summit, they demanded three cents a pound. Even at the higher rate, many of them quit. Coalman carried the final 120 pounds of hardware himself in one last load.

It was nearly October by the time all of the cabin materials were assembled on the summit. The summer's good weather was failing fast. Together with one other worker Coalman quickly set to work nailing the cabin together. An ice storm pinned them down inside their tent for three days, encrusting the canvas with a four-foot-thick shell of rime. They chipped their way out, chiseled ice off the unfinished cabin, completed all but the cupola, and retreated for the winter.

The following summer Coalman packed up an additional two thousand pounds of supplies. During the two-month fire season of 1916 he finished the cupola, reported a total of 131 fires, and welcomed countless climbers with hot coffee. The next summer, in 1917, he brought a phonograph and sometimes invited visitors to come inside and dance. In 1918, on his 586th trip up Mt. Hood, Coalman was swept into a crevasse by a falling rock. He crawled out and made it down the mountain, but could never climb again.

The daring young men who staffed Coalman's cabin for the next fifteen

Black Butte's 1923 lookout is modeled after the 1916 lookout atop Mt. Hood.

summers also learned that the mountain could be an angry master. Charles Phelps, for example, was staffing the lookout one September evening in 1924 when lightning smashed the windows and set the building on fire. Phelps escaped through a cupola window, only to find himself in the thick of a howling, subzero blizzard whiteout. While he was groping his way down the mountain, a lightning bolt set off a rockfall that cascaded past his head. He dropped down an ice chute and sprained his leg. That night he cowered in the smoky fumarole of an ice cave inside the volcanic crater. When the storm finally subsided at dawn, he painfully dragged himself back up the cliffs to the cabin. There he discovered that the blizzard had put out the fire. The broken windows, however, had filled the cabin with a seven-foot snowdrift. He dug out the telephone and told his supervisor to send a rescue party and a new lookout staffer. Then he made himself a cup of coffee and began gathering his things to leave the mountain forever.

Staffers on Mt. Hood were often surprised by unusual visitors. In 1919 a badger appeared at the door of the cabin. The lookout staffer was new that summer and decided he could use a pet for company, so he trapped the fiercely growling animal in a makeshift cage. Three days later, however, it pried its way free from the cage while the staffer was out. The badger tore up the furnishings in a frenzy, ate several pounds of lard, vomited about the cabin, and crawled into the bed to sleep. When the staffer returned, he immediately threw his "pet" outside. Still, the badger hung around the cabin another three days, apparently hoping for more treats.

Chipmunks and mice were common sights at the summit post. Less common was the black bear that climbed up Mt. Hood in September 1923, ambled past the cabin, and climbed down a different way. Who can say why it went over the mountain? One summer in the 1930s, three domestic sheep appeared on the summit. Climbers tried to drive them down without success. A few days later the sheep left on their own.

Human visitors seemed to arrive in bursts. An *Oregonian* story in late July, 1932, inspired a stream of climbers to scale the peak. The article reported that the Mt. Hood lookout staffer that summer, Mack Hall, was so hungry for eggs that he was willing to pay thirty-five cents a dozen for them. The first to respond to this plea was a twenty-year-old bank messenger named Barney Young. Barney read the story in the newspaper when he came home from work. He immediately drove to Government Camp, climbed to the summit in the dark, and woke the lookout at midnight to present him with a dozen fresh eggs. Mission accomplished, Barney climbed back down to his car and returned to Portland in time for work the next morning. Within a week, other visitors had provided Hall with a total of thirteen dozen eggs. He began joking that he didn't need eggs so much as a haircut, in the hopes that a barber might climb up Mt. Hood next.

Although duty on Mt. Hood paid $300 for a sixty-day season—twice the rate of other lookout stations—staffers spotted relatively few fires. The mountain is so tall and stormy that they often saw nothing more than the tops of clouds for days at a time. The building was abandoned in 1935 and blew off the summit in a 1941 storm. Since then the ruins of the old lookout building have become part of the Eliot Glacier. The stories from Mt. Hood, however, have become part of the inspiration for later lookout staffers throughout the state.

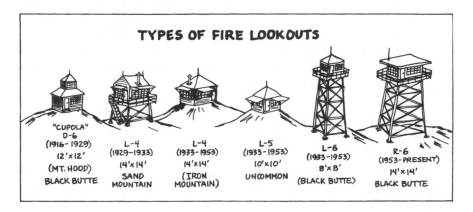

TYPES OF FIRE LOOKOUTS

"CUPOLA"
D-6
(1916-1929)
12'x12'
(MT. HOOD)
BLACK BUTTE

L-4
(1929-1933)
14'x14'
SAND
MOUNTAIN

L-4
(1933-1953)
14'x14'
(IRON
MOUNTAIN)

L-5
(1933-1953)
10'x10'
UNCOMMON

L-6
(1933-1953)
8'x8'
(BLACK BUTTE)

R-6
(1953-PRESENT)
14'x14'
BLACK BUTTE

Black Butte

Plunked in the midst of the Central Oregon plateau, Black Butte looks like a misplaced mountain. The weather here seems out of place too. Black Butte's climate is so dry that the mountain usually appears black, even when the Cascade Range is snowy white.

Black Butte's unusual location and unusually sunny weather make it an ideal fire lookout site. As early as 1910 rangers built a simple "squirrel's nest" platform here by nailing a few planks between two adjacent tree-tops. That platform is gone, but four later structures remain. As a result, Black Butte's summit has the best collection of historic lookout buildings in Oregon. Visitors should be forewarned, however, that the admission to this panoramic collection is steep: a hiking trail that gains 1500 feet of elevation in two miles.

Black Butte from Santiam Pass.

As you drive across the flats of Central Oregon toward this symmetrical volcano, you might well wonder why it erupted here. The more famous High Cascades peaks formed along a fault that has been leaking lava for millions of years. But Black Butte grew along a different, parallel crack to the east. This fault also uplifted Green Ridge's scarp to the north, leaving the Metolius Valley as a long trough. Black Butte began to erupt quite recently, perhaps only 20,000 years ago. It quickly built up a 3000-foot pile of cinders, one of the tallest such cones in the state. The eruption also buried the Metolius River, creating Black Butte Ranch's swampy meadows on one side of the mountain and Metolius Springs on the other, where the river now emerges.

On the drive to the trailhead you'll spiral halfway up the butte on a controversial gravel road. In 1925 the Bend *Bulletin* argued editorially that a road should be built all the way to the summit as a tourist attraction. Opponents scoffed at that proposal, just as they had objected to the news-paper's earlier 1919 plan to build a Skyline Road along the crest of the Cascade Range from Crater Lake to Mount Hood.

The idea of a road up Black Butte reemerged in 1952, when the Forest Service put most of the ponderosa pine here up for sale. The Forest Service stipulated that the winning bidder would have to build a road to within a thousand vertical feet of the butte's summit. Sawmill owners complained that "Black Butte will look like a stripped ape if it is logged," and added that the butte needed the proposed road "like a boar needs two tails." The Forest Service received no bids and withdrew the sale. A decade later, however, the determined rangers tried again. By then the price of timber was higher. The Brooks Scanlon Company agreed to cut the larger trees and build the road that leads to the current trailhead.

Today as you set off on the trail you'll quickly leave the logged land behind and hike into a stand of old-growth ponderosa pines. Notice how the pines' bark looks as though it is composed of thousands of orange jigsaw puzzle pieces. The odd pattern helps the trees survive fires. When the bark gets singed, the outer "puzzle pieces" flake off, helping the trees

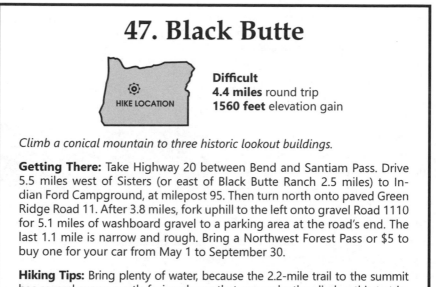

47. Black Butte

Difficult
4.4 miles round trip
1560 feet elevation gain

HIKE LOCATION

Climb a conical mountain to three historic lookout buildings.

Getting There: Take Highway 20 between Bend and Santiam Pass. Drive 5.5 miles west of Sisters (or east of Black Butte Ranch 2.5 miles) to Indian Ford Campground, at milepost 95. Then turn north onto paved Green Ridge Road 11. After 3.8 miles, fork uphill to the left onto gravel Road 1110 for 5.1 miles of washboard gravel to a parking area at the road's end. The last 1.1 mile is narrow and rough. Bring a Northwest Forest Pass or $5 to buy one for your car from May 1 to September 30.

Hiking Tips: Bring plenty of water, because the 2.2-mile trail to the summit has several sunny, south-facing slopes that can make the climb a thirsty trip. If you still have energy when you get back to your car, continue downhill on a restored old trail for 2.8 miles to a lower trailhead on gravel Road 1430, just off paved Road 14. Ceramic insulators on trees remain from the old lookout's phone line along the way.

Season: Snow blocks the trail from mid-November through June. The flowers are best in July.

While You're in the Area: Stop at Santiam Pass to see an abandoned railroad grade (Hike #31). For a scenic drive, detour south on old Highway 242 across McKenzie Pass, where trails explore a lava landscape (Hikes #20 and 21).

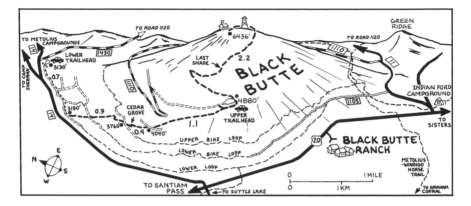

keep cool. The needles of a ponderosa pine are also well adapted to fend off fire. Especially on older trees, the clumps of needles are so high and so widely spaced that flames have a hard time spreading from limb to limb.

After a mile the path crosses a treeless slope where serviceberry bushes bloom white in June. Expect other wildflowers here too: big yellow balsamroot, purple larkspur, and red paintbrush. Far below you'll see the green meadows and golf courses of Black Butte Ranch. Originally an 1870s homestead, this ranch was developed as a resort and vacation home community in 1970 by Brooks Resources, a subsidiary of the company that logged the lower slopes of Black Butte.

Next the path climbs steeply to a broad ridge with wind-stunted whitebark pines. As you follow this ridge up to the summit, you'll notice silvery snags to the right—evidence of a forest fire that almost caught the lookout staff off guard. A lightning storm in the fall of 1981 sparked several small forest fires on the flanks of Black Butte. Before fire crews could arrive, the blazes merged. The lookout staffer watched in horror as the fire raced up toward the summit. Miraculously, the fire petered out just short of the lookout buildings.

At the top the trail detours around the staffed lookout tower to find the butte's best viewpoint, at a cupola-style lookout cabin from 1923. Ahead, Cascade snowpeaks from Mt. Hood to the Three Sisters line up as if for inspection, with Three Fingered Jack saluting front and center.

The 1923-vintage lookout building here was modeled after Lige Coalman's Mt. Hood cabin. As in that earlier lookout, a ladder inside leads up to a tiny second-story room surrounded by windows. In all, two hundred cabins of this style were built on Northwest peaks.

A tall, skinny tower was built just east of the cupola cabin in 1934 to improve fire surveillance. Pack horses brought over a thousand loads up the butte with the necessary building materials. Then a crew from the Civilian Conservation Corps assembled the 82-foot tower and the little eight-foot-square cabin at its top. The tower closed in 1990 and collapsed

Black Butte's 1934 tower collapsed in 2001.

under the weight of winter snow in December 2001.

Today the lookout staffers on Black Butte use two more recent buildings. They live in the log cabin that you can see near the old cupola lookout. This one-room building was constructed in Sisters, disassembled, and flown to Black Butte by helicopter in 1980. A helicopter also brought Black Butte's sturdy, modern lookout tower in 1995. This 62-foot tower is topped with a practical, flat-topped lookout building of the type favored by the Forest Service since the 1950s.

Life on a lookout tower has always required a certain amount of discipline. The duties of a lookout staffer haven't changed much since they were spelled out in a 1920s Forest Service handbook. The first rule in the book was simple: "Keep all windows clean inside and out at all times." The most demanding requirement, however, was that staffers spend at least twenty minutes of each daylight hour watching for fires. This meant that staffers could never wander far from their posts. During thunderstorms their watch was supposed to be continuous, without even breaks for meals. A logbook had to be kept, noting every lightning strike and smoke plume. Inspectors sometimes arrived unannounced to make sure the rules were followed. Among other things, the inspectors checked that the staffer had a fireman's pack always at the ready. A two-day supply of water and a ten-day supply of chopped wood had to be on hand at all times.

The rules also insisted that lookout staffers be courteous to the public. This duty proved especially trying for Carl Demoy, the man who staffed the Black Butte lookout for twenty-five summers. Carl worked in the little eight-foot-square lookout building atop the old 1934 tower. In later years he complained increasingly that tourists kept climbing up to peer in his windows. He put up a sign, "Danger—Do Not Climb," but they ignored it. He sat on the trap door at the top of the stairs, but they pushed on it from underneath and shouted. He hauled up a bucket of rocks and rolled them down the stairs at visitors. Finally the district ranger hiked up to investigate charges that Carl had poured a "yellowish liquid" on ascending intruders.

Do not attempt to climb the lookout tower on Black Butte. In fact, all the buildings here are off-limits to the public. And remember to bring your own drinking water, because the staff here has none to spare. In some ways, living on a lookout tower is like living in a fishbowl—isolated, yet maddeningly exposed to display. Before you tap on the window of a lookout, remember Carl Demoy.

Iron Mountain

Iron Mountain's lookout site is one of the Old Cascades' most popular hiking goals, but most people hike to it the hard way, from the bottom of the mountain. To cut the work in half, drive instead to the shortcut once used by the lookout staffers themselves—a gravel trailhead halfway to the top.

This shorter route still shows off the spectacular plant life that has made Iron Mountain famous. The trail begins, for example, in an ancient forest that includes shaggy-barked Alaska cedars, otherwise rare in Oregon.

Iron Mountain from Cone Peak's meadow.

Iron Mountain hosts a total of seventeen different types of trees, more than any other peak in Oregon. Fully sixty of the plant species here are considered rare or unusual in the Western Cascades. When the trail switchbacks up out of the forest, you'll enter a natural rock garden of early-summer wildflowers: fuzzy cat's ears, purple larkspur, yellow stonecrop, red paintbrush, and pink penstemon.

Finally you'll reach a deck at the lookout site, atop a cliff of red volcanic rock. To the east, all the major Cascade peaks are visible from Mt. Hood to Diamond Peak. To the west, look for Rooster Rock's crag and, on a clear day, the distant hump of Marys Peak (Hike #5) in the Coast Range.

The first lookout station here was simply a firefinder table mounted on a stump in 1929. A tent nearby had a telephone for reporting fires. In 1933 workers from the Civilian Conservation Corps set about building a more permanent lookout base. They used two hundred sticks of dynamite to blast off the peak's summit crag. They leveled the remaining stub by hand. Then they packed in a lookout kit on twelve mules. The kits for that particular, pointy-roofed model of lookout cabin, called the L-4 , cost $500. The company that sold the kits packaged them in bundles that were designed to fit on pack animals. Over a thousand L-4 cabins were placed on Northwest peaks between 1929 and 1953.

The first L-4 cabin on Iron Mountain collapsed under the heavy snows of 1976. High winds blasted much of the ruin off the peak. The next summer a helicopter brought in a replacement, a flat-topped lookout building that had been sitting idle on another peak nearby. That building was finally dismantled in 2007. Today, only a railed viewpoint platform remains.

Be cautious near the summit cliffs. A lookout staffer fell to his death here in the summer of 1990. Despite an investigation, no one has ever discovered whether the staffer slipped off the cliff, was pushed, or

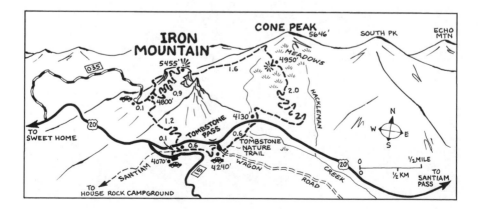

intentionally jumped. Although an accidental death seems most likely, staffers at other lookouts have been driven to odd actions. One young man began setting fires so he would have something to report. The footprints he left at the fire site tipped off investigators. Another staffer was found on top of his tower's roof, preparing, he said, to "rescue Lois Lane."

Iron Mountain is not a place to try flying, even if you're looking for an alternate route down from the lookout site. Instead consider hiking back on a longer trail that circles the mountain. This scenic five-mile

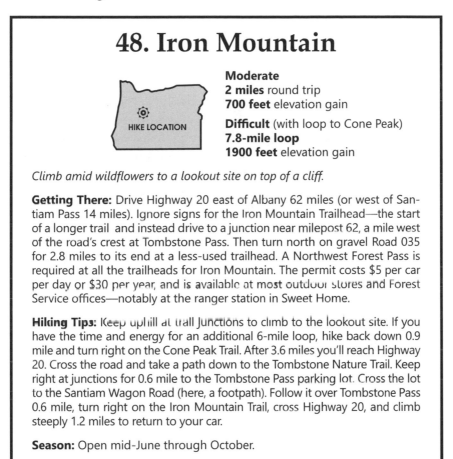

48. Iron Mountain

HIKE LOCATION

Moderate
2 miles round trip
700 feet elevation gain

Difficult (with loop to Cone Peak)
7.8-mile loop
1900 feet elevation gain

Climb amid wildflowers to a lookout site on top of a cliff.

Getting There: Drive Highway 20 east of Albany 62 miles (or west of Santiam Pass 14 miles). Ignore signs for the Iron Mountain Trailhead—the start of a longer trail and instead drive to a junction near milepost 62, a mile west of the road's crest at Tombstone Pass. Then turn north on gravel Road 035 for 2.8 miles to its end at a less-used trailhead. A Northwest Forest Pass is required at all the trailheads for Iron Mountain. The permit costs $5 per car per day or $30 per year, and is available at most outdoor stores and Forest Service offices—notably at the ranger station in Sweet Home.

Hiking Tips: Keep uphill at trail junctions to climb to the lookout site. If you have the time and energy for an additional 6-mile loop, hike back down 0.9 mile and turn right on the Cone Peak Trail. After 3.6 miles you'll reach Highway 20. Cross the road and take a path down to the Tombstone Nature Trail. Keep right at junctions for 0.6 mile to the Tombstone Pass parking lot. Cross the lot to the Santiam Wagon Road (here, a footpath). Follow it over Tombstone Pass 0.6 mile, turn right on the Iron Mountain Trail, cross Highway 20, and climb steeply 1.2 miles to return to your car.

Season: Open mid-June through October.

While You're in the Area: The historic Santiam Wagon Road beside Iron Mountain passes several other interesting destinations that you can drive or hike to see. To the west of Tombstone Pass the old road passes a cave at House Rock Campground (Hike #22). To the east the wagon road just misses Clear Lake (Hike #52) before climbing past Sand Mountain's lookout tower (Hike #50) near Santiam Pass.

loop traverses to the wildflower meadows of Cone Peak, descends to the historic Santiam Wagon Road (see Hike #22), and returns to your car via a lower portion of the Iron Mountain Trail. The extra spiral around the mountain takes two hours, but after the steep little climb to the lookout, it's a nice way to unwind.

The Watchman

High on Crater Lake's western rim, The Watchman's lookout tower commands an eagle's-eye view across the amazingly blue lake to Wizard Island. The steep little climb up The Watchman is one of the most popular paths in the national park.

The Watchman won its name in 1886, when national park promoter William Gladstone Steel (see Hike #42) brought a U.S. Geological Survey crew to Crater Lake to measure the lake's depth. Part of the team set up a survey point on The Watchman to track the precise location of the rest of the team, who were out on a boat sounding the lake with a reel of piano wire. Other names that stuck from that 1886 expedition are Cleetwood Cove (for the boat) and Dutton Cliff (for its captain). The surveyors in the boat recorded a depth of 1996 feet, although sonar has since established a maximum lake depth of 1943 feet.

The Watchman Trail begins at a large, rail-fenced parking area on Crater Lake's Rim Drive. Look here for the fuzzy seedheads of western pasque flower and the blue trumpets of penstemon. The wide path is actually a

Crater Lake from The Watchman's fire lookout.

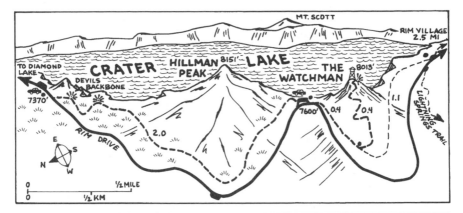

49. The Watchman

HIKE LOCATION

Moderate
1.6 miles round trip
420 feet elevation gain

A 1931 lookout tower on Crater Lake's rim offers spectacular views.

Getting There: From Crater Lake National Park's Rim Village, take the Rim Drive clockwise 4 miles to the trailhead, at a large viewpoint parking lot on the right with a rail fence. If you're coming from Diamond Lake, turn right when you reach the Rim Drive junction and continue 2.2 miles to the parking lot on the left. In either case, you'll have to pay the park's entrance fee, about $10 per car for a week-long pass, or $20 for an annual pass.

Hiking Tips: Note that pets are banned on all park trails. From the parking area, follow a paved sidewalk south along the highway 100 yards to find the actual trailhead. At the quarter-mile mark, you'll pass a snowfield. Just beyond, turn left at a junction and climb 0.4 mile to the summit lookout tower.

If you'd like more exercise and different views after climbing back down to the trailhead, hike right on past your car. This trail skirts Hillman Peak for 2 miles to the Devils Backbone, a volcanic dike that protrudes from the lake's rim cliffs as a craggy wall.

Season: Open mid-July through October.

While You're in the Area: Visit Crater Lake Lodge for a walk up Garfield Peak (Hike #42) or hike down to the lakeshore for a boat trip to Wizard Island's trails (Hike #4).

portion of the long-abandoned 1917 rim road. It traverses a rockslide of giant cream-colored boulders. These rocks are dacite, originally part of a 50,000-year-old lava flow on Mt. Mazama's shoulder. After Mazama's cataclysmic decapitation 7700 years ago, the old lava flow was left as The Watchman, a crest on the gaping caldera's rim.

Hikers in tennis shoes are often surprised to find a snowfield lingering across part of the trail until August. The patch of snow doesn't seem so startling if you consider that fifty feet of snow fall here each winter. In fact, you wouldn't even be able to drive to the trailhead if it weren't for the

The fire lookout on The Watchman.

highway crew that starts plowing out the 35-mile Rim Drive around Crater Lake each April, peeling back the snowpack with two D-7 Caterpillar bulldozers. By the time the crew's 900-horsepower rotary snowplow finishes the road-clearing job, it's usually July.

Turn left at a junction just beyond the snow and climb the final half mile amid struggling mountain hemlock, white lupine, and patches of pinkish five-petaled phlox. The stone-and-wood summit tower was built in 1931-1932. It's still sometimes staffed in summer with rangers who help spot fires and answer hikers' questions. Soak in the view from the lookout's stone patio.

The Watchman's lookout was probably the only one in the country to include a flush toilet. The ground floor of the structure, carefully built of stone, housed a restroom and a cistern until the 1940s. A gasoline pump at Lightning Springs, at the base of the mountain, pumped water a mile up to the tower. Twice a week, park rangers would put in a gallon of gas, start the pump, and leave it running. The pump usually ran out of gas when the cistern was about full. Don't expect toilet facilities today.

This was also one of the first lookouts to use a radio instead of a telephone. On hikes to other lookouts, you'll still sometimes see remnants of heavy-gauge telephone wire strung from O-shaped ceramic insulators in trailside trees. It was 1930 when the Forest Service first experimented with a new wireless radio system. The test site they chose was the Dog Mountain lookout in the Columbia Gorge. The staffer there, Bob Walker, used the new radio system to report that a fire was racing up the mountainside toward him. He quickly buried the radio in a blanket, took his pet nanny goat, and ran down the mountain's far side. A week later when the fire's ashes had cooled, Walker hiked back up to the lookout with his goat, dug up the radio, and reported that the old telephone system's wires had been snapped by falling trees in the fire. The next year, the Forest Service began replacing all their lookout telephones with the new wireless sets.

Today The Watchman's radio mostly helps the rangers keep tabs on the hikers who climb to visit the lookout. Now that the natural role of fire in Northwest forests is better understood, wildfires within the national park are generally allowed to burn. Ideally, small wildfires are supposed to sweep through the woods every few years, burning the brush, rejuvenating the wildflowers, and cleaning up the dead wood without getting hot enough to torch the larger trees. The problem now is that a century of overzealous fire suppression has left the forest littered with woody debris. To restore the natural system, rangers actually go out and set fires, carefully burning away the overgrown underbrush. Ironically, the lookout towers that once guarded the woods from fires are now sometimes used as spotting posts to watch over the progress of the forest's controlled burns.

Sand Mountain

Fewer than one in eight of Oregon's original lookout towers have survived, and all but a few of those stand abandoned. Nostalgia for the old towers runs particularly high among the children of the original staffers. Don Allen, for one, grew up spending summers on top of Sand Mountain, a cratered cinder cone near Santiam Pass.

Allen still remembers the Airstrip Fire of 1967, for example, when 7,600 acres of nearby forest burned. The fire stopped just short of Sand Mountain's summit, sparing the old lookout tower, but a blacker day was yet to come. The following summer a careless staffer accidentally started a cabin fire that burned down the lookout building after all. A trailer with a pop-up cupola served here briefly after that, but was removed by 1972. For Don Allen, it seemed that Sand Mountain's old magic was simply gone.

Twenty years later, Allen founded the Sand Mountain Society, a group dedicated to rebuilding a tower with painstaking historical accuracy. Volunteers—many with lookout experience on other summits—joined in the effort. They salvaged a 1931-vintage L-4-style tower that originally had been built on Whisky Peak in the Rogue River National Forest. They reconstructed furniture based on early photographs. They installed an antique Osborne firefinding table for locating smoke plumes.

Now the volunteers take turns staffing the finished tower each summer, welcoming visitors. And they actually do spot quite a few otherwise unreported wildfires, because this little cinder cone offers one of the most comprehensive panoramas in the entire Central Oregon Cascades.

The switchbacking trail up to the restored lookout tower is not much more than a quarter mile long. At the top you'll gain an impressive view of Mt. Washington rising above Big Lake. To the right of that spire-topped peak you'll see the snowy Three Sisters huddling together. To the left, look for the tip of Black Butte's cone (Hike #47) peeking out across Santiam Pass. Then turn around and look west. In that direction, lava flows snake from the base of Sand Mountain to Clear Lake (Hike #52). The lava dammed the McKenzie River 3000 years ago, creating Clear Lake. In the Old Cascades beyond, look for Iron Mountain's distinctive thumb (Hike #48) and the Three Pyramids' peaks.

After soaking up the view, take a path that loops around the crater rim. Watch for well-camouflaged, thumb-sized horned toads scampering among the cinders. Don Allen sheepishly recalls catching these lizards for pets when he was small. If you talk to other volunteers at Sand Mountain, you'll learn that the loneliness of lookout life inspired staffers all over the state to try taking in unlikely pets. The man who worked in the Red Butte

Sand Mountain's restored lookout.

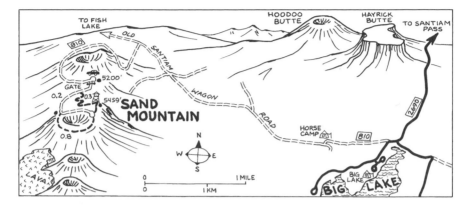

50. Sand Mountain

HIKE LOCATION

Easy
1.3-mile loop
400 feet elevation gain

Hike along a cinder cone's rim to a restored 1931 lookout tower.

Getting There: Drive Highway 20 to Santiam Pass, turn south at the Hoodoo Ski Area sign, and follow the paved Big Lake Road 3.1 miles to a major fork. Keep right toward Big Lake Campground, but after another 200 yards turn right again onto dirt Road 810. This remnant of the Old Santiam Wagon Road remains open to cars, but may be impassable in wet weather. Drive passenger cars with caution to avoid large rocks and ruts. Follow Road 810 as it jogs to the left at a primitive horse camp 0.9 mile from the Big Lake Road. At the 1.5-mile mark, go straight at a fork. After 2.4 miles, go straight at a 4-way junction. Finally, 2.9 miles from the paved road, turn left toward the lookout and climb 1.5 miles to a parking area at a locked gate.

Hiking Tips: Hike up the closed road 200 yards and turn left on a trail switchbacking up to the tower. After soaking up the view, hike on to the closed road's upper terminus and continue on a path around the crater rim.

Season: Open July through October.

While You're in the Area: Two other visitable lookout sites are visible from Sand Mountain: Iron Mountain (Hike #48) and Black Butte (Hike #47). You might also stop at the Santiam Pass railroad grade (Hike #31) or explore the Santiam Wagon Road at House Rock's cave (Hike #22).

lookout of the Umpqua National Forest, for example, once tried to catch a cute bobcat kitten in a gunny sack. He wound up with forty stitches worth of claw marks. At the Reynolds Ridge lookout, a staffer amused himself with a captive mole. It responded by biting him on the nose. The staffer's nose became so infected that his eyes swelled shut. Finally he had to call for two men to come carry him out twenty miles on a stretcher to a hospital.

Perhaps the strangest pets of all were the spiders trained by a bored Oregon State University student. In 1926 Bill Ruhmann took a summer job at the lookout on Roman Nose Mountain, a peak in the Siuslaw National Forest. By the end of summer Ruhmann claimed to be on such good terms with eight spiders in his cabin's wall that they would come out whenever he tapped on the wall with a stick. Then he would carry them one at a time to a window, drop them onto the flies that he allowed to gather there, wait for them to feed, and gently carry them back to their home in the wall.

Horned toad at Sand Mountain.

Today the idea of such intense isolation has developed its own rare appeal. Don Allen, for example, now lives in Portland, surrounded by the city's hectic pace of business appointments and commuting pressures. You can almost see the tension roll off his shoulders as he walks the trail to the Sand Mountain tower. The only sound is the crunch of boots on cinders. When he suddenly stops, the silence is overwhelming. He kneels to catch one of the scampering horned toads in his hand. A bug-eyed, warty reptile peers out from behind Allen's thumb like a miniature triceratops. Allen smiles and lets the horned toad scamper on. Then Allen stands up again, but he doesn't hurry on his way up to the lookout tower. He just stands there, gazing out across the old volcano's rim, breathing deep the chill, pure air of another age.

CHAPTER XIII

Rags and Riches

The Great Depression withered Oregon's economy for a decade. Between 1929 and 1933, stock prices plummeted eighty percent. By then, a third of the work force had been left jobless and half of the banks had failed. As the soup lines lengthened, desperation spread throughout the cities. In the forests, however, a courageous optimism gradually began to take hold. Starting in the darkest days of 1933, federal work programs such as the Civilian Conservation Corps (CCC) employed thousands to build trails, scenic roads, picnic areas, and lodges in the backwoods. Today these monuments of hope remain at some of Oregon's most popular destinations — including Silver Falls State Park, Clear Lake, and Timberline Lodge.

Silver Falls Park

On a single hike through Silver Falls State Park's forested canyon you can visit ten spectacular waterfalls, five of them more than 100 feet tall. The path even leads through mossy caverns *behind* the falls' shimmering silver curtains. But the hike is also a window onto the historic efforts of the Civilian Conservation Corps. Nearly three thousand of the Depression-era "tree troopers" worked here, with a new crew of two hundred arriving every six months between 1935 and 1942. These energetic young men helped rescue the park's landscape from years of commercial exploitation.

Start your hike at the South Falls parking area, a key battleground in the long-running fight between developers and preservationists. The picnic lawns and the parking lot you see here were once crisscrossed by the dirt streets of a poor backwoods town. Platted in 1888, Silver Falls City grew to include two sawmills, a church, a post office, a one-room schoolhouse, and an eight-room hotel. In the town's early years, the nearby forests were surveyed by an ambitious young engineer from Newberg, Oregon: future U.S. President Herbert Hoover. Within a generation, however, most of the forests had been cut. Farmers tried to plow the stump fields, but the short growing season and thin soils yielded little return.

In 1900, a Silverton photographer named June Drake began suggesting that the land surrounding Silver Falls' waterfall-draped canyon should be preserved as a park. Drake's early black-and-white photos of the spectacular falls have since become classics. In 1926, Drake finally succeeded in convincing the National Park Service to investigate the area. But the inspector they sent only shook his head.

South Falls at Silver Falls Park.

"If the region were still virgin," the park inspector wrote his superiors in Washington, D.C., "there is no doubt [the waterfalls'] merit would warrant very careful consideration as to national park value but, unfortunately the region has heard the sound of the axe for many years, a large majority of the big trees having been felled so that the remaining timber is practically all second growth. Worse, there are large areas of stark stumpage staring one in the face from every angle. From the brink of one of the best falls one looks across a canyon up a slope that is absolutely bare except for hundreds of thousands of stumps that from a distance look like so many dark headstones."

As you set out from the South Falls parking lot, you may have trouble believing that the national park inspector was describing the same place. The forest has regrown so thoroughly that the ancient stumps are now hard to spot. Walk down along the creek a few hundred yards to an overlook of 177-foot South Falls, where the creek suddenly vanishes over a cliff edge into the misty treetops. Standing here, you may have trouble believing something else: that a person once canoed off this cascade and lived.

The daredevil in question was Al Faussett, and his 1928 canoe stunt was part of the increasing commercialization that accompanied the National Park Service's rejection. The owner of South Falls, D.E. Geiser, hired a local woman to charge visitors ten cents apiece. On summer weekends, several hundred people might drive up for an outing. To lure bigger crowds,

Geiser began floating old cars down Silver Creek. Picnickers had to pay an extra ten cents each to watch the automobiles hurtle over South Falls.

Hoping for an even larger crowd, Geiser announced that the renowned Al Faussett would paddle over South Falls in a canvas canoe. Faussett had already made headlines by canoeing over Oregon City's Willamette Falls and Mt. Rainier's Snoqualmie Falls. Here, however, the stunt man faced a special problem. If you peer over the stone wall, you'll notice that South Falls splashes onto boulders at the shallow edge of a plunge pool. How on earth could a canoe survive such a landing?

After considering this problem, Faussett built a cantilevered ramp at the top of South Falls that extended the stream twenty feet out into the air. Then he rigged up a cable to help guide him toward the pool. Next he festooned his specially-built canvas canoe with a protective layer of inner tubes. Finally, after Geiser had given the crowd plenty of time to place bets, Faussett paddled downstream. The canoe sailed off the ramp as planned, but then the guide wire snagged in a tree. The canoe spun and crashed.

Faussett eventually recovered from his injuries in a hospital. Today, with a tip of the hat to the old daredevil, the park staff sometimes hosts Al Faussett Days, a festival in which fleets of canoes are floated over the falls. For the modern-day version of Faussett's stunt, however, the canoes are biodegradable miniatures, and no riders are allowed.

To continue your hike, follow the wall to the right and take a paved path down into the falls' canyon. Both the stonework wall and the trail itself date to the 1930s, when the federal government stepped in to help the state develop a park. President Franklin D. Roosevelt announced in 1935 that Silver Falls would be one of his largest Recreational Demonstration Projects. Nationwide, this program bought up 400,000 acres of poor farmland, relocating subsistence farmers to greener pastures. Here the program bought miles of stump-dotted fields. Over the next seven years, the Civilian Conservation Corps set about undoing the damage of the past half century.

The CCC workers became known as FDR's "Forest Army." Although not part of the War Department, the CCC camps were each directed by an Army officer. The program only accepted unemployed single young men, primarily from families on relief. In the camps, military order reigned. After working in the forest all day, the men returned to camp to take night classes in math, business, leadership, and literacy. Each man received $30 a month. Of this, $25 had to be sent home to his family. In the Depression, even such modest sums had substantial buying power. One Oregon CCC veteran recalls that the paychecks allowed his mother to buy a house with a $150 down payment.

When you hike the CCC trail down to a dripping cavern behind South Falls, however, the thundering cataract overhead is likely to turn your thoughts back to nature's handiwork instead of man's. In fact, the waterfalls of this park have an unusual story of their own to tell.

All of the falls in Silver Falls Park spill over what once were beachfront lava flows. Fifteen million years ago, before Oregon's Coast Range arose from the sea, the Columbia River reached the Pacific Ocean just a few miles west of here. Over the next millennia a series of basalt lava flows from Eastern Oregon surged down the Columbia's canyon, gradually pushing the river north to its present location. In the process, eight

---

51. Silver Falls Park

HIKE LOCATION

Easy (to South Falls)
1-mile loop
300 feet elevation gain

Moderate (to Drake Falls)
5-mile loop
600 feet elevation gain

Walk behind the waterfalls in Oregon's largest state park.

Getting There: From Salem, drive 10 miles east on North Santiam Highway 22, turn north at a sign for Silver Falls Park, and follow Highway 214 for 16 miles to the large park entrance sign at South Falls. (If you're coming from the north, drive Interstate 5 to Woodburn exit 271 and follow Highway 214 southeast through Silverton for a total of 30 miles.) When entering the South Falls parking complex, follow signs to Picnic Area C and park at the far end of the lot. Expect a $5 parking fee. Pets are not allowed.

Hiking Tips: Follow the creek downstream a few hundred yards to the top of South Falls. Then follow the paved path downhill and behind the falls. When you reach a junction by a footbridge, turn right for the easy, 1-mile loop back to your car. For a longer loop, go straight on an unpaved path along the creek another 3.1 miles, passing 4 more falls. Then turn right across a footbridge at a sign for Winter Falls. When you reach the highway, turn right on a level path through the woods 1.3 miles to the South Falls area, the lodge, and your car.

Season: The park is open year-round, but mid-winter storms can leave the trails icy or muddy.

While You're in the Area: If you've brought a bicycle, try the paved, mostly level path that loops 5 miles through the woods from the lodge at South Falls. Another bike path follows Silver Creek up to the park's 97-site campground.

distinct lava layers buried what is now the park. Because thousands of years passed between the eruptions, each rock layer had time to collect soil and grow forests before the next lava flow came. When Silver Creek cut through this geologic layer cake, it left waterfalls pouring from each of the hard lava tiers. Meanwhile, the waterfalls often gouged out the soft soil layers underneath, exposing caverns.

For proof of this geologic tale, look up at the roof of the misty cavern behind South Falls. The circular indentations in the ceiling are *tree wells*, casts that were left when lava hardened around burning tree trunks millions of years ago.

Just beyond South Falls you'll come to a trail junction at a footbridge. Only cross the bridge if you want to hurry back to your car. Otherwise continue downstream on an unpaved path that leads past more waterfalls. On this route you'll have the option of a three-mile, five-mile, or seven-mile loop, depending on which side trail you take back to the South Falls area.

Whichever loop you choose, you'll pass the historic Silver Falls Lodge when you return to South Falls at the end of your hike. Built by the CCC crews in 1940, the lodge features massive stonework walls, log rafters, and heavy myrtlewood furniture. The rustic styling recalls Timberline Lodge (Hike #53), and in fact the two projects shared the same architect (J. Elwood Isted) and the same interior decorator (Margery Hoffman Smith). Today the lodge houses an information center and snack bar.

Virtually all of the furniture for Silver Falls Lodge was crafted from two gigantic myrtlewood logs, each five feet in diameter and forty feet long. Donated by a timberman from the Southern Oregon coast, the logs

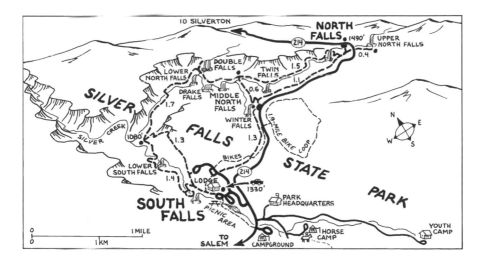

were cut in Brookings and kiln dried in Corvallis before being hauled to the site in CCC trucks. Altogether the two logs provided enough material for twenty-five tables (with three-inch-thick tops), eighty-two matching chairs, eleven benches, and a large bureau. Total cost for the magnificent myrtlewood furniture was a mere $500. Because much of this furniture mysteriously vanished over the years, however, park officials now welcome tips that could lead to the missing pieces.

Once the United States joined World War II in 1941, Congress quickly disbanded the CCC to free up manpower for grimmer battles. FDR's "Forest Army" withdrew from Silver Falls, but they left behind a park that was well on its way to recovering from the ravages of past commercial enterprises. Nearly a million visitors each year now come to admire the woodsy trails and silvery falls of Oregon's largest state park.

Clear Lake

The Civilian Conservation Corps bolted together picnic tables not only at Silver Falls, but also at hundreds of other sites in the Cascades' forests. One of the prettiest is Clear Lake, an astonishingly transparent pool with an eerie, underwater forest. Today a three-hour hike around Clear Lake's shore takes you past huge springs, old growth trees, lava beds, and an old-timey resort with rental rowboats.

As you drive the meandering one-lane road down to Clear Lake from Highway 126, you'll be following a portion of the route opened by CCC crews in 1934. Their narrow road to Clear Lake replaced a fisherman's trail from the Santiam Highway. The Highway 126 connection to McKenzie Bridge was not completed until the 1960s.

Park at the lake's picnic area, where a massive log shelter and stone fireplace remain as evidence of the CCC's solid construction style. Then set off on a trail through the Douglas fir and mountain hemlock forest that rings the lake. Expect glimpses through the woods to the spire of Mt. Washington and the snowy tips of the Three Sisters. Also take time to notice the white woodland wildflowers. The forest floor here is carpeted with bunchberry, a low, six-leaved wildflower that's in the same *Cornus* genus as dogwood trees. Like its much larger dogwood relatives, this dainty plant produces a white, cross-shaped bloom in June and a little bunch of red berries in fall.

After two miles you'll cross some of the rugged lava flows that left the strange, underwater forest. Three thousand years ago, an eruption poured liquid lava down from the base of Sand Mountain (see Hike #50). The lava dammed the McKenzie River and backed up Clear Lake. The water in the

52. Clear Lake

HIKE LOCATION

Moderate
5.4-mile loop
100 feet elevation gain

Circle a glass-clear lake with an underwater forest.

Getting There: From Eugene, start by driving Highway 126 east 70 miles. If you're coming from Albany, drive Highway 20 east 73 miles to the Y-junction with Highway 126 and turn right for 3.7 miles. In either case, watch for a "Clear Lake Resort and Picnic Area" sign between mileposts 3 and 4. Then take a paved side road 0.4 mile downhill and turn right to the picnic area's parking loop.

Hiking Tips: Walk past a log picnic shelter and continue on a trail around the lake counter-clockwise. Expect some traffic noise for the hike's first mile. Keep left at all junctions to circle the lake to the Clear Lake Resort, 200 yards from your car. The resort has no telephones, and the only power is produced by a generator, so bring flashlights if you plan to stay overnight. For reservations and prices, call Linn County Parks at 541-967-3917 or check *www.linnparks.com*.

Season: Open May to mid-November.

While You're in the Area: For a longer hike, simply follow the McKenzie River Trail downstream. It continues 24 miles past Clear Lake, almost to McKenzie Bridge. Both that trail and the Clear Lake loop are open to mountain bikes. For a quick sample of the McKenzie River's scenery, drive Highway 126 toward Eugene 2 miles to a viewpoint of 100-foot Sahalie Falls.

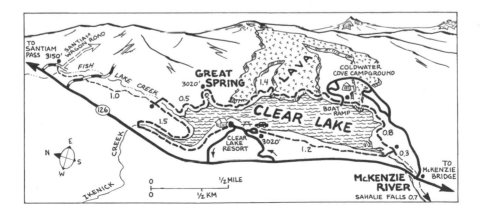

Rowboats at Clear Lake Resort.

new lake was so clear, cold, and calm that the forest here was drowned intact. Today the needles and most branches are gone, but many of the trunks remain. The wood is not petrified. The nearly freezing water has simply suspended decay for three millennia. Boaters can still see ghostly tree snags a hundred feet below the lake's surface. Scuba divers in insulated suits sometimes swim through the forest like giant, slow-motion birds.

At Great Spring the lakeshore trail detours around a rushing river that is only three hundred feet long. The stream emerges from a pool in the lava and flows straight into the lake. Though chilly, the spring's constant 38-degree Fahrenheit temperature keeps Clear Lake from freezing even in the coldest winter weather.

After another half mile you'll cross a footbridge over Fish Lake Creek, an inlet stream that flows only during the spring snowmelt. Then follow the lakeshore path around an arm of the lake to the Clear Lake Resort, near your car.

The tiny Clear Lake Resort offers a half dozen primitive cabins, a few groceries, a dock, and a cafe where hikers can restock on coffee and apple pie. Even if you're short on time, don't miss the chance to rent a rowboat at the lodge's dock. This is the only practical way to see the underwater forest. When the wind is calm and the light is right, there is nothing quite as peaceful as drifting across the green-glass water of Clear Lake, watching trout drift among the broken snags of a forest three thousand years old.

Timberline Lodge

Mt. Hood's Timberline Lodge began as a make-work project in the depths of the Great Depression. But by the time President Franklin D. Roosevelt dedicated this elegantly rustic hotel in 1937 it had become a grand expression of Northwest art. Today, the hotel has become one of Oregon's top tourist attractions. Still, surprisingly few visitors venture into the scenic alpine landscape that lured hotel builders here in the first place. So after you tour Timberline Lodge, leave time to hike a mile up the mountainside. There you'll find the Silcox Hut, a miniature of the old hotel with an even better view.

As you drive up to Timberline Lodge from Government Camp, the forest dwindles to a few spindly firs and then gives way to tundra. When you reach the gray shingled hotel you may well be above the clouds. Building anything at this elevation would be a challenge. Building a hotel was a monumental task.

In 1935, FDR was looking for monumental tasks. Despite the optimism generated by the Civilian Conservation Corps in 1933, the Depression had continued to worsen. The President responded by launching an even larger employment program, the Works Progress Administration. Later renamed the Works Projects Administration, the WPA would hire not only jobless young men, but also craftsmen, artists, builders, and engineers who

Timberline Lodge.

would otherwise be on the relief rolls. FDR hoped that meaningful work would restore the people's confidence, and that the extra income would enable them to buy goods and revive the moribund economy.

The Timberline Lodge project alone employed 7250 Northwest artisans. As you climb the stone steps and enter the carved front door, you'll see their labor-intensive handiwork everywhere. Ahead of you, note the massive hexagonal hearth, with three fireplaces on each floor. The 92-foot-tall chimney required 400 tons of native stone. Look behind the fireplace to find a display about Timberline's past. Then, as you go up the stairs, run your hand over the banister's carved animal figures—a sleeping bear, a beaver, and an owl—polished by the hands of countless visitors. Upstairs you'll see the six massive ponderosa pine pillars that support the lobby roof. Only hotel guests are allowed in the wings to see the individual rooms, but they too exhibit unique craftsmanship. The Trillium Room, for example, features the three-petaled lily in its artwork. The Zigzag River Room has motifs of river ripples and fish designs.

Timberline Lodge's artistic ambiance is a far cry from the atmosphere of the earlier "Timberline Hotel" that once stood near here. That more

Lounge at Timberline Lodge.

primitive hostelry consisted of an 8-by-16-foot hut. Built in 1924 by a McMinnville dentist, the hut had a flimsy porch and a lunch window where a cup of coffee cost an exorbitant ten cents. Although technically a branch of the larger Government Camp Hotel at the base of the mountain, the hut had so little space that overnight guests had to sleep on blankets in three nearby tents. The hut closed in 1930 and was crushed by winter snows. All that remains today are fragments of the foundations, half a mile west of Timberline Lodge.

Still, the example of the little hut at timberline had encouraged people to consider grander development schemes for Mt. Hood. In 1927 a group of prominent Portland businessmen formed a Mount Hood Committee that recommended building a tram, tourist hotel, campground, and gas station. The Forest Service rejected the plan as a "profit-making eyesore." A few years later the committee returned with a proposal for a nine-story, glass-and-concrete skyscraper. This blueprint was likewise dismissed as "impertinent to the mountain scenery."

Finally, architects developed a more rustic design. This time the government bought in. With the headline, "WPA Will Build Mt. Hood Hotel," the *Oregonian* broke the news on December 15, 1935 that Roosevelt had authorized $275,513 for a 300-bed hotel with a road, trails, ski jumps, swimming pool, tennis courts, and parking lot. Workers started clearing snow from the site on June 1, 1936, the same day that the CCC's new Mt. Hood Loop Highway officially opened. Two weeks later the building's cornerstone was laid, and soon 380 WPA workers were on the job. They built massive stone walls that weighed six tons per running foot. They hoisted gigantic beams for the lobby ceiling. By September 14, when the first snow of autumn fell, the cedar shakes of the roof were in place. The 750-pound bronze weather vane, its design hurriedly based on an Indian motif found in a Campfire Girls' handbook, had to be mounted in a blizzard.

Work continued through the winter in shops set up inside old Portland school buildings. Women dyed old Army uniforms and woolen blankets with earth tones, cut them into strips, and hooked them into 119 rugs. Other artisans prepared a hundred pairs of appliqued sailcloth curtains and 152 bedspreads. Craftsmen hammered out wrought-iron hardware, stitched leather lampshades, and built 820 pieces of specially designed furniture. When snow melted from Mt. Hood in the spring of 1937, trucks began hauling the furnishings up to the lodge. By then, cost overruns had tripled the building's price tag to nearly $1 million.

After touring the hotel's lobby, walk out through the rarely used, ceremonial front entry. The ten-foot-tall door weighs 1100 pounds—including 400 pounds of wrought iron—yet it can be opened with a single finger. Step out onto the balcony to enjoy the view of Mt. Jefferson and the Three Sisters.

On this balcony you are standing where FDR delivered the lodge's dedication speech on September 28, 1937. The President and his wife Eleanor had arrived in Portland in their private railroad car early that morning. They rode with Oregon governor Charles Martin in an open car to Bonneville Dam, which FDR dedicated at 9:30 am. Then the ninety-member entourage drove on through Hood River to Timberline Lodge, where a crowd of twelve hundred had gathered. At 1:12 pm, FDR stepped up onto the balcony to give his speech, broadcast live by radio. Meanwhile the horizon sparkled as fire lookout staffers on fifteen Oregon peaks blinked acknowledgment with flashing mirrors. Afterwards, the President and his entourage sat down to an Oregon banquet of salmon, tomato rosettes, and huckleberry pie before driving back to Portland.

In fact, the lodge wasn't quite finished in time for its dedication. Only a few rooms had been hurriedly readied for FDR's inspection. Four months passed before the hotel actually opened to the public on February 5, 1938. To make sure all went well at that event, organizers borrowed the managerial staff of Portland's Multnomah Hotel. Buses brought 150 guests up from Government Camp. That night, two and a half hours of vaudeville acts kept the guests entertained.

Managers soon began wondering how they would entertain guests once the novelty of the new hotel wore off. The proposed pool had not yet

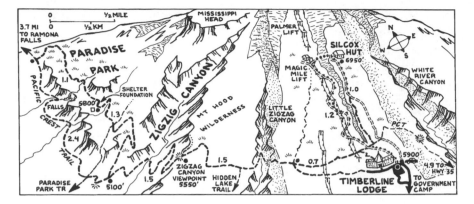

been built, and the tennis courts had been canceled. What was there for visitors to do up on this barren mountainside?

To see one of the solutions they devised, walk out the back door of the lobby, cross the patio, and hike two hundred yards uphill toward the mountain. Here you'll find the Timberline Trail, a 39.3-mile loop built by the CCC around Mt. Hood. Realizing that most hikers would need five days to complete the circuit from Timberline Lodge, the CCC crews built four smaller shelters along the route. The stone hut at Paradise Park was destroyed by a falling tree in the 1990s, but the dirt-floored, ten-foot-square shelters at McNeil Point, Cairn Basin, and Cooper Spur have survived.

Even if Timberline Lodge guests could be convinced to go hiking in summer, what could they do in winter? The answer was to install a mile-long ski chairlift—the first of its kind in America. Skiing was considered such a novelty at the time that the King of Norway was invited to come demonstrate the strange sport for Timberline guests.

The original Magic Mile ski lift has long since been dismantled, but you can sample its views by hiking to the Silcox Hut, the stone building that served as the lift's upper terminus from 1939 to 1962. Reopened as a chalet in 1992, the hut now offers overnight bunks for groups and a limited cafe in the tradition of the Swiss Alps. To find it, turn right on the Timberline Trail and then turn uphill on the Mountaineer Trail. This braided path climbs past wind-gnarled firs and August-blooming blue lupine.

Don't be surprised if you're passed by mountain climbers on this trail. Mt. Hood has become one of the most frequently climbed snowpeaks in the world, and this is the most popular route to the 11,240-foot summit. In 1893, Portland's outdoor club, the Mazamas, chose to hold its organizational meeting on the top of Mt. Hood. On that day, 155 men and 38 women climbed to the summit to elect William Steel the club's first president.

Since then everyone seems to have gotten in on the act. Hood has been scaled by a courageous double amputee and a frivolous prankster in high heels. Klindt Vielbig trekked to the top in 1964 with a gibbon named Kandy. A typical ascent from Timberline to the summit takes seven hours, but Gary Leech set a still-unmatched record by dashing up in just 85 minutes.

Unless you've brought mountain climbing gear, make the Silcox Hut your turnaround point. The squat, stone-walled hut is named for the Forest Service chief who approved the Magic Mile chairlift idea. When the lift opened in 1939 this building housed an engine and turnaround wheel. In those days, the single-passenger chairs crept uphill so slowly the ride took eleven minutes. In 1962, the old lift was replaced by a double-seater a few hundred yards to the west—and that lift was replaced in the 1990s by a high-speed lift with four-passenger chairs. Meanwhile the Silcox Hut

53. Timberline Lodge

HIKE LOCATION

Moderate
2.2-mile loop
1100 feet elevation gain

Tour a rustic 1937 lodge, and then climb to a hut high on Mt. Hood.

Getting There: From Portland, follow "Mt. Hood" signs 55 miles east on Highway 26. At the far end of Government Camp, turn left for 6 miles to Timberline Lodge's parking lot.

Hiking Tips: After touring Timberline Lodge, walk out the back door, cross the patio, and hike two hundred yards uphill toward the mountain. Turn right on the Timberline Trail—which also serves as the Pacific Crest Trail. The path is confused here, but contour a few hundred yards across a snow gully and climb to a small ridge. At a signpost, turn uphill to the left on the Mountaineer Trail. Follow this braided path 0.6 mile and then join a dirt road for the remainder of the climb to the Silcox Hut. To return on a loop, contour 100 yards across a snowfield from the Silcox Hut to the new Magic Mile chairlift and follow a service road back down to the lodge.

Season: Open mid-July through October.

While You're in the Area: For a different hike from Timberline Lodge, follow the Timberline Trail the other direction (west) for 2.2 miles to an overlook of 700-foot-deep Zigzag Canyon. Also consider exploring the Barlow Trail (Hike #18) near Government Camp.

The Silcox Hut.

became a snow-filled ruin, abandoned for decades. Finally a volunteer group restored it to its present splendor. They hired a blacksmith to forge chandeliers and replacement hardware in the Timberline tradition. Today the hut mostly serves as a day lodge, but bunks are available too.

While you're admiring the stark mountain scenery at this elevation, you might consider that the landscape here is entirely the product of recent volcanism. The silvery snags you passed on the trail up are trees killed by the hot blast of a small eruption in the 1790s. The ground itself on this side of the mountain is a debris fan from a much larger, Mt. St. Helens-style blast two thousand years ago. In that eruption, a gigantic avalanche wiped the mountain's slope clean as far as Government Camp. Afterwards, a lava dome slowly rose to plug the vent. The dome remains as Crater Rock, the monolith looming above you just in front of the actual summit.

Mt. Hood is a gigantic work in progress—a construction project with a timeline of millennia. As you hike back down from the Silcox Hut, the wide-angle scenery makes it easy to scan the world from this broader perspective. From here, a stock market crash seems less substantial than a cloud. Time itself ticks at a different pace.

Perhaps this was the real reason President Roosevelt asked the unemployed millions of the Great Depression to come work in the great outdoors: to open America's eyes to the higher view at timberline.

CHAPTER XIV

War!

When Japanese warplanes attacked the Pearl Harbor naval base on December 7, 1941, American strategists suddenly realized that Oregon's thinly defended coast might be the next front line of World War II. The military quickly established lookout posts and machine gun nests along Oregon beaches. They trained fire lookout staffers to recognize Japanese aircraft. They removed road signs from coastal highways to confuse invaders. By day, anti-submarine bombers and blimps patrolled the shore. By night, coastal cities blacked out their lights to hide from aerial attack. Anti-Japanese hysteria ran so high that few protested when the government violated citizens' constitutional rights by moving 117,000 Japanese-Americans away from the Pacific Coast, often to bleak internment camps in the desert.

Desperate for a victory in the early days of the war, President Roosevelt ordered a daring aerial raid on the Japanese homeland. On April 18, 1942, with no practical means for a return trip, Lieutenant Colonel James Doolittle launched sixteen heavy B-25 bombers from the short flight deck of the aircraft carrier *Hornet*. The planes bombed Tokyo and other cities, and landed as best they could in China.

Doolittle's raid shook Japanese morale. The Japanese military resolved to retaliate by striking the American mainland. Military strategists knew such an attack would not be easy. No foreign force had succeeded in attacking the continental U.S. since the War of 1812. The Japanese had no bases or aircraft carriers close enough to launch a raid like Doolittle's. But they had one weapon the U.S. could not yet match: the submarine.

At that time Japanese submarines carried more than just torpedoes. Most had deck cannons that could hurl a five-and-a-half-inch shell nine miles. Forty-two of the submarines could also carry a small, disassembled airplane in a waterproof deck hangar. Before radar, the Japanese routinely used these planes to spot targets for the submarine's torpedoes. To fly the plane, the crew had to bolt on its wings and pontoons, and then launch it from a catapult. When the plane returned, a derrick hoisted it aboard, where the crew quickly took it apart until the next flight.

Early in 1942 a brave young Japanese air officer named Nobuo Fujita proposed to his superiors that the little reconnaissance airplanes be modified to carry two 168-pound bombs. He recommended that the planes drop their bombs on key defense installations from the Panama Canal to Seattle's Boeing Field. He volunteered to fly such missions himself.

At first Fujita's commanders rejected his proposal as too risky. They pointed out that his airplane's sluggish 150-mile-per-hour top speed would make it an easy target for American fighter planes. Instead they ordered Fujita's submarine, the *I-25*, to use only its deck gun and torpedoes to harry Oregon's coast during the summer of 1942. But by the time the *I-25* made its next tour that fall, the commanders had changed their minds. Fujita would be allowed to fly against the Americans after all.

Today you can hike to the sites of the submariners' two unprecedented attacks on the United States: a beachfront dune at Fort Stevens shelled by the *I-25's* deck gun, and a redwood forest near Brookings bombed by Fujita's airplane.

Fort Stevens

Fort Stevens was built near the end of the Civil War to guard the mouth of the Columbia River against rogue Confederate warships. That threat proved imaginary, and the fort's guns were not used. Even when a genuine threat appeared in World War II, the artillery here remained silent. Since then the old military reservation has been converted to an eleven-square-mile state park. Today a network of trails through the coastal forest connects the park's top attractions: a military museum, several abandoned bunkers, the state's largest campground, and an ocean beach with the rusting remains of a shipwreck.

You might start with a visit to the park's military museum, where you'll find displays of uniforms, armaments, and historic photographs. In summer the museum hosts a variety of activities: Civil War reenactments, blacksmithing demonstrations, walking tours of underground bunkers, and tours of the park from the back of a 1950s Army truck.

To start your own hike through the park, however, drive to the park's day use entrance and park in the Battery Russell parking area. Walk from a display board up a staircase to the top of the enormous concrete ramparts. Circular tracks remain where the massive guns once swiveled. Dank bunkers once held stockpiles of the guns' ten-inch shells.

The Army built Battery Russell in 1904 in an attempt to modernize Fort Stevens. The battery's ten-inch "disappearing" guns used the latest design. When a gun fired, the recoil rolled it backwards on a track to a protected location out of sight of enemy battleships.

When the gun needed to fire again, a counterweight rolled it back into position. The guns fired 500-pound shells that could hit a thirty-foot-wide target nine miles away. A well-trained crew could fire a round every thirty-two seconds. But because the guns had been developed before the invention of airplanes, their "disappearing" system was useless against aircraft. And because of breakdowns, only two of the battery's original eight guns still worked by 1942.

From the battlements you can see a slate-blue stripe of ocean beyond the shore pine and the Scotch broom of the sandy woods. Imagine standing here on the night of June 21, 1942. It is overcast, nearly midnight. Then you notice a small, distant flash on the dark horizon. After a few seconds, a worrisome, thin whistle comes from the sky. Suddenly lightning seems to silhouette the trees, the ground shakes, and a deafening blast rips through the air. Hardly a hundred yards away, the backstop of a baseball diamond vanishes in a fiery crater.

Nobuo Fujita's submarine, the *I-25*, had approached the mouth of the Columbia River that night beneath a fishing fleet. The captain correctly guessed that there would be no mines near fishing boats. He surfaced about eight miles off the shore of Fort Stevens, which he thought might be a submarine base. He turned the ship toward the open sea, so its deck gun faced the shore. Then, while Nobuo Fujita carried shells to help, the gunner fired seventeen rounds at random toward the dark shore.

The explosions stampeded Fort Stevens' soldiers out of their barracks. One man ran out the door into a parked truck and cut his forehead. His bloodied face nearly panicked the others into believing the Japanese had already landed. At Battery Russell, the crew scrambled to battle stations, eager for the order to return fire. Meanwhile their officers quickly collected telephone reports of the flashes' location at sea. They decided that the enemy vessel stood just beyond Battery Russell's nine-mile range. If their guns fired short of the ship, they would merely reveal the bunker's location. Then the Japanese gun, with its superior range, would be able to pick off Battery Russell at will. The bunker's telephone rang again. This time it was the machine gunners at the beach, begging for permission to fire.

To see the gun positions on the beach, set out on a wide, sandy trail from Battery Russell's concrete rampart. At first the path follows the crest of an ancient sand dune overgrown with a forest of spruce, shore pines, and wild lily-of-the-valley. Then you'll duck through a tunnel under a road and follow a paved bike path to the broad sand flats of Clatsop Beach.

The first thing you'll notice on Clatsop Beach is the rusting skeleton of a shipwreck. The *Peter Iredale* beached here in 1906 when her captain missed the Columbia River bar. All hands were rescued, but the insurance

underwriters did not think the ship itself was worth repairing. By then, steamships were more common than ships with sails. So a salvage company stripped everything of value, including much of the metal plating. Surf, weather, and rust have whittled away at the rusting remains ever since.

Sunbathers and beachcombers now invade this popular beach each summer, but in 1942 the sand here was a no-man's-land. Obser-

The Peter Iredale *shipwreck.*

vation towers with searchlights and machine guns scanned the beach. On the night of June 21, the lookouts here were the closest witnesses of the Japanese attack. When they called for permission to return fire, the officers told them their machine guns could not possibly reach a target so far out to sea.

The next morning the military determined that the Japanese shells had done no significant damage. No one had been hurt. The officers' decision not to fire back had been technically justified. But morale at Fort Stevens dipped. Soldiers felt frustrated that they had not been allowed to fire. And

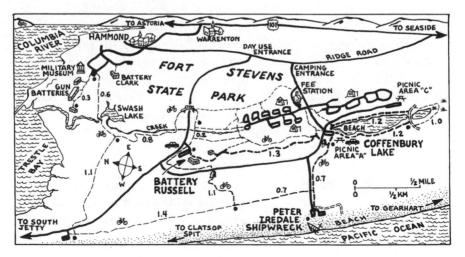

the officers began to realize that fixed gun batteries could no longer be relied upon to defend the Pacific Coast against attack. The defense effort began to shift toward the use of aircraft.

Meanwhile, Fujita's submarine had swiftly retreated. The crew celebrated the success of their attack on the United States mainland and sailed back to Japan for new orders.

54. Fort Stevens

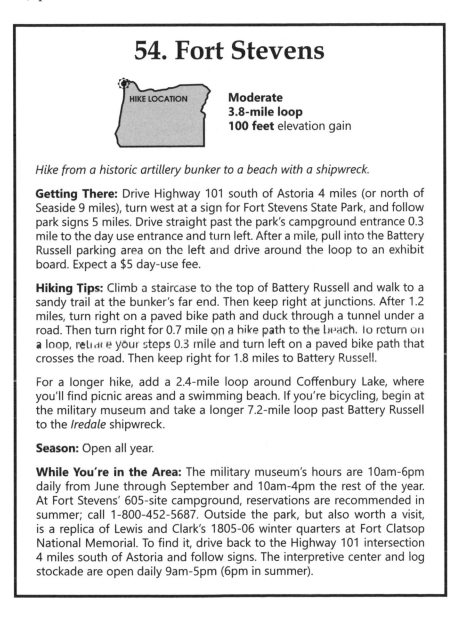

HIKE LOCATION

Moderate
3.8-mile loop
100 feet elevation gain

Hike from a historic artillery bunker to a beach with a shipwreck.

Getting There: Drive Highway 101 south of Astoria 4 miles (or north of Seaside 9 miles), turn west at a sign for Fort Stevens State Park, and follow park signs 5 miles. Drive straight past the park's campground entrance 0.3 mile to the day use entrance and turn left. After a mile, pull into the Battery Russell parking area on the left and drive around the loop to an exhibit board. Expect a $5 day-use fee.

Hiking Tips: Climb a staircase to the top of Battery Russell and walk to a sandy trail at the bunker's far end. Then keep right at junctions. After 1.2 miles, turn right on a paved bike path and duck through a tunnel under a road. Then turn right for 0.7 mile on a hike path to the beach. To return on a loop, retrace your steps 0.3 mile and turn left on a paved bike path that crosses the road. Then keep right for 1.8 miles to Battery Russell.

For a longer hike, add a 2.4-mile loop around Coffenbury Lake, where you'll find picnic areas and a swimming beach. If you're bicycling, begin at the military museum and take a longer 7.2-mile loop past Battery Russell to the *Iredale* shipwreck.

Season: Open all year.

While You're in the Area: The military museum's hours are 10am-6pm daily from June through September and 10am-4pm the rest of the year. At Fort Stevens' 605-site campground, reservations are recommended in summer; call 1-800-452-5687. Outside the park, but also worth a visit, is a replica of Lewis and Clark's 1805-06 winter quarters at Fort Clatsop National Memorial. To find it, drive back to the Highway 101 intersection 4 miles south of Astoria and follow signs. The interpretive center and log stockade are open daily 9am-5pm (6pm in summer).

Wheeler Ridge Bomb Site

Nobuo Fujita found a royal summons waiting for him when his submarine returned to Japan. With growing excitement, Fujita read that he was ordered to Tokyo to see Prince Takamatsu, the younger brother of Emperor Hirohito. When Fujita arrived for the royal audience, the prince told him that his suggestion of bombing the U.S. mainland had been accepted after all. But instead of bombing a spectacular military target like the Panama Canal, as Fujita had originally proposed, he was ordered to bomb a remote part of Southern Oregon's forests.

"Forests?" Fujita later recalled thinking in dismay. "My dreams came to earth! Any cadet could bomb a forest!" He began to feel better about his task only when a commanding officer explained, "The northwest United States is full of trees. Once a fire gets started in the deep woods it is very hard to put out. Sometimes whole towns are burned. If we could start some big fires it would cause the Americans much trouble."

The *I-25* submarine set sail right away. When it surfaced off Southern Oregon, however, the weather was so stormy that Fujita's launch had to be delayed. While he waited, Fujita wrote out his will and carefully placed it in a small box with a clip of his hair, to be given to his wife in the event he did not return. A week later, on September 9, 1942, the rain stopped. The crew assembled the plane in the predawn twilight. Fujita stowed his family's 400-year-old samurai sword beside his cockpit seat for good luck. Then the crew catapulted his airplane into the air.

As you drive to the Wheeler Ridge Bomb Site Trail, you might imagine Fujita's plane flying overhead. The little aircraft passed the Cape Blanco lighthouse and headed fifty miles southeast. Fujita later recalled that the sun rose "like a Chinese lantern" over Oregon that morning. Green ridges protruded like sleeping giants from a featherbed of white fog.

When you turn at Brookings to drive up the Chetco River you'll see a large green mountain ahead: Mt. Emily. In 1942 Howard Gardner staffed a cupola-style fire lookout building on Mt. Emily's summit. As the sun came up on September 9, he was just lighting his woodstove to cook breakfast when he heard a sputtering engine sound, like an old car backfiring. He looked out the window and noticed a strange little airplane circling the foggy forests below. Although he had been trained to recognize the silhouettes of enemy bombers and fighters, he had never seen anything like this pint-sized, fabric-covered plane. He flipped on his radio and raised the Gold Beach ranger station dispatcher at 6:24am. "Gold, this is five-six,

A Japanese submarine-launched airplane.

reporting one aircraft. Single engine, with pontoons. Type unknown. Flying low. Seen east two miles. Was circling, now headed northwest."

The dispatcher sleepily relayed the report to the Army Air Force's command center in Roseburg, where it was laid aside with a shrug. A floatplane straying across the Siskiyou wilderness? Gardner went back to his breakfast.

Meanwhile, Fujita dropped his bombs on Wheeler Ridge. He looked over his shoulder to make sure they had exploded. One, at least, had left flickering flames in the forest. Satisfied, he turned the plane around and headed for the submarine's rendezvous coordinates.

As Fujita's plane flew back past the Cape Blanco lighthouse, a soldier at a coastal observation post spotted the aircraft and telephoned his headquarters in Bandon. The Bandon officer relayed the report to the Roseburg central command. With this confirmation, the center sent P-38 fighter pilots scrambling for their planes. But because of confusion over the sighting's location—south of the city of North Bend—the fighters roared off toward Bend, a city 150 miles inland, where there were no submarines.

Fujita's plane landed safely on its pontoons beside the *I-25*. After the plane had been disassembled and stowed, the captain decided to try torpedoing two merchant ships Fujita had noticed nearby. But as the sub cruised on the surface toward the ships, a warplane suddenly appeared overhead. This was not one of the wayward P-38 fighters, but rather an A-29 bomber on a routine anti-submarine patrol from McChord Field near Tacoma. The submarine captain quickly ordered his ship to dive. It was fifty-five feet below the surface when the bomber's first 300-pound charge detonated. The sub rolled with the blast, and the lights went out. The radio man shouted that his room had been damaged. The captain kept diving. Two more bombs shook the walls before the sub reached 220 feet. Then the captain set the sub on the ocean floor and waited.

By noon Howard Gardner at the Mt. Emily lookout still had heard nothing more about his strange aircraft sighting, so he wasn't thinking about bombs. When the fog finally cleared he noticed a tiny plume of white smoke lingering over Wheeler Ridge. He routinely called in the fire to the ranger at Gold Beach. The ranger there mused that recent rainstorms should have left fire danger near zero. He speculated that the smoke might be a "sleeper" fire from the previous week's lightning. The ranger ordered Gardner and Keith Johnson, the eighteen-year-old staffer in the neighboring Bear Wallow fire lookout, to go check it out. And so, with sixty pounds of firefighting, survival, and radio gear in his backpack, Gardner bushwhacked eight arduous miles to meet Johnson on Wheeler Ridge.

Today the path to the site on Wheeler Ridge is much easier. The trailhead is located about where Gardner met his colleague Johnson. Gardner climbed a tree to get a bearing on the smoke plume. Then he and Johnson tromped through the woods for a closer look. As you hike the modern trail you'll notice that the forest here is strange mixture of trees: tanoaks, pines, six-foot-thick Douglas firs, and redwoods up to twelve feet in diameter. Rhododendrons twist amid the trunks with jungly blooms.

When Gardner and Johnson reached the source of the smoke they were puzzled to find what must have looked like an alien landing site. Scattered fires smoldered in a scorched fifty-foot circle. In the middle, shattered tree trunks surrounded a small pit. Gardner radioed to report that they could put out the fires without difficulty. He added, however, that the cause had definitely not been lightning. It looked suspiciously like a bomb crater.

When Gardner returned to his fire lookout that night, the FBI was on the radio demanding more details. The next day a swarm of soldiers, officers, and federal agents struggled through the steep forest to the site. They dug up a shell casing with Japanese markings and immediately ordered the entire operation hushed up. The public must not be allowed to panic. For the first time in history, an enemy had succeeded in dropping a bomb on the United States mainland.

After waiting twenty days in the ocean off Cape Blanco, Fujita and the submarine's captain decided to strike again. Fujita launched his plane and dropped two more incendiary bombs, this time on the forest near Grassy Knob, just ten miles inland from Cape Blanco. Neither of the bombs exploded. The fire lookout staffer on Grassy Knob radioed in a description of the pontoon plane. But this time Fujita switched off his engine and glided silently back over the beach to his submarine, so the coastal observers missed him. The FBI concluded that the floatplane might not have come from a ship at all. Perhaps the parts for the plane had been smuggled to a secret Japanese base at a wilderness lake and assembled for launch there. Agents spent the autumn hiking to remote lakes in the Siskiyou Mountains. They found no trace of an air base.

Meanwhile, Fujita's submarine sailed up the Oregon Coast torpedoing ships. In the next week it sank two merchant freighters. Near Astoria on October 11 it blew up a submarine—although this later proved to be a Russian vessel. Fujita returned to Japan so proud of the mission's success

55. Wheeler Ridge Bomb Site

HIKE LOCATION

Easy
1.6 miles round trip
100 feet elevation gain

A bomb crater in a redwood forest marks a 1942 Japanese attack.

Getting There: In Brookings on the Southern Oregon coast, drive Highway 101 to the south end of the Chetco River bridge, take South Bank Road inland 5 miles, fork right onto gravel Mt. Emily Road, and follow "Bombsite Trail" signs for 13 twisty, uphill miles to the trailhead sign. Parking is easiest at a pullout 0.2 mile before the trailhead.

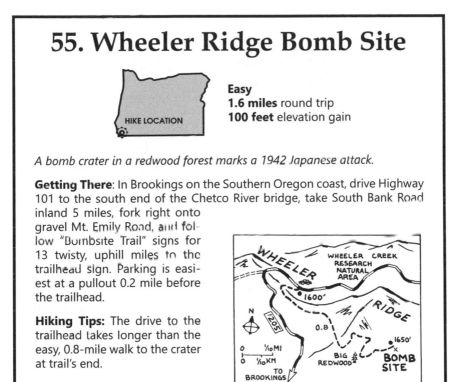

Hiking Tips: The drive to the trailhead takes longer than the easy, 0.8-mile walk to the crater at trail's end.

Season: Open all year.

While You're in the Area: Visit some of the other places Fujita saw as he flew his bombing raid: the Cape Blanco lighthouse (Hike #36), Humbug Mountain (Hike #13), and the Rogue River (Hike #29).

that he wept when his ship pulled into port. "I tried to hold back my tears with binoculars, pretending to be a lookout as we tied up at the dock." The Japanese nation hailed Fujita as a hero.

But Nobuo Fujita's impact on Oregon was far from over, as you'll see when you reach the shallow bomb crater at the end of the trail. The next chapter of the story begins in 1962, twenty years after Fujita's bomb attack. In a daring move intended to bury old grudges, the Brookings' Jaycees invited the retired Japanese pilot to the town's Azalea Festival that year. Veteran groups complained angrily that America should honor its own heroes, not those of the enemy. Fujita himself was unsure of the Jaycees' motives. Since the war, his initial pride in the aerial attack had changed to regret and then shame. He suspected the invitation might be a ploy to put him on trial as a war criminal.

Nubuo Fujita planting a redwood in 1992.

In preparing for his 1962 trip to Oregon, Nobuo Fujita carefully packed the 400-year-old samurai sword he had carried on his missions twenty years before. If the Americans proved unable to forgive him, he would use the sword to commit the Japanese ritual suicide known as *seppuku*. When he arrived in Oregon, however, he was welcomed as an ambassador of good will. Touched, Fujita presented his cherished samurai sword to the people of Brookings as a token of reconciliation. It still hangs on display in the Brookings city library.

Fujita's story next jumps forward thirty years to 1992, when the Forest Service was building a trail to the bomb site for the fiftieth anniversary of the attack. The rangers invited Nobuo Fujita back to Oregon as the guest of honor at the trail's grand opening. Although Fujita was eighty years old, he agreed to come to America once again. He hiked the new trail and planted a redwood seedling in the bomb crater as a token of peace.

After Nobuo Fujita passed away in 1997 at the age of 85, his daughter fulfilled his last request by scattering some of his ashes here. She found— as you will when you reach the shallow crater—that her father's redwood tree had taken root and prospered. Since then, it has been designated one of Oregon's "heritage trees." Nobuo Fujita's message of regret and peace lives on.

CHAPTER XV

The Legacy

Sometimes the spirit of Oregon seems to have survived best on wilderness trails. When the sun flashes from an obsidian chip in the forest duff, you can almost hear the muffled *tink!* of a Nez Perce boy learning to knap obsidian rocks into arrowheads. When the wind whistles through the empty windows of an abandoned lookout tower at twilight, you can almost smell the woodsmoke of the lonely staffer's cast-iron stove. Every hike is a journey through time.

Cities may be the billboards on which civilization writes, erases, and rewrites its frenzied messages. But the world spins more slowly the farther one walks from town. In the wilderness, old lessons remain as if suspended in amber. The land's genetic treasures have survived best here too. Bug-eyed flying squirrels, insect-eating pitcher plants, and fierce native trout retreat to the wilds as if to an inner sanctum.

Wilderness may be the most important legacy that Oregonians will leave. But like any inheritance with multiple heirs, it's prone to dispute. Perhaps no other controversy has so divided the state as the war for the wilds. At times, wilderness trails have become battle lines splitting families and friends. In few places are those battle scars as deep as in Oregon's Opal Creek Wilderness.

Opal Creek

Fifty thousand people a year now hike to see the Opal Creek Wilderness. *Audubon* magazine ranks it with the Grand Canyon as one of the nation's top ten "paradises preserved" in the 20th century. Politicians and Forest Service administrators stumble over each other to take credit for setting aside the 35,000-acre area, with its hundreds of waterfalls and its centuries-old forest.

But just nine years before the area's official dedication in 1998, antiwilderness protesters shut down the State Capitol, demanding that Opal Creek's trees be cut. Salem's streets were gridlocked with hundreds of log trucks, effigies of spotted owls hanging from their mirrors. In the thick of that melee, politicians and bureaucrats backed away from Opal Creek as if from a yellowjacket nest.

To see what the furor was about, hike into the new Wilderness Area yourself. And to understand how it all started, you might want to try looking at the mossy old woods through the eyes of the young boy who accidentally launched Opal Creek's war on a summer night in 1960.

"When I was twelve years old," George Atiyeh recalls, "I spent the summer at my family's old Jawbone Flats mining camp with my great uncle Jim Hewitt. He was an ornery, surprisingly sophisticated old curmudgeon. We all called him Grampa. He put a limit on how far out in the woods a boy like me could wander. But one day I started bushwhacking up Opal Creek. Before long I'd left my boundary far behind. Finally I came to Cedar Flats, a grove of giant trees beside the mossy creek. I sat down there among the cedars and had an experience I still can't explain. I felt I was talking to those old guys. They filled me with an amazing, spine-tingling sense of peace."

By the time George finally hiked home that evening he had missed dinner. "I got chewed out pretty bad. But afterwards I told everyone about this beautiful place I'd found. Grampa nodded that he knew all about it."

Among those listening was the boy's uncle, Victor Atiyeh, later the governor of Oregon. George remembers his uncle commenting, "I hate to burst your bubble, but you know the Forest Service guy we're letting stay in Cabin Number Nine? He's surveying a road that will go right up Opal Creek and log off that whole valley."

A sudden surge of anger and defiance brought the boy to his feet. "They can't log those trees! I won't let 'em do it! I swear I'll stop 'em!" George recalls telling his relatives. "I'd grown up in a family that logged and mined for a living, but the idea that someone was going to kill those cedars was like telling me they were going to shoot my dog."

"Grampa didn't say a word. But Uncle Victor shook his head. 'You're just a boy,' he said. 'There's nothing you can do about it.'"

To find out what George and his "Grampa" did about it, drive up the Little North Fork Santiam River to the trailhead gate and start walking the old road toward Jawbone Flats. Before long you'll cross Gold Creek on a sixty-foot-high bridge. This creek won its name in 1860 when prospectors staked gold mining claims here. The miners built a dozen cabins and riddled the hillside with tunnels before the boom faded. In 1933 the government set up a small Civilian Conservation Corps camp at the mouth of Gold Creek. The cabins were rotting away when "Grampa" Jim Hewitt began buying up the old claims.

By the time George Atiyeh visited Jawbone Flats in 1960, "Grampa" controlled three thousand acres of properties, scattered along five miles of the valley. Here at Gold Creek, his holdings lay squarely across the only feasible access road for the Forest Service to reach Opal Creek. From 1960 until he was moved to a nursing home in 1969, "Grampa" stubbornly stymied logging crews with a series of legal and physical roadblocks. After that, it would be young George's turn to take up the battle.

When you hike beyond Gold Creek you'll skirt dramatic riverside cliffs. Then the route winds through an old-growth grove with some of the area's most impressive big trees. At the hike's two-mile mark, stop to inspect the rusting machinery of Merten Mill on the right. This little sawmill operated briefly during the Great Depression, using a steam-driven winch and capstan salvaged from the battleship *USS Oregon*. The mill folded after two of its lumber trucks fell off the narrow canyon road. Now the mill's grassy site serves as a camping area for backpackers, with a 1933-vintage plank shed as an emergency shelter. A short side trail behind the shed leads down to Sawmill Falls, a thirty-foot cascade pouring into a deep green pool. On a hot summer day it's a great place for a chilly swim.

Jawbone Flats in 1990.

Another mile of hiking up the road brings you to Jawbone Flats. The rustic mining camp preserves twenty buildings that date from 1929 to 1932. The entire settlement now belongs to the Opal Creek Ancient Forest Center, a non-profit group that runs an old-growth study center and rents out cabins. Electricity is still generated by the half-mile-long water flume that powered the camp's ore mill. In the middle of Jawbone Flats a store sells maps and souvenirs to hikers. Across the road on the right is a board-and-batten lodge, built on the site of "Grampa" Hewitt's original home.

After "Grampa" was gone, George Atiyeh stepped in as caretaker in 1969. He had not forgotten his vow to protect Opal Creek. By then George was twenty-one, shaken by Army service during the Vietnam War and inspired by the radical student protesters he'd met at the University of Oregon. When he and friends discovered a Forest Service crew was surveying a new logging road toward Opal Creek, they donned camouflage gear and haunted the workers as non-violent guerrillas. George and his friends slipped through the forest, pulling up survey stakes behind the workers' backs. They poured snow into the gas tanks of the crews' motorcycles. Finally the Forest Service employees were so angry that they stormed into Jawbone Flats with guns at the ready. The Forest Service men threatened to burn the place down if the harassment didn't stop.

"Tempers were out of hand on both sides," George recalls. "They were cold, tired, hungry, and wet. All of us were edgy. My friend aimed his rifle. Bloodshed was just seconds away. I kept my gun in my holster, but looked the men in the eye and told them they were on private property. I took their weapons, dumped out the bullets, and returned them empty. They left peaceably, but I knew the trouble had only begun."

A few days later fifteen police officers circled Jawbone Flats, set up a machine gun by the road, and demanded surrender. George and his friend came out unarmed. Whisked away to the Marion County jail, George despaired that he—and the Opal Creek forests—faced a grim future.

To George's surprise, local North Santiam Valley citizens raised money for his bail. A grand jury reviewed his case and set him free. George's friend faced trial, but a jury found him innocent too. In fact, the judge threatened the *Forest Service* men with jail if they didn't change tactics.

"It was a turning point in my life," George recalls. "I realized that the system could work after all." That winter at Jawbone Flats, George began studying Forest Service regulations and mining laws. For the next fifteen years he tied up the planned Opal Creek timber sales with the government's own red tape, filing one appeal after another. Victory seemed at hand in 1984. That year he convinced his uncle, then Oregon's governor, to ask Senator Hatfield to put Opal Creek in a comprehensive wilderness bill.

But instead of adding Opal Creek to the 1984 wilderness bill, Hatfield released the entire area for logging. Desperate, George pleaded to environmental groups for help. They told him the only way left to save Opal Creek was to bring hikers there to see it. The valley needed a trail. Without a path, they said, Opal Creek's ancient forest might as well be invisible.

And so George volunteered to build a trail. The Forest Service promptly rejected his offer. They did not want hikers in a timber sale area. George decided he had no choice but to take matters into his own hands once again.

As you walk from Jawbone Flats to Opal Pool you'll be following the route taken by a furtive band of illegal trail builders in 1986. In just three days, the environmental guerrillas roughed out a "bear trail" to the ancient trees at Cedar Flats. Then the activists issued invitations to reporters, Congressional staffers, and state legislators. Within weeks the *Oregonian*

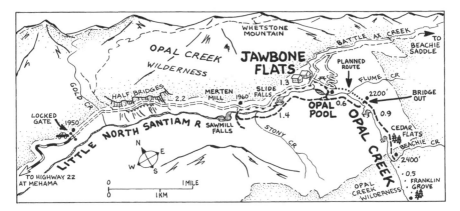

56. Opal Creek

HIKE LOCATION

Moderate
7.1-mile-loop
200 feet elevation gain

A once-controversial Wilderness surrounds a 1930s mining camp.

Getting There: Drive east from Salem on North Santiam Highway 22 for 23 miles to Mehama's second flashing yellow light. Opposite the Swiss Village Restaurant, turn left on Little North Fork Road for 15 paved miles and an additional 1.3 miles of gravel. At a fork, veer left on Road 2209 past the sign "Road Closed 6 Miles Ahead." Then drive 6 miles to the locked gate. Residents of Jawbone Flats are allowed to drive the dirt road ahead; others must park and walk. A Northwest Forest Pass is required here. It costs $5 per car per day or $30 per year, and is available at most outdoor stores and Forest Service offices—notably the ranger station in Detroit.

Hiking Tips: Walk past the road's gate 2.2 miles. Beyond Merten Mill the road forks at the start of the loop. Keep left on the road a mile to Jawbone Flats. To rent one of 4 cabins here that sleep 2-16 people, or to rent a lodge that sleeps 18, call 503-892-2782 or check *www.opalcreek.org*. When hiking through Jawbone Flats, respect the residents' privacy by staying on the road. Cross a bridge on the far edge of the settlement and turn right at a building with a humming water-power generator. After another 0.2 mile, turn right on a short trail to Opal Pool. Then take a bridge across the creek to a junction with the Opal Creek Trail. Turn left if you'd like to explore further up Opal Creek; otherwise, turn right to return to your car.

Season: Open all year, except in winter storms.

ran a glowing article on the marvels of Opal Creek, hailing it as an uncut jewel hardly an hour's drive from Portland.

The Forest Service vowed to prosecute whoever had built the unauthorized trail. "I just told them I'd seen a herd of bears going up there," George laughs.

The controversial trail succeeded in swinging public attention to Opal Creek's plight. State legislators proposed a new preservation bill, timber companies orchestrated massive anti-wilderness demonstrations in Salem, and the national media picked up the story. Suddenly the moss-draped forests of Opal Creek were appearing on newsmagazine covers, TV specials, and newscast backdrops. An avalanche of nationwide support swept the wilderness effort to victory.

In recent years the Forest Service has updated its approach to wilderness, increasingly recognizing the importance of old-growth forests. The agency is also planning to replace much of Opal Creek's original "bear trail" with an improved path. Until then, hiking up the creek to Cedar Flats remains a bit of an adventure.

If you do reach the giant cedar trees, be sure to pause long enough to sit among the ancient trunks. This is the mystic grove where a twelve-year-old boy once dreamed away an afternoon. Great, curving limbs droop overhead to frame the mossy earth with a pillared shelter. The air tastes crisp and fresh as split apples. Jungly leaves filter the distant sunlight to a soothing green glow. The creek's whitewater seems to whisper that this will all never end.

Today George Atiyeh lives in Elkhorn, Oregon, a small town within earshot of the roaring Little North Santiam River. He reflects on his thirty-eight-year struggle with a touch of regret. "Opal Creek created a lot of dissension, even among the friends I grew up with. I'm sorry it came to that. Those wounds will be slow to heal. And the fight is far from over. Ancient forests are still being clearcut. Everywhere you look, humanity is having a devastating impact on the land. The planet is resilient, but unless we act responsibly, we may not be here when it finally recovers."

George glances to his daughters, sitting nearby, and his quiet words seem meant for them. "One person *can* make a difference. If you know in your heart that something is right, don't let anyone tell you it's impossible."

•§•

Acknowledgments

Oregon history is the story of people, and the creation of this book called on the talents and memories of many. I would particularly like to thank those who checked the manuscript: Janell Sorensen, Terence O'Donnell, Nancie Fadeley, Wes Sullivan, George Atiyeh, John Hook, Martha Bayless, Lee Kirk, Howard Wade, Brenda Shaw, Paul Hash, and Pat Murphy.

My research relied heavily on the Oregon Collection at the University of Oregon's Knight Library, the Oregon Historical Society library, the Eugene Public Library, and the University of Oregon Map Library.

For years I have received the help of countless staffers from the Forest Service, Bureau of Land Management, Oregon State Parks, National Park Service, and the many other agencies that oversee Oregon's trails. These dedicated people have taken the time to check the maps and text for nearly a thousand hikes described in my books and articles.

Specific thanks go to Beth Hege Piatote. The quotation by Soy Redthunder on page 170 originally appeared in her article, "A Circle of Hands," in the spring 1998 issue of *Oregon Quarterly*.

Finally, I'd like to thank the readers and hikers who have volunteered suggestions and stories about the trails in my hiking guidebooks over the years. I only regret that I could not recount more of the tips and tales you have shared about Oregon's past.

Photography credits: Oregon Historical Society—cover and page 165 (OrHi52504), cover and page 173 (0163N850), back cover and page 103 ((OrHi21572), page 2 (OrHi36316), page 28 (OrHi35789), page 40 (OrHi59338), page 45 (OrHi11707), page 47 (OrHi65079), page 65 (OrHi36626), page 84 (CN012658), page 87 (OrHi35288), page 95 (OrHi5282), page 104 (OrHi63575), page 108 (OrHi178), page 136 (OrHi4672), page 141 (OrHi44244), page 159 (OrHi48460), page 211 (OrHi5578), page 217 (OrHi5699), page 222 (OrHi14129), page 228 (OrHiCN006375), page 237 (OrHi37649), page 243 (OrHi38587), page 246 (OrHi88716), and page 247 (OrHi36867). Janell Sorensen—author photo on page 320.

Hiker's Checklist

Ready to hit the trail? Here are a few tips to help make sure your outing is safe and enjoyable.

The Boxed Inserts

First, take a close look at the boxed inserts throughout this book. Each of these numbered descriptions rates the difficulty of the hike. **Easy** hikes are less than four miles round-trip and gain less than 500 feet in elevation. Never very steep, they make good first-time trips for novices, and generally can be undertaken in tennis shoes. Trips rated as **Moderate** range from one to six miles round-trip. The longer hikes in this category are not steep, but shorter trails may gain up to 1000 feet of elevation. Hikers on these trips must be in good condition and will need to take several rest stops. **Difficult** trails, suitable only for experienced hikers, may range from two to ten miles round-trip, and may gain up to 2000 feet of elevation.

The **elevation gains** listed in the boxed inserts tell much about the difficulty of a hike. Those who puff climbing a few flights of stairs may consider even 500 feet of elevation a strenuous climb, and should watch this listing carefully. Note that the figures are for each hike's *cumulative* elevation gain, adding all the uphill portions, even those on the return trip.

The **hiking season** of any trail varies with the weather. In a cold year, a trail described as "Open May through October" may not yet be clear of snow by May 1, and may be socked in by a blizzard before October 31. Similarly, a trail that is "Open all year" may close due to storms.

Collect Only Memories

Visitors to historic sites must take great care not to disturb the areas' archeological value. On nearly all of the trails in this book, collecting arrowheads, bottles, or other cultural artifacts is prohibited by federal law. Report to authorities anyone you see digging without a permit. Never touch petroglyphs; even making a rubbing can cause permanent damage.

Sawmill Falls on the trail to Opal Creek.

Wild Animals

Part of the fun of hiking is watching for wildlife. Lovers of wildness rue the demise of our most impressive species. Grizzly bears are extinct in Oregon. Black bears, cougars, and wolves are so profoundly shy that most Oregonians will never see one. No one has been killed by any of these animals in the history of the state. Similarly, rattlesnakes are truly rare in Oregon. Insects pose a more realistic hazard. Expect mosquitoes at high elevations in July. As a precaution against ticks, hikers should check their cuffs and collars after walking through dry forests or grass.

Drinking Water

Day hikers should bring all the water they will need—roughly a quart per person. A microscopic paramecium, *Giardia,* has forever changed the old custom of dipping a drink from every brook. The symptoms of "beaver fever," debilitating nausea and diarrhea, commence a week or two after ingesting the paramecium. If you're backpacking, bring an approved water filter or purification tablet, or boil your water five minutes.

Proper Equipment

Even on the tamest hike a surprise storm or a wrong turn can suddenly make the gear you carry very important. Always bring a pack with the ten essentials: a warm, waterproof coat, drinking water, extra food, a knife, matches in a waterproof container, a fire starter (butane lighter or candle), a first aid kit, a flashlight, a map (topographic, if possible), and a compass.

Before leaving on a hike, tell someone where you are going so they can alert the county sheriff to begin a search if you do not return on time. If you're lost, stay put and keep warm. The number one danger in the woods is *hypothermia*— being cold and wet too long.

Courtesy on the Trail

As our trails become more heavily used, rules of trail etiquette have become essential. Please:

- Pick no flowers. Many rare species are protected by law.
- Leave no litter. Eggshells and orange peels can last for decades.
- Step off the trail on the downhill side to let horses pass.
- Do not shortcut switchbacks.

Groups to Hike With

If you enjoy the camaraderie of hiking with a group, contact one of the organizations that leads trips to the trails in this book. None of the groups requires that you be a member to join scheduled hikes, and trip fees are rarely more than a dollar or two. Hikers generally carpool from a preset meeting place. If you have no car, expect to chip in for mileage.

Chemeketans. Three to eight hikes a week, based in Salem. Cabin near Mt. Jefferson, meetings at 360½ State Street, Salem. Founded 1927. Info at *www.chemeketans.org.*

Deschutes Land Trust. Five to ten free hikes a week, based in Bend. Office at 210 NW Irving Ave., Bend, OR 97701. Call 541-330-0017 or check *www.deschuteslandtrust.or/events.*

Mazamas. Three to ten hikes a week, based in Portland. Cabin at Mt. Hood, office and meetings at 527 SE 43rd Ave., Portland, OR 97215. Founded 1894. Contact 503-227-2345 or *www.mazamas.org.*

Obsidians. Two to five hikes a week, based in Eugene. Monthly potluck meetings at Eugene lodge. Write P.O. Box 51510, Eugene, OR 97405, or check *www.obsidians. org.*

Sierra Club. Weekly hikes in many parts of the state, except in winter. Check *oregon.sierraclub.org.*

Trails Club of Oregon. Hikes on Saturdays and Sundays, based in Portland. Cabins at Mt. Hood and Columbia Gorge. Founded 1915. Write P.O. Box 1243, Portland, OR 97207. Call 503-233-2740 or check *www.trailsclub.org.*

For More Information

To check on permit requirements, trail maintenance, snow levels, or other questions, call directly to the trail's administrative agency. These offices are listed below, along with the hikes in this book for which they manage trails.

Hike	Managing Agency
6	Bandon Chamber of Commerce 541-347-9616
36	Cape Blanco State Park 541-332-2973
9	Cape Perpetua Visitor Center 541-547-3289
14	Champoeg State Park 503-678-1251
55	Chetco Ranger District 541-412-6000
43, 44	Columbia Gorge Nat'l Scenic Area 541-308-1700
4, 42, 49	Crater Lake National Park 541-594-3000
31, 56	Detroit Ranger District 503-854-3366
11	Ecola State Park 503-436-2844
33	Eugene District BLM 541-683-6600
54	Fort Stevens State Park 503-861-3170 x21
40	Friends of Shore Acres 541-756-5401
29	Gold Beach Ranger District 541-247-3600
13	Humbug Mountain State Park 541-332-6774 x0
23	Josephine County Parks 541-474-5285
1, 2	Lakeview District BLM 541-947-2177
20, 21, 50, 52	McKenzie Ranger District 541-822-3381
24	Medford District BLM 541-618-2200
19	Middle Fork Ranger District 541-782-2283
27	North Fork John Day Ranger District 541-427-3231
41	Oregon Caves National Monument 541-592-2100
37, 38	Oregon Historical Society 503-222-1741
8, 15, 32, 35, 39, 46	Oregon State Parks 800-551-6949
17	Oregon Trail Interpretive Center 541-523-1843
3	Prineville District BLM 541-416-6700
16	Salem Parks Department 503-588-6261
12	Sauvie Island Wildlife Area 503-621-3488
51	Silver Falls State Park 503-873-8681
26	Siskiyou Mountains Ranger District 541-899-3800
47	Sisters Ranger District 541-549-7700
5	Siuslaw National Forest 541-750-7000
22, 49	Sweet Home Ranger District 541-367-5168
28	The Nature Conservancy 541-770-7933
45	The Nature Conservancy 503-802-8100
30	Wallowa Mountains Visitor Center 541-426-5546
7	Wash. Dept. of Natural Resources 360-902-1000
10	Washington State Parks 360-902-8844
25	Wild Rivers Ranger District 541-471-6500
34	Yaquina Head ONA (BLM) 541-574-3100
18, 53	Zigzag Ranger District 503-622-3191

For Further Reading

Other Works by William L. Sullivan

The author of this book has also written a comprehensive series of "100 Hikes" books describing the trails of Oregon, as well as two adventure memoirs about Oregon, several works of fiction set in Oregon, an Oregon road map's travel guide, and a wilderness guidebook for the state. All of these are available at bookstores, or online at *www.oregonhiking.com*.

- *100 Hikes in Northwest Oregon.* Eugene: Navillus Press.
- *100 Hikes/Travel Guide: Central Oregon Cascades.* Eugene: Navillus Press.
- *100 Hikes/Travel Guide: Oregon Coast & Coast Range.* Eugene: Navillus Press.
- *100 Hikes in Southern Oregon.* Eugene: Navillus Press.
- *100 Hikes/Travel Guide: Eastern Oregon.* Eugene: Navillus Press.
- *A Deeper Wild.* Eugene: Navillus Press.
- *Atlas of Oregon Wilderness.* Eugene: Navillus Press.
- *Cabin Fever: Notes From a Part-Time Pioneer.* Eugene: Navillus Press.
- *The Case of D.B. Cooper's Parachute.* Eugene: Navillus Press.
- *Listening for Coyote: A Walk Across Oregon's Wilderness.* Corvallis: OSU Press.
- *Oregon Favorites: Trails & Tales.* Eugene: Navillus Press.
- *Oregon's Greatest Natural Disasters.* Eugene: Navillus Press.
- *Oregon Topo-Travel-Reference Map.* Eugene: Imus Geographics.
- *Oregon Trips & Trails.* Eugene: Navillus Press.
- *The Oregon Variations: Stories.* Eugene: Navillus Press.

Bibliography

This book is not intended as a comprehensive history of Oregon, or even of the featured locales. If the selection of stories presented here has piqued your interest, however, more exhaustive works are available on specific subjects. The list below includes the most significant materials used in the book's research.

Chapter I: The First Tracks

Aikens, C. Melvin and Dennis L. Jenkins, eds. *Fort Rock Archeology Since Cressman.* Eugene: University of Oregon, 1994.

Allison, Ira S. *Pluvial Fort Rock Lake.* Portland, Department of Geology and Mineral Industries, 1979.

Bedwell, Stephen. *Fort Rock Basin: Prehistory and Environment.* Eugene: University of Oregon, 1973.

Brogan, Phil F. *East of the Cascades.* Portland: Binfords & Mort, 1964.
Cressman, Luther S. *A Golden Journey: Memoirs of an Archeologist.* Salt Lake City: University of Utah, 1988.
Ferguson, Denzel and Nancy. *Oregon's Great Basin Country.* Bend: Maverick, 1978.

Chapter II: Angry Spirits

Beckham, Stephen Dow. *The Indians of Western Oregon.* Coos Bay: Arago Books, 1977.
Clark, Ella E. Indian *Legends of the Pacific Northwest.* Berkeley: University of California, 1953.
Drucker, Philip. *Indians of the Northwest Coast.* Garden City, New York: Natural History, 1955.
Hall, Roberta L. *The Coquille Indians.* Lake Oswego: Smith, Smith and Smith, 1984.
Jennings, Jesse D. "Prehistory." *Handbook of North American Indians, Vol. II.* Warren d'Azeredo, ed. Washington D.C.: Smithsonian, 1986.
Judson, Katharine Berry, ed. *Myths and Legends of the Pacific Northwest.* Chicago: A.C. McClurg, 1910.
Lopez, Barry. *Giving Birth to Thunder, Sleeping With His Daughter: Coyote Builds North America.* New York: Avon, 1977.
Mackey, Harold. *The Kalapuyans.* Salem: Mission Mill Museum, 1974.
Ramsey, Jarold, ed. *Coyote Was Going There: Indian Literature of the Oregon Country.* Seattle: University of Washington, 1977.

Chapter III: The Explorers

Bucy, David E.M. *The Guide to Cape Perpetua.* Corvallis: Northwest Natureworks, 1987.
Cleaver, J.D. *Island Origins: Sauvie Island.* Portland: Oregon Historical Society, 1986.
Johansen, Dorothy O. and Charles M. Gates. *Empire of the Columbia: A History of the Pacific Northwest, Second Edition.* New York: Harper & Row, 1967.
Lockley, Fred. *Conversations With Bullwhackers.* Mike Helm, ed. Eugene: Rainy Day, 1981.
Lucia, Ellis. *Tough Men, Tough Country.* Englewood Cliffs, New Jersey: Prentice Hall, 1963.
Miller, Emma Gene. *Clatsop County, Oregon: A History.* Portland: Binfords & Mort, 1958.
Moody, Ralph. *Gateways to the Northwest, Vol. II: The Old Trails West.* Sausalito: Comstock, 1963.
Rowell, Frank A. *The Treasure of Neakahnie Mountain.* Berkeley: West Coast Print Center, 1976.
Schwantes, Carlos Arnaldo. *The Pacific Northwest: An Interpretive History.* Lincoln: University of Nebraska, 1996.

Chapter IV: The Settlers

Brosnan, Cornelius J. *Jason Lee: Prophet of the New Oregon.* New York: Macmillan, 1932.
Corning, Howard McKinley. *Willamette Landings: Ghost Towns of the River.* Portland: Oregon Historical Society, 1967.
Fadeley, Nancie Peacocke. *Mission to Oregon.* Eugene: Fadeley, 1976.
Hussey, John A. *Champoeg: Place of Transition.* Portland: Oregon Historical Society, 1967.
Johansen, Dorothy O. and Charles M. Gates. *Empire of the Columbia: A History of the Pacific Northwest, Second Edition.* New York: Harper & Row, 1967.
United Methodist Archives. 680 State Street, Suite V-60. Salem, Oregon 97301

Chapter V: Wagon Wheels

Brogan, Phil F. *East of the Cascades.* Portland: Binfords & Mort, 1964.
Grauer, Jack. *Mount Hood: A Complete History.* Gresham: Grauer, 1975.
Haines, Aubrey L. *Historic Sites Along the Oregon Trail.* St. Louis: Patrice, 1981.
Hanley, Mike. *Owyhee Trails.* Caldwell: Caxton, 1975.
Hatton, Raymond R. *Oregon's Sisters Country.* Bend: Maverick, 1996.
Jensen, Veryl M. *Early Days on the Upper Willamette.* Oakridge: Upper Willamette
    Pioneer Association, 1970.
Nielsen, Lawrence E. *Pioneer Roads in Central Oregon.* Bend: Maverick, 1985.
Peterson, Pete. *Our Wagon Train Is Lost.* Eugene: New American Gothic, 1975.
Potter, Miles F. *Oregon's Golden Years.* Caldwell: Caxton, 1982.

Chapter VI: Gold!

Lockley, Fred. *Oregon's Yesterdays.* New York: Knickerbocker, 1928.
Potter, Miles F. *Oregon's Golden Years.* Caldwell: Caxton, 1982.
Weis, Norman D. *Ghost Towns of the Northwest.* Caldwell: Caxton, 1993.

Chapter VII: Trails of Tears

Ashworth, William. *Hells Canyon.* New York: Hawthorn, 1977.
Beckham, Stephen Dow. *The Indians of Western Oregon.* Coos Bay: Arago Books,
    1977.
    — *Requiem for a People.* Reprint, Corvallis: Oregon State University, 1996.
Lockley, Fred. *Conversations With Bullwhackers.* Mike Helm, ed. Eugene: Rainy
    Day, 1981.
Peterson, Emil R. and Alfred Powers. *A Century of Coos and Curry: History of
    Southwest Oregon.* Portland: Binfords & Mort, 1952.
Ramsey, Jarold, ed. *Coyote Was Going There: Indian Literature of the Oregon Coun-
    try.* Seattle: University of Washington, 1977.
Reyes, Chris, ed. *The Table Rocks of Jackson County.* Ashland: Last Minute, 1994.
Wood, Erskine. *Days With Chief Joseph: Diary and Recollections.* Portland: Oregon
    Historical Society, 1970.

Chapter VIII: The Iron Horse

Brogan, Phil F. *East of the Cascades.* Portland: Binfords & Mort, 1964.
Hatton, Raymond R. *Oregon's Sisters Country.* Bend: Maverick, 1996.
Nash, Wallis. *Oregon: There and Back in 1877.* Reprint, Corvallis: Oregon State
    University, 1976.

Chapter IX: Beacons to Sea

Beckham, Stephen Dow. *Cape Blanco Lighthouse.* North Bend: Coos Bay BLM, 1995.
Finucane, Stephanie. *Heceta House.* Waldport: Siuslaw National Forest, 1980.
Gibbs, James A. *Tillamook Light.* Portland: Binfords & Mort, 1953.
Minor, Rick. *Yaquina Head: A Middle Archaic Settlement on the North-Central Oregon
    Coast.* Eugene: Heritage Research Associates, 1991.

Chapter X: Boom Years

Beckham, Stephen Dow. *The Simpsons of Shore Acres.* McMinnville: Arago, 1971.
Douthit, Nathan. *The Coos Bay Region 1890-1944: Life on a Coastal Frontier.* Coos
    Bay: River West, 1981.

Labbe, John T. *Fares, Please! Those Portland Trolley Years.* Caldwell: Caxton, 1980.
MacColl, E. Kimbark. *The Growth of a City: Power and Politics in Portland, Oregon 1915 to 1950.* Portland: Georgian, 1979.
Maddux, Percy. *City on the Willamette: The Story of Portland, Oregon.* Portland: Binfords & Mort, 1952.
O'Donnell, Terence. *Portland: A Historical Sketch and Guide.* Portland: Oregon Historical Society, 1976.
Webber, Bert. *What Happened at Bayocean.* Fairfield, Washington: Ye Galleon, 1973.

Chapter XI: The Horseless Carriage

Jones, Philip N., ed. *Columbia River Gorge: A Complete Guide.* Seattle: Mountaineers, 1992.
Smith, Dwight A., et al. *Historic Highway Bridges of Oregon.* Portland: Oregon Historical Society, 1989.

Chapter XII: The Fire Line

Grauer, Jack. *Mount Hood: A Complete History.* Gresham: Grauer, 1975.
Kresek, Ray. *Fire Lookouts of the Northwest.* Fairfield, Washington: Ye Galleon, 1984.

Chapter XIII: Rags and Riches

Rose, Judith, ed. *Timberline Lodge: A Love Story.* Portland: Graphic Arts Center, 1986.
Sisney, Paul. *Silver Falls State Park: A History.* Salem: Written Well, 1995.

Chapter XIV: War!

Kresek, Ray. *Fire Lookouts of the Northwest.* Fairfield, Washington: Ye Galleon, 1984.
Webber, Bert. *Retaliation: Japanese Attacks and Allied Countermeasures on the Pacific Coast in World War II.* Corvallis: Oregon State University, 1975.

Chapter XV: The Legacy

George, Anthony. *The Santiam Mining District of the Oregon Cascades.* Salem: Solo Press, 1985.

General Oregon Resources

Alt, David D. *Roadside Geology of Oregon.* Missoula: Mountain Press, 1978.
Bishop, Ellen Morris and John Eliot Allen. *Hiking Oregon's Geology.* Seattle: Mountaineers, 1996.
Friedman, Ralph. *Tracking Down Oregon.* Caldwell: Caxton, 1978.
— *Oregon for the Curious.* Caldwell: Caxton, 1979.
— *A Touch of Oregon.* Reprint, Sausalito: Comstock, 1974.
Holbrook, Stewart. *Far Corner: A Personal View of the Pacific Northwest.* New York: Ballantine, 1952.
McArthur, Lewis A. *Oregon Geographic Names.* Portland: Oregon Historical Society, 1996.
Nordhoff, Charles. *Northern California, Oregon and the Sandwich Islands.* 1874, reprint Berkeley: Ten Speed, 1974.
Orr, Elizabeth et al. *Geology of Oregon, Fourth Edition.* Dubuque: Kendall/Hunt, 1995.

Index

About the Author

William L. Sullivan is the author of seventeen books about Oregon. He writes outdoor columns for the Eugene *Register-Guard* and the Salem *Statesman-Journal*. A fifth-generation Oregonian, he received his English degree at Cornell University, studied linguistics at Germany's Heidelberg University, and completed an M.A. in German at the University of Oregon.

In 1985 he set out to explore Oregon's wilderness on a 1,361-mile solo

William L. Sullivan at his log cabin.

backpacking trek from the state's westernmost point at Cape Blanco to Oregon's easternmost point at the bottom of Hells Canyon. His journal of that two-month adventure, published as *Listening for Coyote*, was chosen by the Oregon Cultural Heritage Commission as one of Oregon's "100 Books," the most significant books in the state's history. Since then he has written a series of *100 Hikes* guides, for which he hiked virtually every trail in Oregon.

Sullivan's hobbies include backcountry ski touring, playing the pipe organ, reading foreign language novels, and promoting libraries. He and his wife Janell Sorensen live in Eugene but spend summers without roads or electricity in a log cabin they built by hand along a wilderness river in Oregon's Coast Range. Sullivan's memoir of his adventures at that cabin retreat is entitled *Cabin Fever: Notes From a Part-Time Pioneer*.